Scripting Languages

Automating the Web

O'REILLY™

WORLD WIDE WEB JOURNAL

SCRIPTING LANGUAGES: AUTOMATING THE WEB **Volume 2, Issue 2, Spring 1997**

Editor: Rohit Khare

Managing Editor: Donna Woonteiler

News Editor: Dave Sims

Production Editor: Nancy Crumpton

Technical Illustrator: Chris Reilley

Software Tools Specialist: Mike Sierra

Quality Assurance: Clairemarie Fisher O'Leary

Cover Design: Hanna Dyer

Text Design: Nancy Priest, Marcia Ciro

Subscription Administrator: Marianne Cooke

Photos: Cip Ayalin

 This book is printed on acid-free paper with 85% recycled content, 15% post-consumer waste. O'Reilly & Associates is committed to using paper with the highest recycled content available consistent with high quality.

ISSN: 1085-2301

ISBN: 1-56592-265-4   4/1/97

W 3 C   G L O B A L   T E A M

W3C Administration

Jean-François Abramatic
  W3C Chairman and Associate
  Director, MIT Laboratory for
  Computer Science
  jfa@w3.org

Tim Berners-Lee
  Director of the W3C
  timbl@w3.org

Vincent Quint
  Deputy Director for Europe
  Vincent.Quint@w3.org

Nobuo Saito
  W3C Associate Chairman
  and Dean, Keio University
  nobuo.saito@w3.org

Tatsuya Hagino
  hagino@w3.org
  Deputy Director, Asia

User Interface

Vincent Quint
  Domain Leader
  Vincent.Quint@w3.org

Bert Bos
  bert@w3.org

Ramzi Guetari
  guetari@w3.org

José Kahan
  Jose.Kahan@w3.org

Yves Lafon
  lafon@w3.org

Håkon Lie
  howcome@w3.org

Chris Lilley
  chris@w3.org

Dave Raggett
  dsr@w3.org

Irène Vatton
  Irene.Vatton@w3.org

Daniel Veillard
  Daniel.Veillard@w3.org

Technology and Society

Jim Miller
  Domain Leader
  jmiller@w3.org

Eui-Suk Chung
  euisuk@w3.org

Daniel Dardailler
  danield@w3.org

Philip DesAutels
  philipd@w3.org

Joseph Reagle
  reagle@w3.org

Ralph Swick
  swick@w3.org

Architecture

Dan Connolly
  Domain Leader
  connolly@w3.org

Anselm Baird-Smith
  abaird@w3.org

Jim Gettys
  jg@w3.org

Philipp Hoschka
  Philipp.Hoschka@w3.org

Ora Lassila
  lassila@w3.org

Henrik Frystyk Nielsen
  frystyk@w3.org

Cross Areas and Technical Support

Janet Bertot
  bertot@w3.org

Stephane Boyera
  Stephane.Boyera@w3.org

Daicho Funato
  daichi@w3.org

Tom Greene
  tjg@w3.org

Rohit Khare
  khare@w3.org

Sally Khudairi
  khudairi@w3.org

Arnaud Le Hors
  lehors@w3.org

Stéphan Montigaud
  montigaud@w3.org

Luc Ottavj
  ottavj@w3.org

Administrative Support

Pamela Ahern
  pam@w3.org

Beth Curran
  beth@w3.org

Susan Hardy
  susan@w3.org

Josiane Roberts
  Josiane.Roberts@inria.fr

Yukari Mitsuhashi
  yukari@w3.org

W 3 C   M E M B E R S

Adobe Systems Inc.

Aérospatiale

AGF.SI

Agfa Division, Bayer Corp.

Alcatel Alsthom Recherche

Alfa-Omega Foundation

Alis Technologies, Inc.

America Online, Inc.

American International Group Data Center, Inc. (AIG)

American Internet Corporation

Apple Computer, Inc.

Architecture Projects Management Ltd.

AT&T

Attachmate Corporation

BELGACOM

Bellcore

Bitstream, Inc.

British Telecommunications Laboratories

Bull S.A.

Canal +

Canon, Inc.

Cap Gemini Innovation

Center for Mathematics and Computer Science (CWI)

CERN

CIRAD

CNR—Instituto Elaborazione dell'Informazione

CNRS

Commissariat a L'Énergie Atomique (CEA)

CompuServe, Inc.

Computer Answer Line

CosmosBay

Council for the Central Laboratory of the Research Councils (CCL)

CyberCash, Inc.

Cygnus Support

Dassault Aviation

Data Research Associates, Inc.

Defense Information Systems Agency (DISA)

Delphi Internet

Deutsche Telekom

Digital Equipment Corporation

DigitalStyle Corporation

Eastman Kodak Company

École Nationale Supérieure d'Informatique et de Mathématiques Appliquées (ENSIMAG)

EDF

EEIG/ERCIM

Electronic Book Technologies, Inc.

ENEL

Enterprise Integration Technology

ERICSSON

ETNOTEAM S.p.A.

First Floor, Inc.

First Virtual Holdings, Inc.

Folio Corporation

Foundation for Research and Technology (FORTH)

France Telecom

FTP Software

Fujitsu Limited

Fulcrum Technologies, Inc.

GCTECH, Inc.

GEMPLUS

General Magic, Inc.

Geoworks

GMD Institute FIT

Grenoble Network Initiative

GRIF S.A.

Groupe ESC Grenoble

Harlequin Inc.

HAVAS

Hewlett Packard Laboratories, Bristol

Hitachi, Ltd.

Hummingbird Communications Ltd.

IBERDROLA S.A.

IBM Corp.

ILOG, S.A.

InContext Systems

Industrial Technology Research Institute

Infopartners S.A.

INRETS

Institut Franco-Russe A.M. Liapunov

Intel Corporation

Intermind

Internet Profiles Corporation

Intraspect Software, Inc.

Joint Info. Systems Comm. of the UK Higher Ed. Funding Council

Justsystem Corporation

K2Net, Inc.

Kumamoto Institute of Computer Software, Inc.

Lexmark International, Inc.

Los Alamos National Laboratory

Lotus Development Corporation

Lucent Technologies

Mainspring Communications, Inc.

Matra Hachette

MCI Telecommunications

Metrowerks Corporation

Michelin

Microsoft Corp.

MITRE Corporation

Mitsubishi Electric Corporation

MTA SZTAKI

National Center for Super-computing Applications (NCSA)

National Security Agency (NSA)

NCR

NEC Corporation

Netscape Communications

NeXT Software, Inc.

NHS (National Health Service, UK)

Nippon Telegraph & Telephone Corp. (NTT)

NOKIA Mobile Phones

Novell, Inc.

NTT Data Communications Systems Corp.

Nynex Science & Technology, Inc.

O'Reilly & Associates, Inc.

O2 Technology

Object Management Group, Inc. (OMG)

OCLC (Online Computer Library Center, Inc.)

Omron Corporation

Open Market Inc.

Open Software Foundation

Oracle Corp.

ORSTOM

Pacifitech Corporation

PointCast Incorporated

Pretty Good Privacy, Inc.

Process Software Corp.

Prodigy Services Company

Progressive Networks

Public IP Exchange, Ltd. (PIPEX)

R.I.S. Technologies

Raptor Systems, Inc.

Reed-Elsevier

Rice University for Nat'l HCPP Software

Riverland Holding NV/SA

Royal Hong Kong Jockey Club

Security Dynamics Technologies, Inc.

Sema Group

SICS

Siemens-Nixdorf

Silicon Graphics, Inc.

SLIGOS

SoftQuad

Software 2000

Sony Corporation

Spry, Inc.

Spyglass, Inc.

STET

Sun Microsystems Corporation

SURFnet bv

Swedish Institute for Systems
Development (SISU)

Syracuse University

Tandem Computers Inc.

Teknema Corporation

Telequip Corporation

Terisa Systems

The Hong Kong Jockey Club

Thomson-CSF Ventures

TIAA-CREF

TriTeal Corporation

U.S. Web Corporation

UKERNA

Unwired Planet

Verity, Inc.

Vermeer Technologies Inc.

VTT Information Technology

Wolfram Research, Inc.

WWW. Consult Pty Ltd.

WWW—KR

Xerox Corporation

Xionics Document Technologies,
Inc.

C O N T E N T S

This issue's cover image Copyright © 1997 Photodisc, Inc.

C O N T E N T S

C O N T E N T S

When Tim Berners-Lee released his first version of the Web, it quickly developed a reputation as a versatile and convenient tool for accessing mission-critical data at the European Laboratory for Particle Physics (CERN). The Web tools he developed were widely hailed as the best way to access the CERN-wide telephone directory. Not for publishing papers, not for promoting HTML, not for inventing a unified Internet addressing scheme—the early Web was renowned as a gateway for the *Ph* phone directory system.

Of course, the impact of Tim's innovations became clearer as they spread among sister institutions and through the outside world for more "traditional" Web applications. But is it really an accident that the Web took off as a "mere" gateway to another information system? This issue, *Scripting Languages: Automating the Web*, testifies that, in fact, gateways and automated information services are a critical element of the Web. The Web's ability to integrate other Internet services and information sources under its common user interface and transport protocol is the central synergy argument behind its explosive growth. Successful Web clients, such as NCSA Mosaic, incorporated the same lesson by offering unified "front-ends" to a whole collection of services. Successful Web programmers learned quickly how to use interactive scripting and automated database reporting to publish catalogs and transaction systems. Successful Web designers leverage the latest-and-greatest client scripting tools to animate and customize Web pages. This issue is about that entire spectrum of interactive automation technology.

Automatability

Broadly construed, W3C's mission is to realize the full potential of the Web. MIT LCS Director Michael Dertouzous began writing about some of that potential before the Web was ever imagined. In his new book, *What Will Be*, he captures 15 years of speculations about the Information Marketplace, where computers do the drudge work of the Information Age just as bulldozers did for the Industrial Age. The key is automating and eliminating the tedious, unsophisticated analysis we currently waste human talents on: filtering and sorting, searching and sampling, bidding and settlement. Computers cannot replace the creative spark—reading, writing, seducing—but they are there to do our bidding for systematic actions. The Web, as the first system worthy of being judged as a marketplace, is also emerging as a computing platform in its own right.

The philosophical insight the Web rests upon is automatability—not automation. The Web is a successful social system because it's community insists on standards for how to instrument the Web, rather than on particular languages or APIs. Using the standard <OBJECT> and <SCRIPT> tags, anyone can extend HTML to cope with a new embedded-object model or scripting language. Using CGI, webmasters are free to provide extended functionality with any tools they'd like. Automatability is about making some common semantic understanding visible to the infrastructure for the next layer of experimentation. Even Cascading Style Sheets are a form of automation, by mechanically applying its idiosyncratic formatting rules to standardized HTML semantics—after all, CSS1 is only one of many formatting contenders like JavaScript Style Sheets (JSS) and Document Style Semantics and Specification Language (DSSL).

W3C's Role

The World Wide Web Consortium's dedication to technical diversity over automatable standards mirrors that of the Web community's. In the context of *Scripting Languages: Automating the Web*, it means that W3C focuses on horizontal enabling technology—such as how to embed any script in HTML—rather than vertical languages and tools. This is not just a sign of officious neutrality between sparring members, but a genuine and principled stance. Namely, W3C is in no position to annoint winners and losers for the wild and wooly Web market, nor should anyone else at this nascent stage of Web growth. Furthermore, the Web inherently supports diversity and vigorous community-formation; it is in the collective interest (if not particular companies' interests) to remain neutral.

W3C came to a similar conclusion regarding its Mobile Code activities: many Members fervently advocated technologies like Java, ActiveX, Curl, Inferno, even Kaleida's ill-fated ScriptX. W3C's contribution was to step back and "route around" the messy market debate by concentrating on enabling hooks like the <OBJECT> tag and better labeling and digital signaure support for *any* piece of mobile code. Today, that approach applies to a similar battle for "Dynamic HTML"—VBScript versus JavaScript versus WebScript versus . . . and the list goes on.

Degrees of Freedom

The Web is a genuine computing platform because it can reach far beyond file distibution to expose several automatable "pivot points" in the design of an archetypal transaction. We can add scriptable and extensible behavior to the Web in the following ways:

1. As a user front-end

2. Within the Web client-user interface

3. Within the Web server programming interface

4. As a back-end gateway to other services

Adding intelligence at each of these junctures can help us build powerful, lively, efficient, and versatile information services over the Web. Best of all, these services are composable: no sooner than one server publishes a whiz-bang airline reservation interface than another can provide a multi-airline low-fare search engine and a third can automatically author and publish a low-fare newsletter.

In this issue, we are proud to present work at each of these pivot points. Up front, we asked Larry Wall and Tom Christiansen about the pervasive impact of Perl on Web automation, as well as reporting on the joint W3C/IETF work towards smart clients for distributed authoring and versioning. "W3C Reports" describes client innovations in *Amaya* and new specifications for integrating scripting into HTML. Nine "Technical Papers" collectively address scripting language options for clients and server extensibility.

Looking Ahead

The *World Wide Web Journal* continues to refine its editorial balance. This issue extends our commitment to staying relevant to wide technical readership. As you may know, this Journal was launched with some intention of being a traditional, refereed academic journal. Like most Web institutions though, the Journal has evolved into a new and relatively unprecedented form under the Web's intense pressure for timeliness, scope, and breadth. The Journal has shifted to a more strongly thematic, more accessible format with articles ranging from how-to through to advanced R&D. Those changes, beginning with the Winter 1997 issue, "Advancing HTML: Style and Substance," have paid off on the bottom line, too.

Among the people that reviewed papers and helped with this issue were Ron Petrusha, Andy Oram, Frank Willison, and Linda Mui of O'Reilly & Associates and Dave Sims of Songline Studios. Some of the articles in this issue also appear in Web Review, an online magazine for Web developers and designers, at *http://webreview.com*. We'd also like to thank Jukka Korpela for his comments on the article *What's New in HTML 3.2: Formalizing Enhancements to HTML 2.0*, which appeared in the Winter 1997 issue. His letter and response from author Chuck Musciano, along with errata, archives of past issues, and news of forthcoming issues can be found at *http://www.w3.org/pub/WWW/Journal*. We welcome your comments and suggestions.

We have similarly high hopes for this issue and Summer 1997's "Web Security: A Matter of Trust." ■

Rohit Khare
khare@w3.org
March 1997, Cambridge, Massachusetts

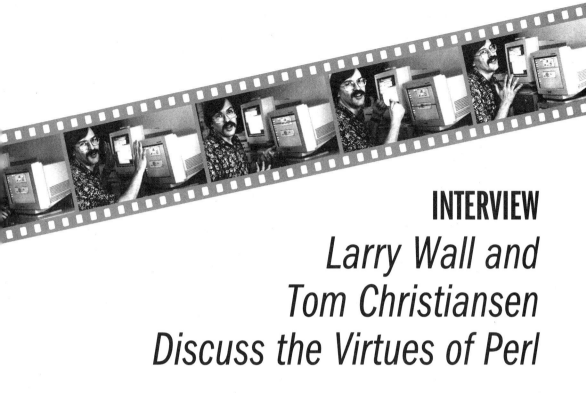

INTERVIEW
Larry Wall and Tom Christiansen Discuss the Virtues of Perl

Larry Wall (shown above) has been developing free software for years, and developing a following that is unlike any other. Once confined to the world of UNIX, Larry and his fellow Perl hackers now find themselves in the middle of something much bigger: the World Wide Web. Perl is the language of choice for Webmasters everywhere. Quietly and almost invisibly, it has been getting jobs done on the Web. In this interview, Dale Dougherty talks to Larry Wall and Tom Christiansen about the language, the culture, and the community of Perl.

DD: *If I'm not a programmer, is Perl a good place to start? Tom?*

TC: It certainly can be a good place to start. The amount of Perl it takes to do CGI programming or Spider work, or the simple text munching and document preparation that Perl affords you, really isn't too tough. It's especially nice because we have some canned libraries and modules and scripts to help you so you don't have to do it on your own. Real smart people sat around in ivory towers for years doing the hard work—now you get to use the fruits of their labors.

LW: On top of that, let me add that there's a cultural thing going in the Perl culture which allows you to use a subset of Perl. If you use a subset of C++ corresponding to C then people tend to laugh at you: I didn't really like that. So I sort of laid down the law and said that anyone can use a subset of Perl and that's okay—it's officially okay. We will encourage you to do that because it's a natural language concept. We don't expect a five-year-old to speak with the same diction that we expect from a 50 year old. By the same token, use a subset of Perl that is appropriate to the task, and if you learn something more later on, that's okay. We don't expect you to know it all.

What Kind of Language is Perl?

DD: *Okay, let's talk about Perl as a language. Where does it fit? It's talked about as a scripting language, and obviously came out of UNIX. Larry, you take pride that it breaks the mold of traditional computer languages.*

LW: It came to me way back when—it seems like a long time ago now, but I was working in the UNIX universe, and the UNIX universe at that time consisted of C and Shell—not to be confused with "C-shell." And either you programmed in C or you programmed in Shell. The revelation that came to me one day was that these were not two halves of a whole, but rather two extremes on a two-dimensional graph.

C was good at getting down into the innards of things, but wasn't very good at whipping things up quickly. Whereas Shell was good at whipping things up quickly, but couldn't get down into the nitty-gritty stuff. So, if those are two-dimensional on a graph, then there's this big blank area out there where, well, where Perl is now. So that's the origin of Perl.

When I decided to fill that [blank area], it occurred to me that I should design the language I wanted. Rather than just designing another language—we already have enough languages—I'd bring to it my unique background in linguistics, in music or art. So I took equal parts of computer science and linguistics and art and common sense. I'm very much

into synthesis, so the language that I designed is more synthetic.

An Expressive Language

DD: *You talk about a program as a work of art, rather than a mathematical construct. That might appeal to a set of people who develop Web pages and think in terms of expressiveness rather than simply elegant expression.*

LW: Traditional languages, the typical computer science-style language, has tried for the most part for minimalism. That is, they try to express in the least number of features everything that you might want to do.

DD: *C, for instance, is an example of a minimalist language. It has a very spare syntax, but is very difficult to learn, and you don't have very much help along the way. Why is Perl easier to learn and use than C?*

TC: That's easy. Perl is a lot easier to learn than C.

C is not like a lot of languages if you look at all the world's languages. But the languages that they teach you in school and that you're expected to use in the industry, from FORTRAN and Pascal to C and C++, all of these share in common the mis-feature of forcing the programmer to worry about all kinds of things that get in the way of expressing what you're trying to do. They get in the way of actually executing the algorithm.

You have to worry about two things that are just nuts: one is memory allocation and the other is data typing. And everything from FORTRAN to C++ bogs you down in that.

Now there are a lot of other languages in the world. Dennis Ritchey has said that, "People need to understand that C and Pascal are really the same language." Even if they are by Dennis' criteria, nonetheless Perl does things differently. It takes care of this crazy memory allocation business and also fluid data typing.

When you're dealing with text processing especially, the atomic chunk of data is a bunch of text. It is not a string, a data, or a 13-bit floating-point number. It is just a thing, and Perl is conducive to dealing with chunks the way a human thinks of it instead of bending over backwards to make it easy on the computer. We [should] optimize for human time above computer time, although we try to optimize computer time when we get a chance. The person has to come first.

It's All About Shortcuts

LW: Let me put a more philosophical spin on that. Perl is a language that is about shortcuts, and shortcuts are about going at an angle, in metaphorical terms.

Computer scientists have a term that they like to throw around, called "orthogonality," and that's what they mean when they talk about minimal languages. They visualize a problem space as having a certain number of dimensions, and they want to be able to give you coordinates to, say, go left 15 feet, and north so many feet, etc. They think that somehow or another that is making things easier for the computer and the human, but I don't buy that.

If you're in a park and you want to visit the restroom you don't go left 15 feet and 25 feet due north. You make a bee-line straight for the restroom. Humans love to take shortcuts, they love to optimize. What I've done is [like this]—there's a university somewhere where the first year they built it, they just planted grass; they didn't put in any sidewalks. Then the next year when they saw where all of the paths were worn, they put in all of the sidewalks where they already knew people wanted to go. Now those sidewalks did not go at right angles all of the time. What I'm trying to do with Perl is formalize the shortcuts people want to take.

TC: This is the difference between version 4 of Perl and version 5. In version 4, there weren't a lot of facilities for certain kinds of things that people were expecting to do—some more structured data types, etc. So Larry planted this sod that he called EVAL, so anytime people needed to use something in the language that wasn't there they just hacked it up with EVAL. Whereas with version 5, he watched what people were using EVALs for and now we don't need to do it because we have the underlying facilities—those diagonal tracks through the path—that's why we have multi-level data, etc.

DD: *You'd like to say that Perl is a diagonal language, not an orthogonal language.*

Gluing Things Together

DD: *Perl is interfacing with the OS . . .*

TC: It's interfacing with everything.

DD: *. . . as a "glue" language. What is it gluing together?*

LW: Anything that the user wants to glue together.

TC: Processes, system calls, files, remote connections, database functions, etc.

DD: *Why do you think this "glue" language, like Tim O'Reilly said, has become the work-horse of the Web?*

LW: I think it's sort of a matter of humility. There are many languages out there that came from various ivory towers, and they tend to keep to themselves and hold themselves aloof to the rest of the world—they don't want to sully their purity.

TC: Perl supports no purity.

LW: The Perl purity test not withstanding, however . . .

DD: *The people who use Perl kept finding problems to solve. The Web was a new problem space. Users tried it and found that it worked for them and began applying it. Obviously the early servers were all UNIX-based and there was a need to have some level of dynamic execution when the HTML document was fetched from the server.*

TC: They realized that in order to do dynamic pages they had to have some program executing, typically a CGI program. Perl is certainly the language of choice for CGI programming. With Perl, you could do rapid prototyping of tools for Web servers.

Perl's a good choice because you want to get your CGI script up on the Web server, and then change it again tomorrow. If you're writing an assembler, that's not very pleasant.

Perl is also—unless you work for those people doing the massive search engines who have trigabytes of data—the language of choice for what I call "spider work." This involves going out and finding documents or doing link checkers and all that—anything having both ends—the active content as well as the data analysis, where the data might be a Web document or address.

DD: *Perl's doing lot of the behind the scenes stuff on a Web site, having to do with the process of putting it all together.*

Data Munging

DD: *Let's talk about the data munging. Now we have access to lots and lots of information online, but relatively speaking, other than the browser, poor facilities for processing that data. If you wanted to keep track of something that's happening, and collect data for a report, that would be kind of difficult. Have you seen any applications of Perl in that area?*

TC: Certainly log analyzers were the first things people started to use.

DD: *Good characteristic—lots of data, most of it worthless—where you really want to apply programs to figure out what the patterns are that are worth observing.*

TC: Another interesting use of data munging is when you've got a whole tree that you're trying to maintain, you'd like to get a representation of what connects to what. It's very easy in Perl to go through a whole bunch of files and count up the URLs in each of them and then summarize them. For instance, "these all go to that URL," and figure out the relationships—"this has this many of that, and that has this many of the other thing."

So you're dealing with all kinds of separate little pages and inside them there are little bits of text that you need to pull out. It's not real easy

> *"I didn't design Perl for the Web because I didn't envision the Web—I wish I had. But it was sort of a natural for much of the Web activity because it is, first of all, among many other things, a text processing language."*

to pull them out with tools like *grep* (a UNIX utility) because that's not the level of granularity that you need. After you've started pulling out these pieces and files and collating them to make your charts, then all of a sudden you realize you also need to cross-reference this stuff with things outside my site on the Web. Well, *grep* is not going to go and fetch a URL for you no matter how much you ask it. On the other hand, that's really easy for Perl to do.

LW: I didn't design Perl for the Web because I didn't envision the Web—I wish I had. But it was sort of a natural for much of the Web activity because it is first of all, among many other things, a text processing language. That means taking text apart into little bits. It also means gluing text back together. So it is not only a data reduction language, it can also be viewed as a data production language. And in

fact, in CGI scripts, it is doing more of the production than the reduction.

Dynamic Web Sites

TC: A lot of people use Perl to generate their whole Web site. On *perl.com*, I've got about 3,000 to 3,500 pages that I didn't write—I wrote the program that wrote them. People are always asking me, "Oh, gosh Tom, what Web publishing system did you use to produce these phenomenal documents?" And the answer is, "Perl."

It's a roll-your-own application. There are commercial applications that do specific kinds of tasks, but more often than not, your unique idea of what has to be done doesn't fit into the pigeon holes that the commercial products provide you. So at some level, you have to paste something together yourself, and that's what Perl's great for doing.

LW: And Perl will often be used, not necessarily to write HTML directly, but it may be used to write other languages. Perl is being used to write C, Java, Visual Basic; this is where Perl shines.

DD: *One of the ways I've seen it used is where people create a custom super-set of HTML and then parse that set of tags to make replacements and do other things before sending the page out.*

LW: You can view the chunks of metadata, if you will, to be inside or outside of the document you're trying to produce.

The Culture of Perl

DD: *One thing I want to touch on that you said once, and it's obviously an important element to the success of Perl in the marketplace, is the Perl community. There really is a strong culture around Perl.*

LW: Cultured Perl?

DD: *Very good. We won't say "cult," but we'll say "culture." But it really is amazing and it's something that an individual starting to learn or apply Perl is able to tap. There are a lot of Perl resources online that you may not find for other programming environments.*

LW: Well, it was always part of the plan to build up a culture. I don't believe that a language can exist in isolation. It comes from my linguistics background. The users or speakers of a language evolve it into whatever they want it to be.

There is a lot of input into Perl that I did not put there. People have made many suggestions, and I've taken some of them and have rejected many more, though some people wouldn't think so. Perl is a living language— it's evolving all the time. Although we are now trying to stabilize the Perl core, I put in an extension mechanism into Perl 5 so that people could do this evolutionary thing while at the same time Perl is being stabilized.

Right from the start Perl was designed to evolve. One of the reasons for the funny characters on the front of variables names is because it protected the name spaces of the variables from reserved words and I could add

reserved words without breaking anybody's script. This sort of thing was intentional. Beyond that, I wanted to encourage esoteric input from the community.

I wanted the Perl community to function like a little bit of Heaven, where people are naturally helping each other. People want to help each other. They encourage each other, they give each other cool things . . .

TC: . . . They don't really expect anything in return for giving them those cool things. The free gifts.

LW: And perhaps some of that is from my theological background. But everything is grist for the mill.

The Magic of CPAN on perl.com

DD: *What is CPAN at perl.com?*

TC: It is a bit of Web "magic" that allows me to have a "virtual" transfer rate of 500-600 MB over a modem.

CPAN, not to be confused with the Congressional cable channel C-SPAN, is the Comprehensive Perl Archive Network. It is a collection of useful scripts, tips, tricks, traps, source code, library modules, documentation, precompiled binaries for non-native systems. These exist throughout the world.

perl.com provides you with a virtual interface to the CPAN. When you go to download the latest Perl source, what happens, with a little Apache magic and CGI scripting, is it redirects you to the nearest archive site. It says, "Hmm, he's coming from Taiwan. Perhaps it would be better for him to get the Perl from Taiwan rather than from Swaziland or something." So it does a little bit of origin inference. Of course, name space and DNS reversing is not actually network topology, but it works rather well—especially for people outside North America. Everybody in North America gets thrown in the North American pool. So it just picks the closest place and I do a dynamic redirect to get it from a close site. Which goes much faster than my very . . . slow . . . modem.

DD: *In CPAN, can I find sources for the Windows environment?*

TC: Yes you can. As distributed, Perl builds on virtually any flavor of UNIX, Plan-9, OS2, and VMS. However, in these, let's take CPAN as the top level. Right underneath that, you have a number of directories such as *source, modules, docs,* etc., but the one you're interested in right now is called *ports.* Underneath ports you find things such as MVS, or Amiga, or Windows, NT, Mac (the Mac port tracks very closely along the standard release). The Windows *port* doesn't track quite so closely, but we have reason to believe that as of the 5.004 release we will in fact be tracking very closely. But yes, you can get binaries, especially from the non-UNIX systems, from that *ports* directory. And of course, these can be quite large. Consequently it's extremely important that I redirect you to a faster site.

DD: *Again, at www.perl.com, in addition to the sources, you'll find some index to scripts?*

TC: You'll find a lot of different indexes, in fact, to both modules and scripts. Underneath that top-level CPAN directory there's a directory called *Scripts.* Inside that, they're organized by class, i.e., these are the Web-related scripts, these are the CISININ-related scripts.

Another top-level directory is *Modules.* The modules are not stand-alone programs the way the scripts are; these are the libraries that help you write a Web Spider, or shopping cart for CGI programming, or graphical programming, or database, or all kinds of things.

Java versus Perl

DD: *I'd like to talk about Java and Perl. Obviously we've heard a lot more press about Java and what it's going to do . . .*

TC: They have a marketing organization.

DD: *. . . and how it's going to transform every possible computing environment. Yet, as we've pointed out, it's a fair bet to say that Perl is more widely used on the Web. Here we have a freeware effort, this Perl community, a bunch of individuals working cooperatively very much in the style of the original Internet. Then you have Java, which comes out of Sun Microsystems—it is very much a commercial environment. People are making bets on it, they have a lot at stake. They're trying to say how Java will topple Microsoft, and that Java will do this, and that Java will do that. How does this make you feel?*

LW: It's a bit saddening to see a pretty decent language overhyped like Java has been. I think that Java will find its niche. Like you said, people are interested in seeing that Java is not the one solution. So it will level the playing field again.

DD: *What do you think Java's niche will be?*

LW: Applications development of a portable nature. But there will be people who do Perl also.

TC: I see Java's real niche as replacing, for many people, C++ as an applications language.

LW: Perl has always taken the low road. We don't do a lot of hype—although some people would disagree with that—but we don't have a marketing organization as Tom says.

DD: *Your marketing consists of slogans like, "Perl is the language for getting your job done," and "Perl makes easy things easy, and hard things possible." They are all in your book.*

TC: Perl and Java are fundamentally different languages. I'm not talking about dollar signs or semi-colons. I'm not talking about whether its byte or machine compiled, or just in time or Perl interpreted. What I'm talking about is that Java is a static language where the compiler can make a lot of inferences about whether you've been a good boy or not.

LW: You don't do rapid prototyping in Java.

TC: Ah, no. Where as Perl is a language that is fundamentally dynamic in nature.

LW: Failsoft.

TC: If you make a mistake, it tries its best. It doesn't just blow up and make you re-boot your Windows machine.

DD: *You mean when I download an applet, and it just kinda goes, "Bleah!"*

TC: Well, yeah. Or when you just run a program, if it's not like, "We read in one byte too many; I guess we're going to abort your whole program." Or, "Gosh, we didn't find that module, or that library, or that include file so we're going to die"—no.

Perl can recover from problems. Failures can be made noncatastrophic—it tries its best. Here's a case. You have a CGI program that was written to respond to one version of your form, then you update your form. The program and the form should be in sync but somebody's got a cached version of your form out there on the Web. Their reply comes back and it is an older version, and they're missing one or two fields. Some programs that use RPC calls would just die immediately. You try your best. With Perl, it is very easy making due with what you have.

Perl and Web Databases

DD: *You've talked about data reduction. And then data production in the sense of creating useful reports. It's a glue language.*

LW: I think that the biggest use of Perl nowadays for CGI scripting is to hook up the Web with databases. There is a tremendous amount of activity around using Perl as a database driver.

TC: We're not going to be real concrete on what a database is, though. Because almost anything on the Web is data, and the Web is about getting data from one place to users in another place, and wherever that data is, you can construe that to be a database. And Perl is great glue for connecting the users and the data.

WORK IN PROGRESS
People & Projects at W3C

THE "REAL" WEBTV
PHILIPP HOSCHKA AND REAL-TIME MULTIMEDIA

When Philipp Hoschka updated his Cannes Film Festival Web site last year, he had the opportunity to offer video clips of interviews with the festival's star actors and directors. The only problem was figuring out how he should do that.

Hoschka turned to MBone, a rather "traditional" way to present video on the web. Mbone, of course, is a broadcast system that transmits large amounts of data (like video) so that a minimal amount of bandwidth is actually used. Mbone answered his immediate need of broadcasting video, but still didn't provide the interactive aspect that he's looking to create on the Web.

Now Hoschka's on the forefront of developing new standards for real-time multimedia. As the activity leader of the real-time multimedia project at the World Wide Web Consortium, he's hard at work trying to establish a way for people to send and receive high-quality multimedia online—sort of a CD-ROM or interactive television for the Web. In October, he organized and chaired a W3C workshop, "Real-Time Multimedia and the Web," and he recently formed the "Real-Time Multimedia Working Group."

Hoschka and his new multimedia working group want to make it possible for Web developers to easily express things like, "five minutes into the presentation, show image X and keep it on the screen for ten seconds"—and have viewers download it just as easily. That synchronicity between audio, video, and graphic images is what Hoschka and the new working group will be hashing out in the coming months. He hopes to have the format specification and interoperable applications developed by the end of the year.

The concept of real-time multimedia is a hot one, with software developers, CD-ROM producers, the Web community, and groups working on audio/video-on-demand all scrambling to make their mode of transfer the best. Apple's Quicktime, Macromedia's Director, and Microsoft's Active X have all proposed some means of presenting real-time multimedia on the Web. But none of these is standard, and some (like Director) require knowledge of scripting to create multimedia pieces. With a simpler standard developed, more people will be able to design real-time multimedia presentations with the assurance that they can reach a wider audience more easily.

"People are calling for audio and video integrated into the Web, and also for having some sort of standardized animation format," says Hoschka. What format they use for standardizing the process is yet to be determined. However, each of the communities involved in the working group—coming from the CD-ROM, Web development, and audio/video on-demand industries—have something to contribute. For instance, the CD-ROM community has a lot of experience when it comes to support for creating real-time multimedia content. The Internet-based "audio/video on-demand" proponents can significantly contribute with

regard to transmitting real-time content over the Internet. And the Web community is most experienced with open formats—thus far for static multimedia documents, but soon with dynamic multimedia content.

Without the working group, there is a very real chance that each of these communities would go on developing their own multimedia formats—and form a chaotic mix of non-interoperable solutions to the problem. "Are they all going to have their own format, or are we all going to agree on one?" asks Hoschka. Obviously, he's hoping to have all three communities come to some sort of agreement by next year.

When that happens, it should definitively change the way the Web looks and works. According to a W3C activity statement on real-time multimedia content, "Industry analysts predict . . . that Web content will become similar to the content of today's multimedia CD-ROMs or even today's television programs. In other words, they believe that the Web will be turned into a distribution system for both interactive and continuous multimedia content, or real-time multimedia content."

Hoschka prefers to compare the concept of real-time multimedia to TV, since that's what most people are familiar with. "When you think about it, everybody surfs the TV, and that's where I think the word came from—you "surf" the Web.

"In CNN news broadcasts, if you see something that you want to know more about, there's nothing you can do about it. But if it's on the Web, you can click on it and find out more," says Hoschka. "It's going to be interactive in the same way that the Web is interactive. You can switch between the couch potato mode and the active mode very quickly . . . you can surf in a more meaningful way, because not only can you switch programs, but you can also find out more about what's interesting."

"Implementing the equivalent of a television program with Internet protocols such as today's version of HTTP is close to impossible," says Hoschka. "When many people want to see the same content at the same time, an individual copy has to be sent to each of the receivers. This is very expensive in terms of Internet bandwidth, and does not scale to the millions of people watching a television program."

Hoschka got his start in the field of audio and video transfer on the Web five years ago when he began working at INRIA's Internet research group.

He describes the tension that existed at the time between the classic Internet people and the up-and-coming Web community, and he says INRIA helped close the gap. "[INRIA has] been influential in audio and video on the Web . . . starting in 1992, when people thought the Internet couldn't handle that kind of transfer," says Hoschka. "It was pretty pioneering work, actually."

His interest in the field took a more personal turn in 1995, when he first decided to pay homage to the Cannes Film Festival. "I truly love the film festival . . . so in 1995, I thought, let's do a Web site. I edited it like a madman for ten days," says Hoschka. "I thought I'd be the only one doing it. Then, on the first day, I found there were about five other people who were doing it!"

Still, he was pleased with his results, and received a lot of positive feedback for the project. Then, in 1996, he was contacted by Mayra Langdon Riesman from Film Scouts about including clips of interviews she would conduct during the festival into his Web site. His "CannesCast" currently includes interviews with Rosanna Arquette, James Spader, David Cronenberg, Jennifer Jason Leigh, Robert Altman, and Bernardo Bertolucci.

Though he hasn't announced his plans yet, it appears the gears are turning within Hoschka's head for this coming "CannesCast" in May. While his real-time multimedia group is just getting started, he's already contemplating some changes to the site. "I hope to become more technologically advanced in 1997," he says.

— Kimberly Amaral

COLLABORATIVE AUTHORING
JIM WHITEHEAD AND THE WEBDAV GROUP

Consider this: You and several other coworkers are collaborating on a big report for work. Being the diligent employee that you are, you pull out your copy of the report on a Saturday and start revising it. But before you arrive at work the following Monday, someone else has gotten a hold of the report and made a few changes of her own. Now one of you has to either relinquish your changes or start over from scratch. There's just got to be some other way to develop in this environment. . . .

Enter Emmet James Whitehead, a Ph.D. candidate at the University of California, Irvine who these days finds himself consumed by these kinds of problems. Whitehead is also the chairman of WebDAV: the World Wide Web Distributed Authoring and Versioning group. WebDAV is actually an ad hoc group of developers who work on remote authoring tools, which formed last September. They currently work in cooperation with the World Wide Web Consortium, and are in the process of becoming part of the Internet Engineering Task Force.

Whitehead explains that the purpose of the WebDAV group is "to enhance the Web so that you can do remote editing of Web pages as well as do the browsing of Web pages that you can do now. There is also a collaborative aspect. It will work well for a single person editing Web pages, but it really shines when there are groups of people working on Web pages."

WebDAV technology deals with four main aspects of collaborative or distributed authoring:

- *Overwrite prevention*. If two people are working on the same document, how do you keep them from writing over each other's changes? WebDAV has proposed a "locking" mechanism on documents. So if you open a document with an intent to edit it, whenever someone else tries to edit it, they are "locked out." This insures that a document is only being edited by one person at a time.

- *Name space management*. Think of all the documents you have stored on your hard drive. Now narrow that list down to the documents on one partition, on one drive, or even in one folder. How these documents are arranged, and the grouping of them, is called a "name space." These "name spaces" also exist on the Web—that's how those really long URLs are derived. Using WebDAV technology, you could search an online directory within a certain "name space," locate the file you want, and then move or copy it. You could even copy a file to another URL, so that you can access it at its new location to edit it and have others work on it as well.

- *Metadata*, or information about information, includes descriptions of a document such as the author, date of creation and revisions, and who owns the copyright. This becomes especially handy for anyone who's ever searched for information on a particular star in the sky and come up with three hundred references to Keanu Reeves. The ability to search metadata documents will allow users to look for, say, just the author. This capability narrows searches and most likely will give you more relevant results.

- *Version management*, or revision control, is extremely useful whenever you need access to a version of a document other than the latest one. With version management, you could access an older version of a document and then get a list of all the changes that were made to it. Whitehead explains that this feature is especially needed by the legal community, which compares older versions of a law to the current version.

Whitehead equates all these capabilities to how a library works. Once you check out a library book, it is yours to read and make notes on. When you're finished, simply return it to the library (no late fees required), including all your notes. The document and all the notes are available for others to see, access, and edit as well.

But before more than one person can start editing a document, there has to be a way for everyone to have access to the same document and all its cumulative changes. The best way to do this, of course, is to place that document online, allowing people from across the globe—or the next cubicle over—to pull up that document and start editing it on their screen.

This isn't a new concept. In fact, the original concept of the Web included provisions for people to edit material they found online—not just be passive surfers. As early as 1990, a prototype Web editor and browser was running on NeXT-platform computers, where people could both read and write to Web content. Other browser/editor programs began to emerge: both NaviPress by NaviSoft and FrontPage by Vermeer hit the market in 1995, proclaiming dual browser/editor features. In

early 1996, these were purchased by America Online and Microsoft respectively, demonstrating some major marketing backup for this type of capability.

Once again, the problem of non-standard protocols began to emerge. People using FrontPage couldn't "publish" their creations on an AOLserver, or use AOLpress (another browser/editor tool) with the FrontPage server extensions. More complications are expected to emerge as Novell and Lotus recently announced their plans to offer Web servers with authoring support later this year.

Whitehead and the WebDAV group have already answered some of these concerns. They've come up with the requirements and standard protocol for software companies trying to develop browser/editor software. The aim—like the rationale behind standardizing the rest of the Web—is to allow people using any kind of machine or software to both read a document online, and then edit it. The reader then takes over even more control of the information provided online.

But let's say you're an author who's published something on the Web you don't want edited by others. For that situation, Whitehead explains, the WebDAV group is making sure their extensions can be used with current security extensions that are being developed by others.

The beauty of this entire approach is that it's essentially invisible to the user. No longer do you have to be an HTML or Web guru to edit or make notes on a document someone else has put online. "Using this capability will be largely transparent to users of the program," says Whitehead. "Once you find out what you want to edit, click Open and the program will use the Web to open that document. That document will pop up onto your screen and you can start editing."

You won't even need any new special software for this capability. Whitehead says they hope to have WebDAV technology working with the software you own and are accustomed to—like MicrosoftWord and Excel. WebDAV is working closely with representatives from Microsoft, Netscape, Novell, and Xerox to make this happen. They hope to finish their duties—planning out the specifications for across-the-board distributed authoring—by the first half of this year. Whitehead predicts that in just the first or second quarter of next year, consumers will start seeing products on the shelf that feature WebDAV technology.

"It will provide a standard collaboration infrastructure so people can start a project using their everyday, favorite tools. And if it turns out they have to start collaborating, they don't have to do anything different. They can use the same tools using the Web," says Whitehead.

The idea behind linking documents that weren't designed for the Web came to Whitehead years ago when he was writing software at Raytheon Company in Lexington, MA. "I had this insight that a lot of time was being spent while I was writing software looking up other related pieces of information . . . like making sure that a software met its require-

ments. So there's a lot of going back and forth between documents," he says.

"If all the information could be put online and you could capture the relationships between them and make them browse-able," his job would have been much easier. His situation planted the seed that would become the WebDAV project. It's also closely related to another project he's currently working on at UC Irvine: Chimera. Chimera's purpose is to provide hypertext capability for software development.

Whitehead's path towards both projects has actually been a winding one. During his three-year stay at Raytheon, he wrote software for a German air traffic control system, and the prototype of an airplane landing system. Usually, if someone makes a mistake writing a piece of software, the worst it could do is crash your system. If Whitehead made a mistake on his software, it could crash an airplane.

"Software itself is inherently safe, but when it starts controlling a system that interacts with the world, people could die," says Whitehead. That concern drove him to study security software at UC Irvine with faculty member Nancy Leveson. However, when he got there, Leveson had accepted a position at the University of Washington. Despite this, Whitehead decided to stay in the program and began working on the Chimera project.

Being in southern California has also allowed this 29-year-old some geographic benefits. Some of his favorite activities include "boogie-boarding" and barbecuing. The warm climate also provides the opportunity to garden year-round, something Whitehead has definitely taken advantage of. He formed an organic gardening group at UC Irvine, spending the last days of February planting a lemon tree, and waiting as his lettuce becomes almost ready to harvest. Whitehead admits that while being in graduate school may not be the best paying position in the world, "it gives you the freedom to work on what you like to do." It seems Whitehead is already well on his way toward a successful career doing just that.

– Kimberly Amaral

W3C Publishes Cascading Style Sheets Recommendation

DECEMBER 17, 1996, *Cambridge, Massachusetts*
W3C issues Cascading Style Sheets, Level 1 as a W3C Recommendation. CSS1 is a set of tools to help Web designers specify page presentation properties such as fonts, colors, and margins. One style sheet can apply to all Web pages on a site, simplifying maintenance of large sites. Microsoft and Netscape will both include support for CSS1 in the 4.0 releases of their browsers; several other W3C Members and vendors including Adobe, SoftQuad, and Grif say they will also add support. *http://www.w3.org/pub/WWW/Press/CSS1-REC-PR.html*

Digital Signature Initiative Initial Implementation Phase Meetings

FEBRUARY 4-5, 1997, *Redwood Shores, California*
The Digital Signature Initiative (DSig) is developing signed, machine-readable assertions that can help users decide what to trust on the Web: safe applets, accurate price lists, original press releases, and more. These meetings marked the transition from the design to the implementation of signature labels. Several W3C Members have participated in the decisions to use PICS rating systems and elements of the base digital signature cryptography suite. *http://www.w3.org/pub/WWW/Security/DSig/Overview.html*

W3C Endorses HTML 3.2 as a Recommendation

JANUARY 14, 1997, *Cambridge, Massachusetts*
Developed throughout 1996 by W3C together with industry leaders IBM, Microsoft, Netscape Communications, Novell, SoftQuad, Spyglass and Sun Microsystems, HTML 3.2 adds features already widely deployed in client software, such as tables, applets, text flow around images, superscripts and subscripts, and backwards compliability with earlier HTML standards. W3C continues its work on HTML extensions for multimedia objects, scripting, style sheets, layout, forms, higher quality printing, and math. *http://www.w3.org/pub/WWW/Press/HTML32-REC-PR.html*

Jigsaw 1.0 Released

JANUARY 13, 1997, *Sophia-Antipolis, France*
This marks the first complete release of Jigsaw, W3C's experimental Java-based Web server. It is fully HTTP/1.1 compliant and includes a complete Web caching system, both of which can dramatically increase total Web performance. *http://www.w3.org/pub/WWW/Jigsaw*

World Economic Forum

JANUARY 30–FEBRUARY 4, 1997, *Davos, Switzerland*

Tim Berners-Lee represented W3C at the annual meeting of the World Economic Forum (WEF), a nonprofit organization that brings together leaders in government, business, and academia. The subtitle of the 1997 meeting was "The Networked Society," and one of the highlights was the launch of the world's most exclusive intranet, a global web of WEF movers and shakers. *http:// www.weforum.org/, http://search.nytimes.com/web/docsroot/library/cyber/euro/012597euro. html#1*

Results of Web Performance Study Released

FEBRUARY 1, 1997

After months of detailed research, W3C released its experiments about the combined effect of several recent W3C Recommendations and IETF Proposed Standards on Web performance. W3C demonstrated significant overall timing improvements when using HTTP/1.1 pipelining, PNG, and CSS1 Style Sheets. The report builds on earlier work presented at the San José IETF meeting in December and the London W3C Advisory Committee meeting in January. John Markoff publicized the results in the *New York Times* on February 16, followed by reports on MSNBC and in many trade publications. *http://www.w3.org/pub/WWW/Protocols/HTTP/Performance/Pipeline.html*

Amaya Source Code Public Release (0.95 beta)

FEBRUARY 10, 1997, *Grenoble, France*

Amaya is both a browser and an authoring tool specifically conceived to serve as a testbed client, to experiment and demonstrate new Web protocols and formats as well as new extensions to existing ones. A testbed client must be versatile enough to allow a wide range of experiments and demonstrations, so Amaya was designed as an active client; one that not only retrieves documents from the Web and presents them to the user, but also works as an authoring tool that allows an author to create new documents, to edit existing ones, and to publish these documents on remote Web servers. This issue of the Web Journal includes an introduction to Amaya. *http://www.w3.org/pub/WWW/Amaya*

HTML & CSS Working Group Meetings

FEBRUARY 24, 1997, *Sun Valley, Idaho*
The newly formed HyperText Markup Language and Cascading Style Sheets & Formatting Properties Working Groups have been launched out of the former HTML Editorial Review Board. These two groups are responsible for shepherding the future evolution of these technologies. Several current proposals were discussed, including printing, fonts, aural rendering, and new HTML tags. *http://www.w3.org/pub/WWW/MarkUp/Group/* (W3C Members only)

Automated Firewall Traversal and Collections Using Signed Assertions

FEBRUARY 26, 28, *Cupertino, California*
W3C hosted two meetings about applications of digitally signed assertions at JavaSoft. The first focused on tools and rules administrators expect to make regarding automated trust decisions at the Firewall. The second acknowledges that trust labels work for ensembles of related resources, not lone applets. As part of this project, W3C is developing Web Collections for jointly presenting trust metadata. *http://www.w3.org/pub/WWW/Security/DSig/*

Mathematical Markup Working Group Meeting

MARCH 10-11, 1997, *Cambridge, Massachusetts*
After more than a year of in-depth study of the issues, and the development of several software prototypes, the group has agreed on a core proposal for HTML Math. The proposal provides a language that describes the visual presentation of research-level mathematics. Optional content tagging allows for encoding the mathematical content with sufficient precision that HTML Math can be used for communication between mathematical software, such as computer algebra packages, or for rendering in other media, such as speech synthesis for the visually impaired. *http://www.w3.org/pub/WWW/MarkUp/Math/WG, http://www.ams.org/html-math/*

Synchronized Multimedia Working Group Meeting

MARCH 19-20, 1997, *Cupertino, California*
The recently formed working group aims to describe protocols and formats for synchronized, real-time streaming multimedia on the WWW. The initial meeting at Apple focused on refining the Charter and building upon last summer's Workshop in the same area. Group leader Phillip Hoschka has a W3C Report on the area in this issue and also discusses his plans and goals in this issue's People and Projects. *http://www.w3.org/pub/WWW/AudioVideo/Synch-call.html*

Web Accessibility Initiative Launch

APRIL 6, 1997, *Santa Clara, California*

After careful worldwide groundwork, W3C took a leading role in making the Web more accessible to people with disabilities, including technology, guidelines, and education. US President Clinton endorsed the W3C's Web Accessibility Initiative (WAI) Project and W3C's International Program Office (IPO). WAI was launched in conjunction with WWW6, whose conference theme is also accessibility. *http://www.w3.org/pub/WWW/Disabilities/*

Sixth International World Wide Web Conference

APRIL 7-11, 1997, *Santa Clara, California*

The Sixth annual WWW conference takes place in the heart of Silicon Valley. W3C staff and members, active throughout the conference's history, participate in workshops and tutorials, an official W3C conference track, Developer's Day sessions, and several adjacent W3C Member meetings. *http://www.w3.org/pub/Conferences/WWW6/*

Electronic Commerce Interest Group Meeting
Security Interest Group Meeting

APRIL 11-12, 1997, *Santa Clara, California*

As part of W3C's new Process, Interest Groups allow our Members to study and debate developments in broad areas of Web technology. On Friday, Electronic Commerce issues were discussed in a split meeting at Developer's Day and a private W3C session. Presentations focused on JEPI (the Joint Electronic Payments Initiative), IBM's MiniPay experiment, and others. Similarly, on Saturday, W3C held a Security meeting focusing on certificates, digital signatures, and trust management. *http://www.w3.org/pub/WWW/Payments,   http://www.w3.org/pub/WWW/Security*

W3C Advisory Committee Meeting

JUNE 18-19, 1997, *Tokyo, Japan*

Official member representatives convene to hear updates from the W3C's director and staff on various areas of activity and plans for the future. This meeting marks the debut of our newest host institution, Keio University.

The Web Consortium is dedicated to preserving and enhancing diversity on the Web—not just of human conversations and communities, as reflected by its Technology & Society Domain work on PICS and Public Policy, but of technologies as well. Some technologies are absolute, like URLs and semantic markup; but in others W3C enforces vigilant neutrality. In the fast-moving battle of scripting languages and Web automation tools, W3C's primary goal is to evolve the Web infrastructure to support experimentation.

The HTML Working Group is developing the first line of defense by allowing scripting languages to be transported within HTML documents. The latest Working Draft in this area reflects nearly final consensus from W3C and a host of Member organizations, including Netscape and Microsoft. Dave Raggett's "Client-Side Scripting and HTML" specification clearly demonstrates how to integrate locally executable scripts into today's HTML documents. In the future, the new W3C Document Object Model Working Group may follow up with more detailed specifications detailing how to control HTML elements within a document, something that is currently specific to each scripting language API.

W3C is also pushing its automatability agenda with its flagship Web client, Amaya, *which was recently released to the public complete with source code. Vincent Quint and Irène Vatton's "An Introduction to Amaya" explains how it supports embeddable objects, plug-in formatters, and other extensible features.* Amaya, *as both browser and editor, is part of a new generation of smart Web clients that will become the front line in Web automation. In the future, automatable Web front-ends can work with users to support distributed group collaboration, agents that seek out new information, and "push" messaging.*

Last, Philipp Hoschka reports on W3C's brand new initiatives in supporting real-time information delivery, synchronization, and integration of multimedia within the Web. Just as the disabled, for instance, have a right to expect a Web infrastructure that can deliver alternate forms of content for them, authors have the right to express themselves using appropriate media over the Web—and W3C is committed to providing diversity to enable this. The hottest new technologies are not just static content forms (HTML, PDF, and so on), but dynamic interaction and streaming multimedia. Along with scripting languages, this area will evolve to enliven the user experience, recapturing the expressivity of CD-ROM–based multimedia applications, and creating Web communities rather than merely passive entertainment.

CLIENT-SIDE SCRIPTING AND HTML

Dave Raggett

Abstract

The HyperText Markup Language (HTML) is a simple markup language used to create hypertext documents that are portable from one platform to another. HTML documents are SGML documents with generic semantics that are appropriate for representing information from a wide range of applications. This specification extends HTML to support locally executable scripts including JavaScript, VBScript, and other scripting languages and systems.

Status of This Document

This is a W3C Working Draft for review by W3C HTML-ERB members. It will be made public immediately following a yes vote by the ERB.

Introduction

This specification extends HTML to support client-side scripting of HTML documents and objects embedded within HTML documents. Scripts can be supplied in separate files or embedded directly within HTML documents in a manner independent of the scripting language. Scripts allow HTML forms to process input as it is entered: to ensure that values conform to specified patterns, to check consistency between fields and to compute derived fields.

Scripts can also be used to simplify authoring of active documents. The behavior of objects inserted into HTML documents can be tailored with scripts that respond to events generated by such objects. This enables authors to create compelling and powerful Web content. This specifica- tion covers extensions to HTML needed for client-side scripting but leaves out the architectural and application programming interface issues for how scripting engines are implemented and how they communicate with the document and other objects on the same page.

The SCRIPT Element

The content model for the SCRIPT element (shown in Example 1) is defined as CDATA. In this kind of element, only one delimiter is recog- nized by a conforming parser: the end tag open (ETAGO) delimiter (i.e., the string </). The rec- ognition of this delimiter is constrained to occur only when immediately followed by an SGML name start character (`[a-zA-Z]`). All characters that occur between the SCRIPT start tag and the first occurrence of ETAGO in such a context must be provided to the appropriate script engine.

Note that all other SGML markup (such as com- ments, marked sections, etc.) appearing inside a SCRIPT element are construed to be actual char- acter content of the SCRIPT element and not

Example 1

```
<!-- SCRIPT is a character-like element for embedding script code
     that can be placed anywhere in the document HEAD or BODY -->

<!ELEMENT script - - CDATA>
<!ATTLIST script
      type       CDATA   #IMPLIED -- media type for script language --
      language   CDATA   #IMPLIED -- predefined script language name --
      src        %URL    #IMPLIED -- URL for an external script --
      >
```

parsed as markup. A particular script engine may choose to treat such markup as it wishes; however, a script engine should document such treatment.

The restriction on appearance of the ETAGO delimiter may cause problems with script code that wishes to construct HTML content in the code. For example, the following code is invalid due the to presence of the </EM> characters found inside of the SCRIPT element:

```
<SCRIPT type="text/javascript">
    document.write ("<EM>This won t
    work</EM>")
</SCRIPT>
```

A conforming parser would treat the </EM> data as an end tag and complain that it was an end tag for an element not opened, or perhaps actually close an open element. In any case, it is recognized as markup and not as data.

In JavaScript, this code can be expressed legally as follows by ensuring that the apparent ETAGO delimiter does not appear immediately before an SGML name start character:

```
<SCRIPT type="text/javascript">
    document.write ("<EM>This will
    work</EM>")
</SCRIPT>
```

In Tcl this looks like:

```
<SCRIPT type="text/tcl"> document
    write "<EM>This will work</EM>"
</SCRIPT>
```

In VBScript, you can avoid the problem with the Chr() function—for example:

```
"<EM>This will work<\" & Chr(47) +
    "EM>"
```

Each scripting language should recommend language-specific support for resolving this issue.

The following describe the attributes used with SCRIPT elements, all of which are optional:

TYPE

The Internet media type specifying the scripting language—for instance, **type="text/ javascript"** or **type="text/vbscript"**.

LANGUAGE

Names the scripting language using well-known identifiers—for instance, "JavaScript" or "VBScript".

SRC

The optional SRC attribute gives a URL for an external script. If a SRC attribute is present, the content of the SCRIPT element should be ignored.

HTML documents can include multiple SCRIPT elements, which can be placed in the document HEAD or BODY. This allows script statements for a form to be placed near to the corresponding FORM element. Note that some script engines evaluate script statements dynamically as the document is loaded, so that there is the possibility that references to objects occurring later in the document will fail.

If authors include script elements with different scripting languages in the same document, user agents should attempt to process statements in each such language. This corresponds to programs with some procedures written in one language and others in another language—for example, C and FORTRAN.

Default Scripting Language

The default scripting language in the absence of TYPE or LANGUAGE attributes can be specified by a META element in the document HEAD—for example:

```
<META HTTP-EQUIV="Content-Script-
    Type" CONTENT="text/tcl">
```

where the CONTENT attribute specifies the media type for the scripting language, and the HTTP-EQUIV attribute is the literal string **Content-Script-Type**. If there are several such META elements, the last one determines the scripting language.

In the absence of such a META element, the default can be set by a Content-Script-Type HTTP header in the server response—for example:

```
Content-Script-Type: text/tcl
```

If there are several such headers, the last one takes precedence over earlier ones.

NOTE

In the absence of either a META element or an HTTP header, many user agents assume the default scripting language to be JavaScript.

Self-Modifying Documents

Some scripting languages permit script statements to be used to modify the document as it is being parsed. For instance, the HTML document:

```
<title>Test Document</title>
<script type="text/javascript">
    document.write("<p><b>Hello
        World!</b>")
</script>
```

Has the same effect as the document:

```
<title>Test Document</title>
<p><b>Hello World!</b>
```

From the perspective of SGML, each script element is evaluated by the application and can be modeled as a two-step process:

1. Dynamically defining an anonymous CDATA entity; corresponding to the combined text written by all of the **document.write** or equivalent statements in the script element.

2. Referencing the entity immediately after parsing the script end tag.

HTML documents are constrained to conform to the HTML document type definition both before processing any script elements and after processing all script elements.

The NOSCRIPT Element

```
<!ELEMENT noscript - -
    (%body.content)>
```

The content of this element is rendered only when the user agent doesn't support client-side scripting, or doesn't support a scripting language used by preceding script elements in the current

document. It gives authors a means to provide an invitation to upgrade to a newer browser, and is designed to work with downlevel browsers. The NOSCRIPT element can be placed anywhere you can place an HTML DIV element.

```
<NOSCRIPT>
<P>This document works
    best with script enabled
    browsers
</NOSCRIPT>
```

Examples of Event Handlers using SCRIPT

You can include the handler for an event in an HTML document using the SCRIPT element. Here is a VBScript for a text field:

```
<INPUT NAME=edit1 size=50>
<SCRIPT TYPE="text/vbscript">
  Sub edit1_changed()
    If edit1.value = "abc" Then
      button1.enabled = True
    Else
      button1.enabled = False
    End If
  End Sub
</SCRIPT>
```

Here is the same example using Tcl:

```
<INPUT NAME=edit1 size=50>
<SCRIPT TYPE="text/tcl">
  proc edit1_changed {} {
    if {[edit value] == abc} {
    button1 enable 1
    } else {
    button1 enable 0 }
  }
    edit1 onChange edit1_changed
</SCRIPT>
```

Here is a JavaScript example for event binding within a script: first, a simple click handler:

```
<script language=JavaScript>
  function my_onclick() {
      . . .
  }
  document.form.button.onclick =
    my_onclick
</script>
```

Here's a more interesting window handler:

```
<script language=JavaScript>
  function my_onload() {
```

```
        . . .
    }
    var win = window.open("some/other/
        URL")
    if (win) win.onload =  my_onload
</script>
```

In Tcl this looks like:

```
<script language=tcl>
    proc my_onload {} {
        . . .
    }
    set win [window open "some/other/
        URL"]
    if {$win != ""} {
        $win onload my_onload
    }
</script>
```

Scoping of Object Names

Scripting engines are responsible for binding object references in scripts to objects associated with documents. Script engines may support more than one language. This allows handlers to be written in one language, and the event binding to be defined in another, thereby avoiding the limitations of particular languages.

Some scripting languages like VBScript provide language conventions for binding objects that source events to script functions that handle events. Other languages typically allow you a run time mechanism to set up such bindings, e.g., to register call-backs, or a way to poll for events and dispatch them to appropriate handlers.

How do scripts reference objects? In many cases objects associated with HTML elements such as form fields can be identified by virtue of the document markup, e.g. the tag names and attribute values. HTML ID attributes provide identifiers that are unique throughout a given document, while NAME attributes for elements defining form fields are limited in scope to the enclosing FORM element.

Scripting systems may allow authors to script objects that occur within an object associated with an OBJECT or IMG element. Document

frames allow one document to be nested in another. Script handlers could be placed in a parent document and used to control the behaviour of a child document. Scripts may also be used for objects external to documents, such as the user agent or other applications. A particularly simple form of scripting is to just wire up objects that source events with ones that sink events. One event may be multicast to several recipient objects.

One way to deal with naming is to introduce language-specific naming conventions—for example, `document.form1.button1` as used by JavaScript. Another is to rely on the context in which a SCRIPT element is located to guide search for a named object. For instance, if the SCRIPT element is within a FORM element, objects associated with form elements with matching NAME values may be sought in preference to elements with matching ID values.

Some scripting languages, such as VBScript, limit the scope of references to a given module, but don't provide language specific means for defining modules. If a module is associated with an HTML document then element ID values can be used for binding handlers to objects. If the module is associated with an HTML form, then form field NAME attribute values could in principle be used by the script engine to unambiguously bind handlers to objects by placing the handlers in a SCRIPT element within the associated FORM element.

Intrinsic Events

A number of common events can be handled using attributes placed on the HTML elements associated with the object generating the event. The attribute names for intrinsic events are case insensitive. The attribute value is a scripting language dependent string. It gives one or more scripting instructions to be executed *document. write* or equivalent statements in intrinsic event handlers create and write to a new document rather than modifying the current one.

In the following example, userName is a required text field. When a user attempts to leave the field, the OnBlur event calls a JavaScript function to confirm that userName has an acceptable value.

```
<INPUT NAME="userName"
  onBlur="validUserName(this.value)">
```

Here is another JavaScript example:

```
<INPUT NAME="num"
  onChange="if (!checkNum(this.
    value, 1, 10))
      {this.focus();this.select();}
        else {thanks()}"
  VALUE="0">
```

Scripting language

The scripting language assumed for intrinsic events is determined by the default scripting language as specified above for the SCRIPT element.

SGML parsing of intrinsic event handler attributes

The script attributes for intrinsic events are defined as CDATA. The SGML processing of CDATA attribute values requires that:

1. Entity replacement occur within the attribute value; and

2. The attribute value be delimited by the appearence LIT (") or LITA (')

The literal delimiter that terminates the attribute value must be the same as the delimited used to initiate the attribute value. Given these lexical restrictions, the delimiters LIT or LITA, ERO (entity reference open—&), and CRO (character reference open—&#) may not freely occur as script code within a script event handler attribute. To resolve this issue, it is recommended that script event handler attributes always use LIT delimiters and that occurrences of quote marks (") and ampersands (&) inside an event handler attribute be written as follows:

```
"  should be written as "&quot;"
   or as "&#34;"
&  should be written as "&amp;" or
   as "&#38;"
```

For example:

```
<INPUT NAME="num"
  onChange="if (compare(this.value,
    "help")) {gethelp()}"
  VALUE="0">
```

Note that SGML permits LITA (') to be included in attribute strings quoted by LIT ("), and vice versa. The following is therefore okay:

```
"this is fine " and so is "this"
```

The following is an example of how intrinsic events are specified in the HTML document type definition:

```
<!ATTLIST SELECT
    name       CDATA       #REQUIRED
    size       NUMBER      #IMPLIED
    multiple   (multiple)  #IMPLIED
    onFocus    CDATA       #IMPLIED
    onBlur     CDATA       #IMPLIED
    onChange   CDATA       #IMPLIED
    >
```

The set of intrinsic events

The set of intrinsic events are listed below together with the HTML elements they can be used with. This set is expected to grow slightly:

onLoad

A load event occurs when the browser finishes loading a window or all frames within a FRAMESET. The onLoad event handler executes the scriptlet when a load event occurs. This attribute can only be used with BODY or FRAMESET elements.

onUnload

An unload event occurs when you exit a document. The onUnload event handler executes the scriptlet when an unload event occurs. This attribute can only be used with BODY or FRAMESET elements.

onClick

A click event occurs when an anchor or form field is clicked. The onClick event handler executes the scriptlet when a click event occurs. This event is generated by buttons, checkboxes, radio buttons, hypertext links, reset and submit buttons. This attribute can only be used with INPUT and anchor elements.

onMouseOver

This event is sent as the mouse is moved onto an anchor. This attribute can only be used with anchor and AREA elements.

onMouseOut

This event is sent as the mouse is moved out of an anchor or textarea element. This attribute can only be used with anchor and AREA elements.

onFocus

A focus event occurs when a field gains the input focus by tabbing or clicking with the mouse. Selecting within a field results in a select event, not a focus event. This attribute can only be used with the SELECT, INPUT, and TEXTAREA elements.

onBlur

A blur event occurs when a form field loses the input focus. This attribute can only be used with the SELECT, INPUT, and TEXTAREA elements.

onSubmit

A submit event occurs when a user submits a form. This may be used to control whether the form's contents are actually submitted or not. For instance, JavaScript won't submit the form if a scriptlet for the onSubmit event returns false. This attribute can only be used with the FORM element.

onSelect

A select event occurs when a user selects some of the text within a single or multiline text field. This attribute can only be used with the INPUT and TEXTAREA elements.

onChange

A change event occurs when a form field loses the input focus and its value has been modified. This attribute can only be used with the SELECT, INPUT, and TEXTAREA elements.

NOTE

Some user agents support onMouseover, onMouseOut, and onClick on a much wider variety of elements, not just the elements listed above.

Reserved Syntax for HTML CDATA Attributes

This specification reserves syntax for the future support of script macros in HTML CDATA attributes. The intention is to allow attributes to be set depending on the properties of objects that appear earlier on the page. The syntax is:

```
attribute = "... &{ macro body }; ...
"
```

The remainder of this section describes current practice for the use of script macros, but is not a normative part of this specification.

Current Practice for Script Macros

The macro body is made up of one or more statements in the default scripting language (as per instrinsic event attributes). The semicolon following the right brace is always needed, as otherwise the right brace character (}) is treated as being part of the macro body. Its also worth noting that quote marks are always needed for attributes containing script macros.

The processing of CDATA attributes proceeds as follows:

1. The SGML parser evaluates any SGML entities—for example, >

2. Next the script macros are evaluated by the script engine.

3. Finally the resultant character string is passed to the application for subsequent processing.

Note that macro processing takes place when the document is loaded (or reloaded) but isn't redone when the document is resized or repainted, etc.

Here are some examples using JavaScript. The first one randomizes the document background color:

```
<BODY BGCOLOR= &{randomrbg()}; >
```

Perhaps you want to dim the background for evening viewing:

```
<BACKGROUND SRC= &{if(Date.
    getHours > 18)...}; >
```

The next example uses JavaScript to set the coordinates for a client-side image map:

```
<MAP NAME=foo>
    <AREA SHAPE="rect" COORDS=
        "&{myrect(imageurl)};"
        HREF="&{myurl};">
</MAP>
```

This example sets the size of an image based upon document properties:

```
<IMG SRC=bar.gif WIDTH= &{document.
    banner.width/2}; HEIGHT= 50% >
```

You can programmatically set the URL for a link or image:

```
<SCRIPT>
    function manufacturer(widget) {
        ...
    }
    function location(manufacturer) {
        ...
    }
    function logo(manufacturer) {
        ...
    }
</SCRIPT>
<A HREF= &{location(manufacturer("
    widget"))}; >widget</A>
<IMG SRC= &{logo(manufacturer("widget"
    ))}; >
```

This last example shows how SGML CDATA attributes can be quoted using single or double quote marks. If you use single quotes around the attribute string, you can include double quote marks as part of the attribute string. Another approach is use " for double quote marks—for example,

```
<IMG SRC="&{logo(manufacturer
    (&quot;widget&quot;))};">
```

Using Form Fields Without a NAME Attribute

For an INPUT, TEXTAREA, or SELECT element to be considered as part of a form, when submitting the form's contents, both of the following conditions must apply:

1. The element must have a NAME attribute.

2. The element must be contained by a FORM element.

If either of these two conditions are not met, then the field is not treated as being part of a form. This allows fields such as text fields and buttons to be used together with scripting to build user interfaces independent of the role of these elements for forms.

Deployment Issues

Authors may wish to design their HTML documents to be viewable on older browsers that don't recognize the SCRIPT element. Unfortunately any script statements placed within a SCRIPT element will be visible to users. Some scripting engines for languages such as Java-Script, VBScript and Tcl allow the script statements to be enclosed in an SGML comment syntax, for instance:

```
<SCRIPT LANGUAGE="JavaScript">
<!-- to hide script contents from old
    browsers
  function square(i) {
    document.write("The call passed
        ", i ," to the function.","<BR>")
    return i * i
  }
  document.write("The function
      returned ",square(5),".")
// end hiding contents from old
    browsers -->
</SCRIPT>
```

The JavaScript engine allows the string <!-- to occur at the start of a SCRIPT element and ignores further characters until the end of the line. JavaScript interprets // as starting a comment extending to the end of the current line.

This is needed to hide the string --> from the JavaScript parser.

Down-level browsers will ignore the SCRIPT start and end tags and interpret the <!-- string as the start of an SGML comment. In this way the contents of the SCRIPT element are hidden within an SGML comment.

In VBScript a single quote character causes the rest of the current line to be treated as a comment. It can therefore be used to hide the string --> from VBScript—for instance:

```
<SCRIPT TYPE="text/vbscript">
  <!-- Sub foo()
      ...
          End Sub
  -->
</SCRIPT>
```

In Tcl, the hash character (#) comments out the rest of the line:

```
<SCRIPT LANGUAGE="tcl">
  <!-- to hide script contents from
      old browsers proc square {i} {
    document write "The call passed
      $i to the function.<BR>"
    return [expr $i * $i]
    }
    document write "The function
      returned [square 5]."
  # end hiding contents from old
      browsers -->
</SCRIPT>
```

Some browsers close comments on the first > character; to hide script content from such browsers, you can transpose operands for relational and shift operators (e.g., to use $y < x$ rather than $x > y$) or use scripting language dependent escapes for >. ∎

References

1. HTML 2.0 Proposed Standard—RFC 1866.
2. Berners-Lee, T., and D. Connolly. November 1995. This can be found at *ftp://ds.internic.net/rfc/rfc1866.txt.*
3. W3C Recommendation for HTML 3.2 .
4. Raggett, Dave. January 1997. This can be found at *http://www.w3.org/pub/WWW/TR.*
5. Internet Media Types—RFC 1590.
6. Postel, J. "Media Type Registration Procedure," RFC 1590, USC/ISI, March 1994. This can be found at *ftp://ds.internic.net/rfc/rfc1590.txt.*
7. MIME—RFC 1521.
8. Borenstein, N., and N. Freed. "MIME (Multipurpose Internet Mail Extensions) Part One: Mechanisms for Specifying and Describing the Format of Internet Message Bodies," RFC 1521, Bellcore, Innosoft, September 1993. This can be found at *ftp://ds.internic.net/rfc/rfc1521.txt.*
9. OBJECT Elements.
10. The syntax and semantics for OBJECT are defined in *http://www.w3.org/pub/WWW/TR/WD-object.html.*

Bibliography

1. JavaScript, an overview is available from *http://home.netscape.com/eng/mozilla/Gold/handbook/javascript/index.html.*
2. Visual Basic Script, an overview is available from *http://www.microsoft.com/vbscript/default.htm.*
3. ActiveX Scripting, an introduction to ActiveX Scripting is available from *http://www.microsoft.com/intdev/sdk/.*
4. Tcl, the Tcl FAQ can be found at *http://www.NeoSoft.com/tcl/tclhtml/tclFAQ/part1/faq.html.* You can also look at the tcl news group *comp.lang.tcl.*

About the Author

Dave Raggett (W3C, Hewlett Packard)
MIT Laboratory for Computer Science
545 Technology Square
Cambridge, MA 02139
dsr@w3.org

Dave currently works at the World Wide Web Consortium (W3C) on secondment from Hewlett

Packard's Corporate Research Laboratories in Bristol, England. His work is heavily involved with developing standards for the World Wide Web: as author of the HTML 3.0 draft specification and earlier the HTML+ Internet Draft, as the creator of the Arena browser, and as co-chair of the IETF working group for HTTP. He is also working on ideas for downloadable fonts, style sheets, and non-proprietary public domain protocols for micropayments (without export restrictions).

AN INTRODUCTION TO AMAYA

Vincent Quint, Irène Vatton

Abstract

[W3C Note; February 20, 1997]

Because the Web is based on a client-server architecture, a client and a server are needed both for experimentation and to demonstrate new specifications. Within W3C, Jigsaw plays this role on the server side, while Amaya was developed to play the same role on the client side. This NOTE presents the results of the decisions made in designing Amaya, its key features, and a description of the user interface and software architecture.

Status of This Document

This document is a NOTE made available by the W3 Consortium for discussion only. This indicates no endorsement of its content, nor that the Consortium has, is, or will be allocating any resources to the issues addressed by the NOTE.

A list of current NOTEs can be found at: *http://www.w3.org/pub/WWW/TR/* .

Since NOTEs are subject to change, you are advised to reference the URL for the "latest version."

This document briefly presents Amaya, the W3C testbed client. It explains the motivations for the development of the software as well as its goals. It also presents the main design choices that have been made to reach these goals.

A Multi-Purpose Client

Amaya is both a browser and an authoring tool dedicated to the World Wide Web (see Figure 1). It has been specifically conceived to serve as a testbed client to experiment and demonstrate new Web protocols and formats as well as new extensions to existing ones. This makes its features a bit specific.

A testbed client must be versatile enough to allow a wide range of experiments and demonstrations. That is the reason why Amaya has been designed

as an active client—one that not only retrieves documents from the Web and presents them to the user, but also allows an author to create new documents, to edit existing ones, and to publish these documents on remote Web servers.

To help investigate the impact of new specifications on the many aspects of a Web client, Amaya has been designed with both of the following:

- A WYSIWYG style of interface, which makes it easy to use

- A structured representation of documents, which allows it to stick to the Web specifications

The Web is made of a number of documents linked together. While working on the Web, a user needs to access several documents, especially when following, creating, or modifying links. For that reason, Amaya is able to work on several documents at a time, acting as a browser and as an editor simultaneously: the whole client functionality is available at any time for any document.

In its basic version, Amaya implements many Web protocols and formats:

- It handles HTML documents with their hypertext links.

- It can display pictures in several formats, including PNG.

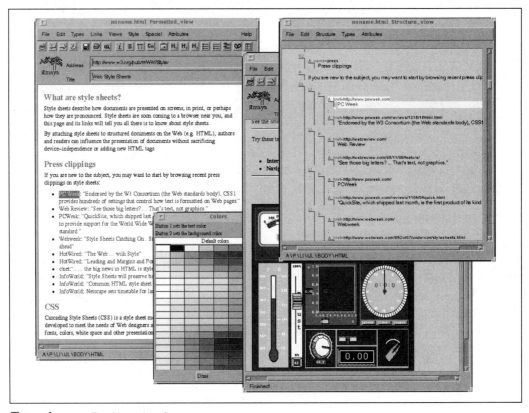

Figure 1   The Amaya interface

- It supports CSS1, which allows it to display documents with style sheets and to create or edit style sheets.

- It accesses remote sites by means of HTTP 1.1, as implemented in *libwww*.

Amaya's Approach to HTML

HTML is the document format for the Web. As a Web tool, Amaya must take all aspects of this format into account. As we know from existing tools, there are different approaches for using HTML in a Web client. Amaya, too, has its own approach, as you'll see below.

As an editor, Amaya processes HTML files in a specific way. An editor based on the WYSIWYG paradigm must allow the user to act on the for-

matted document for altering the HTML source. To allow that feature, the HTML source is treated as a data structure definition. When parsing a source file, Amaya builds an internal representation of the document structure, which is basically a tree. This logical structure is then utilized both for formatting and for editing.

In Amaya, HTML is considered to be an SGML application. The editor always follows the HTML DTD when manipulating the document structure, as such, and performs only valid operations. The advantages of this approach are that it leads to well structured documents and allows other tools to further process the documents safely. The drawbacks are also well known:

1. Manipulations are often complex from the user viewpoint.

2. Documents that are not strictly correct are often rejected.

The latter is a real nuisance, since many documents are syntactically or structurally incorrect on the Web.

To address the first drawback, we have paid particular attention to the user interface. Most commands issued by the user are the same as those proposed by usual word processors, but are interpreted by the editor in terms of the internal document structure. Specific structure manipulation commands are thus avoided, as well as context sensitive menus.

To address the second drawback, the HTML parser has been designed in such a way so that Amaya *never* rejects *any* document. When it parses a document that is not structurally correct, it tries to transform the structure of the document. Sometimes this structure is so bizarre that it's not possible to automatically generate a fully HTML-conformant structure. In that case, the parser still loads the document. If the user attempts to modify it, however, the editor performs only valid operations. Thus, the document structure is improved: even though it is not guaranteed to be *always* correct, it's not worse than its original condition. In addition, the user is not prevented from working on any document.

User Interface

A WYSIWYG Interface

Users are not required to know the HTML or CSS languages in order to author Web pages. Amaya asks them neither to write nor read the documents they create under their HTML syntax. The HTML file is automatically produced by the tool, as well as the CSS syntax.

But Amaya is not simply a word processor with an HTML filter. Because it is intended to implement as many aspects of Web specifications as possible, Amaya should be able to implement every HTML feature. Though it is modeled after HTML, users can interact with it in a very simple and natural way.

For these reasons, the WYSIWYG paradigm has been chosen for the user interface, with a structured model for the internal representation. Documents are presented to the user they would be if displayed by the most popular browsers and the user interacts with the editor on the basis of this external representation. Simultaneously, the editor maintains an internal representation that follows the HTML rules and constraints, as stated in the DTD.

Document elements

A user can manipulate text in the same way as if s/he were using a simple word processor. At any time, the user can select any part of that text and assign to it an HTML type (H1, LI, EM, etc.), by means of the Types menu or of the shortcut buttons. Such a command transforms the selected part into an element of the chosen type. If some other elements need to be created or transformed to keep the document HTML-conformant, these transformations are also performed. Though this allows the author to first type in the contents and to provide structure *afterwards*, the opposite is also possible: the type of an element can also be chosen *before* entering its contents.

In Amaya, this is the only way to manipulate the document structure. The user does not enter or edit tags. Only the editor directly acts on the document structure. When it makes a change, it checks the change against the HTML DTD to make sure that the structure remains correct.

This kind of user interface may require complex structure transformations by the editor. The user may select a passage that has a given structure (say, a bulleted list) and ask for a completely different structure (say, a table). For such complex transformations, the editor cannot rely only on the DTD, since semantics are involved. The problem is solved by a *transformation language*. This language is used to define complex structure transformations. It allows users to define structure patterns and the corresponding transformed structures. With these definitions, the editor may perform any transformation that the user may need and the user may define new transformations as needed.

This approach has a number of advantages:

- The user is not constrained by editing modes—at any time any element type can be created or changed and new elements can be created before of after their contents.

- The document structure can be transformed freely, thus relieving the user from the burden of complex interaction imposed by most structure editors.

- The document is always structurally correct regarding the HTML DTD.

Attributes

In HTML, various attributes can be associated with a number of elements. The allowed attributes depend on the element type, as stated by the DTD. To help the user choose the right attributes, a specific menu offers all attributes that can be associated with the selected element(s), and only those attributes.

Because this menu provides the only way to associate attributes with elements, only valid attributes can be entered. Moreover, because attributes are allowed only predefined values, these values are also proposed in a specific menu so that only valid values are entered.

This enforces the structured approach that guarantees that documents are always structurally correct.

Views

In some cases, the structure of an HTML document may be complex, with a number of nested elements of several types. That complexity may lead to ambiguity; different structures may look very similar when displayed in their formatted representation. As a help to the user in such situations, Amaya can display the actual structure of the document being edited. This is called the *structure view*—it is displayed in a separate window that the user can view simultaneously with the formatted view.

The structure view presents the document's hierarchical structure as an indented list and displays the type and attributes of every element. This view is not a static representation. The user can act on it by selecting any element there and modifying the document exactly in the same way as in the formatted view. In addition, all editing commands are executed in both views simultaneously, whatever the view chosen for issuing the command.

The principle of showing the same document in different windows simultaneously is not restricted to the structure view. An *alternate view* is also available, which shows the document as it would be displayed on a dumb terminal. Like the structure view, the alternate view may be used for editing. It's not simply a preview that allows the document to be checked from a different viewpoint; it's rather a dynamic representation, where the user can make changes.

The concept of a view may be used for showing other aspects of a document. For instance, it is fairly simple to define new views; one can imagine a window showing links, another showing headings (a table of contents), etc.

Links

Links are first class citizens in Web pages and deserve particular attention. Typically, the user need not type URLs to edit links. Instead, the browsing function of Amaya is used to load different documents. Links are then created or modified by simply clicking on the target document or anchor that is displayed on the screen. Thus, the user can see the actual target of a link and avoid any mistake when setting links.

Style Sheets

A Web page is ruled not only by the HTML spec-ification, but it can also include stylistic material that conforms to the CSS (Cascading Style Sheets) specification. The same approach has been taken for CSS as for HTML: the user does not write CSS syntax directly. S/he interacts with a formatted document and immediately sees the result of his/her commands either on the formatted document or in other views. Amaya is in charge of produc-ing the actual CSS syntax.

Since the same result may be achieved by associ-ating style declarations at several locations in an HTML document, the formatted view is not enough—other means must be provided for avoiding ambiguity. In HTML, the structure view fulfills this need by clearly showing where style rules are located (e.g., as Style attributes associ-ated with HTML elements, Style elements in the heading of a document, or a link to a style sheet).

Publishing Documents on the Web

Amaya is not simply a structured editor, but it is a complete Web authoring environment. Users working with Amaya are on the Web and can access any Web resource. The following actions can be performed in a single consistent environ-ment:

- Browsing the Web

- Finding information while writing a docu-ment

- Copying and pasting from any document, directly on the formatted representation

- Creating links and checking these links immediately

In Amaya, the editing and browsing functions are integrated seamlessly in a single tool.

Access to the Web is not restricted to browsing: the document you edit can also be published on remote servers where you are allowed to write. Publishing on the Web is as simple as saving a document to a local file—just type an URL instead of a filename when saving a document, and Amaya does the rest. Included objects such as pictures are also saved and all URLs are updated accordingly if the document has moved from its original location.

Transferring documents and other resources to and from remote servers is performed by *libwww*. Access to these servers is performed exclusively by means of the following HTTP methods:

- GET loads remote documents

- POST/GET send forms

- PUT publishes documents

Amaya also takes advantage of the most advanced features of HTTP, such as content negotiation to retrieve the most appropriate pic-ture format, or maintaining connections to save bandwidth.

Architecture

Amaya's internal design reflects its testbed role. The software architecture allows easy extensions. Several APIs and mechanisms are available to change and extend its functionality with as few modifications as possible within the source code.

To allow its handling of documents in a struc-tured way, Amaya has been designed as an appli-cation on top of the Thot tool kit. Thot is a set of libraries that implement document manipulation functions, based on a structured document model that clearly separates content, structure, and pre-sentation.

The Thot Languages

All editing and formatting functions in Thot rely on the document logical structure. In any applica-tion that uses Thot, a document is represented internally as a tree that assembles typed elements, such as headings, paragraphs, lists, highlighted phrases, and so on. These elements may have attributes that provide more information about the element's role in the document structure, exactly like in HTML and SGML.

Thot provides four languages that are used to write four types of *schemas*. A schema is a set of *rules* that define the behavior of the editor regarding the logical structure of documents, their presentation, their external syntax, or some specific treatments. These languages are described in the sections that follow.

Logical structures: language S

The logical structure of a document is constrained by certain rules. Structure rules specify the available element types and attributes, they indicate how these elements may be assembled to make a valid structure; and they state what attributes can be associated with each element type. In Thot, structure rules are gathered in *structure schemas*. A structure schema defines the logical structure of a document type; it is written in a simple declarative language, called S.

Amaya uses a structure schema to specify the logical structure of HTML documents. This schema is equivalent to the HTML DTD.

Document presentation: language P

The document image displayed in different views is defined by a *presentation schema*, written in language P. A presentation schema specifies the views to be proposed to the user and indicates using *presentation rules,* how the elements and attributes defined in the corresponding structure schema should be displayed in these views.

Amaya uses several presentation schemas, which specify different layouts and styles for HTML documents: one for color screens, one for printers, etc. These schemas define the default presentation to be applied to HTML documents, when no particular style information is associated. If CSS is used, these presentation schemas are dynamically extended with presentation rules that correspond to the CSS rules included in or referred from the document.

External syntax: language T

A structure schema specifies only the internal logical structure of documents, rather than their external syntax. The same structure can be conveyed by different syntaxes, and when the document is saved several syntaxes can be used. The output syntax is defined by a *translation schema*, written in language T. A declarative languages, it specifies how each element and attribute defined by a structure schema should be represented in the external representation.

A translation schema is used in Amaya to define the HTML syntax. Other schemas can be used to save the document in ASCII or in LATEX, for instance.

Application construction: language A

The fourth language of Thot is language A. It is used to define the user interface of an application as well as its specific commands (basic editing commands are provided by Thot). With an *application schema*, written in language A, a developer specifies the menu bar that appears at the top of each view, the contents of the corresponding pull-down menus, and the functions that are called by these menus. An application schema also lets you extend or modify the basic editing functions provided by Thot.

Amaya is a Thot application described in language A. It uses the basic editing functions provided by Thot, to which it adds some particular commands that are specific to the Web and the HTML structure.

Each language has its own compiler. The S, P, and T compilers generate files that are loaded dynamically by the Thot library at running time, while the A compiler generates C code that must be compiled and linked with the modules implementing the application.

Thot libraries

The main Thot library provides developers with an API that allows them to handle all entities and objects that make a document and its environment. There are functions for creating, modifying, deleting, opening, accessing, finding, and moving documents, logical structures, elements, attributes, links, views, etc.

Document manipulation functions

All document manipulation functions are based on the schemas presented above. As an example, an application program need only call two functions (`NewTree` and `InsertTree`) to create a new subtree in the document structure. Function `NewTree` receives as a parameter the type of the element that must become the root of the new tree, and according to the structure schema, it creates all the required elements in the subtree. Function `InsertTree` uses the structure schema to check whether the tree can be inserted at the required place in the document structure and it uses the presentation schema to redisplay only what is needed in all open views. The developer is concerned only with the document logical structure; all the rest is handled by Thot. This makes the development of applications very simple.

Thot also provides a library of graphical user interface functions that, along with language A, makes the development of a user interface very simple as well.

Extension mechanism

A number of standard editing functions are provided by Thot, but these functions may need to be modified, extended, or replaced by the application in some cases. For that reason, application schemas allow developers to specify some specific functions (that they have to write) that must be called before, after, or instead of the standard functions. They can specify different functions that are performed according to the element type or attribute concerned. This allows the behavior of the standard editing functions to change without making any change within the Thot code itself.

For example, activating an element by double-clicking it is a standard Thot function. But when an anchor is clicked in Amaya, a specific function must be performed to get and display the referred document. Language A allows a developer to declare that, when an element of type anchor is clicked, a specific function must be called instead of the standard Thot function. That function, written by the developer, uses the Thot library to access the HREF attribute associated with the clicked anchor, and then uses *libwww* to get the corresponding document, which the Thot library displays.

Amaya as a Thot application

Amaya inherits a lot of functions from the Thot library: text editing, formatting, basic structure manipulations, user dialogue, picture display, are among them. More specific functions are implemented by the following software components:

HTML parser

The HTML parser reads an HTML stream, parses it, and builds the logical structure of the corresponding documents using the Thot API.

CSS parser

The CSS parser reads CSS syntax, contained in a style sheet, in the HEAD of an HTML file or in a STYLE attribute, and generates the corresponding presentation rules for Thot.

User interface

The user interface is partly inherited from Thot, for the most common functions, and partly specified in language A, for the specific Amaya commands.

Specific editing functions

Specific editing functions are declared in language A and implemented on top of the Thot API.

Structure transformations

Simple structure transformations are implemented by the Thot library, based on the structure schema. More complex transformations are described by the transformation language.

libwww

Amaya access remote Web servers through the latest version of *libwww*, which implements HTTP 1.1.

An Open-Ended Architecture

The architecture described in this NOTE allows Amaya to be extended in many ways. Most extensions can be handled very simply, often without programming. Using the Thot library and its API, most basic editing functions are available and can be reused very easily. Using the available declarative languages, many changes to the software can be made simply by changing declarations.

These features have already been used to experiment some proposed extensions to HTML, such as an extended table model or the OBJECT element associated with a plug-in mechanism. An experiment with Web collections is also in progress for printing large documents published as a set of smaller HTML pages. Additional work is planned in the W3C team, but other interested parties are encouraged to use Amaya to experiment with other extensions and develop their own applications. ∎

Further Readings

1. For a description of Amaya's user interface, see *http://www.w3.org/pub/WWW/Amaya/User/Manual.html*

2. Specification of Thot languages (S: structure, P: presentation, T: translation), see *http://opera.inrialpes.fr/thot/languages.html*

3. The Thot API (see http://opera.inrialpes.fr/thot/APIman.toc.html)

4. Amaya's structure transformation mechanism and its language, see *http://www.w3.org/pub/WWW/Amaya/User/Transform.html*

5. How to modify or extend Amaya, see *http://www.w3.org/pub/WWW/Amaya/User/AmayaArchi.html*

6. How to download the source code for Amaya, see *http://www.w3.org/pub/WWW/Amaya/User/SourceDist.html*

7. Other Amaya-related reading, see *http://www.w3.org/pub/WWW/Amaya/User/*

About the Authors

Vincent Quint
W3C/INRIA 2004
Route des Lucioles
B.P. 93 06902
Sophia Antipolis Cedex France
vatton@w3.org

Vincent is Deputy Director for European operations of the W3C. He is a Research Director at INRIA and coordinator of the User Interface areas. Prior to joining the W3C team in February 1996, he led project Opera, which focused on various aspects of electronic documents such as document models and structure, structured editors, hypertext, and digital typography. During the last ten years, he has been deeply involved in the design and development of various systems, including Grif, Thot, and Tamaya. His research interests include document models, document production systems, active documents, document engineering, hypertext, and collaborative work.

Irène Vatton
W3C/INRIA 2004
Route des Lucioles
B.P. 93 06902
Sophia Antipolis Cedex France
vatton@w3.org

Irene is a research engineer based at INRIA in Grenoble, France. She is involved in the development of Amaya, specifically in the user interface. Before joining the W3C team in February 1996, Irene was at project Opera, where she had been working extensively on structured documents and authoring tools. She is the co-author of the Thot library and initialized the development of a prototype Web client, Tamaya, from which the new Amaya tool is derived. Irene holds a Ph.D. from the University of Grenoble.

TOWARD SYNCHRONIZED MULTIMEDIA ON THE WEB

Philipp Hoschka

Introduction

Web technology is limited today when it comes to creating continuous multimedia presentations. For these applications, content authors need to express things like "five minutes into the presentation, show image X and keep it on the screen for ten seconds." More generally, there must be a way to describe the synchronization between the different media (audio, video, text, and images) that make up a continuous multimedia presentation.

There is an imminent danger that a plethora of non-interoperable solutions for integrating real-time multimedia content into the Web architecture will emerge. These different solutions will most likely not result from a healthy competition advancing technological progress. Instead, they will result from a simple lack of communication between the three very different communities involved, namely the Web community, the CD-ROM community, and the community working on Internet-based audio/video-on-demand.

Representatives from each community participated at the recent W3C workshop on "Real Time Multimedia and the Web." In the feedback we received after this event, members of all communities, including several key players, reported that they see W3C as a promising forum for exchanging ideas and for finding consensus on common solutions for integrating synchronized multimedia presentations into the Web.

A synergy of their orthogonal expertise holds the promise that a single, sound technical solution can be found for many of the issues of real-time multimedia content on the Web. Such agreements are the necessary signal for independent content providers to start creating synchronized multimedia content for the Web and, thus, for market growth in this area.

W3C Workshop "Real-Time Multimedia and the Web"

Many of the observations in this paper are based on the results of the W3C workshop on "Real-Time Multimedia and the Web." This workshop took place at the W3C site at INRIA Sophia-Antipolis on October 24 and 25, 1996. All position papers and detailed minutes are available at *http://www.w3.org/pub/WWW/AudioVideo/RTMW96.html.* The workshop was transmitted live on the MBone using IP multicast.

About 70 participants were registered, among them the project manager of Macromedia Director and Shockwave (Jonathan Grayson, Macromedia), the chair of the IETF (Internet Engineering Task Force) working group on conference control (Mark Handley, Information Sciences Institute), a chief architect of Apple Quicktime (Peter Hoddie, Apple), the chair of the MHEG[*]-5 working group (Klaus Hofmeister, GMD[†]), a co-author of Real Time Streaming Protocol (RTSP) (Rob Lanphier, Progressive Networks), one of the editors of the Real Time Transport Protocol (RTP) standard (Henning Schulzrinne, Columbia University), the former chair of the MPEG (Motion Pictures Experts Group) systems group (Jan van der Meer, Philips), and the chair and the deputy director of W3C (Vincent Quint, INRIA). Twenty-five percent of the participants came from the U.S.,

---

[*] Multimedia and Hypermedia Expert Group
[†] Gesellschaft fuer Mathematik und Datenverarbeitung (National Research Lab for Computer Science and Mathematics)

53 percent came from industry, and 47 percent from research organizations.

The first day of this two-day event dealt with multimedia formats. Morning presentations both from industry (Alcatel, Macromedia, Apple) and from research organizations (GMD, University of Massachusetts/Lowell, INRIA Grenoble) set the stage for the discussions in the breakout sessions in the afternoon. The day ended with a session on "wild ideas and strong opinions," featuring talks on integrating games into the Web (University of Oslo), a caching infrastructure (Oracle), and a call for action to browser developers for better integration of live media (University of Ulm).

The hot topic of the second day was audio and video transmission on the Internet. It included a presentation of RTSP by Rob Lanphier, one of the co-authors. RTSP has been proposed by Netscape and Progressive Networks as a standard protocol for accessing real-time multimedia sources on the Internet. The first set of presentations (University of Lancaster, Columbia University, Nemesys) discussed the feasibility of audio/visual transmission on the Internet. This was followed by a session in which interactive television experts (Philips) discussed with Internet experts (Lulea University, UCL) whether digital television services could be realized using Web technology. The second day finished with a discussion on the future directions of W3C work in the area of real-time multimedia on the Web.

Synchronized Multimedia Applications

Many industry analysts predict that the Web will be turned into a distribution system for both interactive and continuous multimedia content, or *synchronized multimedia content*. A typical example of synchronized multimedia are presentations created with tools like Microsoft's Powerpoint or Macromedia's Authorware. Other examples can be found on CD-ROM products like training courses, lexica, "virtual" art galleries, or

CDs of pop groups enhanced by text, images, and video. For instance, in a "guided tour," the screen shows a sequence of different images, text, and graphs, which are explained in an audio stream that is played in parallel.

Actually, many of today's television programs are multimedia presentations and could be produced by using techniques learned in creating multimedia CD-ROMs. Consider a television news broadcast: many parts of the television screen contain text, images, graphs, or other static elements. These static elements could be sent as separate files, together with a schedule that determines at which point in time the content of these files should be displayed on the screen. This may require much less bandwidth than sending the same content as full motion video.

Interestingly enough, the graphic design of some television programs already employs elements of CD-ROM and computer user interfaces—for example, windows pop up in a news broadcast or program items are presented in menu form. The much-heralded integration of television and computers thus seems to be already on its way, at least on the level of graphic design of television programs. Of course, television programs lack the interactivity of Web and CD-ROM content. For example, a user cannot simply interrupt the transmission of a news program by clicking on a photograph to retrieve more information about a person.

Providers of synchronized multimedia content are interested in using the Web for several reasons. First, the Web greatly facilitates updating content. Therefore, more up-to-date information can be offered via the Web than on a CD-ROM. Moreover, distribution of content via the Web is cheaper than distributing CD-ROMs. Finally, consumers that use CD-ROMs do not need to buy a new end-user appliance for accessing the same content via the Internet. Both technologies require the same end-user appliance, namely a personal computer. With the forthcoming high-speed Internet links, it seems likely that in the near future Web technology will assimilate the content that is distributed on CD-ROMs today.

Requirements

A comparison between CD-ROM products and typical Web sites reveals many similarities. First of all, image and text media types are very important for both Web and CD-ROM content. Moreover, the user interfaces are also very similar. On CD-ROMs, the user navigates through the multimedia content using a "point-and-click" interface. On the Web, this sort of interface is achieved by using hyperlinks (URLs), possibly associated with image maps.

However, current Web technology is clearly limited when it comes to creating continuous multimedia presentations. For this, two new components must be added to Web technology: a format for authoring synchronized multimedia content, and support for network transmission of this type of content.

Authors of continuous multimedia presentations have to express things like "five minutes into the presentation, show image X at the lower right corner of the screen. For the next ten seconds, move it to the upper right corner of the screen. While doing this, play the last ten seconds of the Spring concerto from Vivaldi's 'Four Seasons'." In general, the format must allow describing the positioning and the synchronization between the different media (text, images, audio, and video) that make up a continuous multimedia presentation.

Transmitting synchronized multimedia content over the Internet requires meeting the real-time constraints of the presentation; that is, a particular piece of a file has to be available when it is needed in the presentation. Two solutions address this issue:

- Prefetching of files
- Using a streaming protocol

The current transport protocol used by the Web (HTTP) is usable for prefetching files but not as a streaming protocol.

Streaming protocols are particularly important for audio and video files. Popular applications for Internet-based audio/video-on-demand such as RealAudio (*http://www.realaudio.com*) and VDO-Live (*http://www.vdo.com*) rely on streaming protocols to cope with the real-time constraints of audio and video replay. Standard protocols for streaming applications are developed within the IETF (RTP, RTSP).

The Case for a Web-Based Solution

One possible solution for enabling synchronized multimedia presentations on the Web is to use a format that restricts the overlap with existing Web technology to the use of URL-based addressing. This approach has been followed by many products currently on the market. Examples are Macromedia's Shockwave (*http://www.macromedia.com*), Apple's Quicktime plugin (*http://www.apple.quicktime.com*), Microsoft's NetShow (*http://www.microsoft.com/netshow*), and Pointcast (*http://www.pointcast.com/*) when operating in "screen saver" mode.

From the point of view of a content provider, this approach has the advantage that existing authoring tools for some of these formats can be used for creating synchronized multimedia content for the Web. However, it also has a number of drawbacks.

First, the potential audience of the content will have a more difficult time of finding the content, since the text part of the content is in a format unknown to Web search engines, and thus cannot be indexed.

Moreover, the Web allows the creation of new content by reusing existing raw material, which can be stored on different servers all over the Internet. Two of the most successful Web applications, search engines and Web directories, work only because today's Web content is reusable. In contrast, content encoded in CD-ROM formats is generally not reusable because the image, text, and other files used in CD-ROM content are often wrapped into a single file when put on the Web.

Internet-based audio/video-on-demand applications are currently being extended to also "stream" other media types, such as text and images, and not only audio and video. Examples are Netscape's MediaServer (*http://www.netscape.com/comprod/announce/media.html*) and work at Progressive Networks on extensions of the RealAudio product RealMedia Architecture (*http://www.realaudio.com/prognet/rm/index.html*). These applications require a format for synchronizing different media types contained in a presentation, and standard formats for basic data types such as text and images. Work has already started on designing application-specific formats.

The Web community is using open formats that can duplicate some of the functionality of CD-ROM formats today (image maps, HTML, URLs) and is working on formats (layout control, stylesheets, fonts, scripting) that will bring the capabilities of the Web even closer to those of CD-ROM formats. Content providers tend to prefer open formats, since they can be relatively sure that their content will be "durable." If content providers start to produce synchronized multimedia content for the Web, the market for products to author, display, and serve this type of Web content will also grow.

A Plan of Attack

The key to a solution is to make individual elements of an HTML page addressable. For example, each paragraph in a document could have an individual identifier. This allows such expressions as "ten seconds into the presentation, remove the second paragraph from the screen." It also allows control of audio and video files, which can be included in the HTML file using the object element (*http://www.w3.org/pub/WWW/MarkUp/Group/9612/WD-object-961216.html*).

Approaches to address HTML elements in order to use them in synchronized multimedia presentations have already been developed (see Microsoft's proposal for an object model for HTML at *http://www.w3.org/pub/WWW/MarkUp/Group/webpageapi/* or the animation based on the "layer" tag in Netscape 4.0 at *http://home.netscape.com/comprod/products/communicator/index.html*.

In contrast to the rest of the Web formats (HTML, CSS) that are declarative, media synchronization on the Web can currently be expressed only by using a scripting language such as JavaScript or Visual Basic.

Declarative formats have well-known advantages over scripting languages. For instance, script-based content is often hard to produce and maintain. Having to write a program in order to, say, express the synchronization of an audio track with a video track seems overly complicated. Moreover, it is easier to build automated tools for a declarative format than for a scripting language.

Therefore, CD-ROM authoring tools use declarative formats such as Apple's Quicktime as an alternative approach to well-known scripting languages such as Macromedia's Lingo or Apple's Hypercard. Both declarative and scripting approaches have succeeded in the CD-ROM marketplace and are often used side-by-side in a particular multimedia product. Some of the most important contributions in this field have been made by several W3C member organizations.

The ease of building converters can be very important in bringing synchronized multimedia presentations to the Web. Using a declarative approach allows the building of format converters that permit putting existing content on the Web, similar to today's HTML converters for well-known word processors. In the other direction, a simple conversion from a declarative Web format into an existing format may allow the reuse of existing players as display engines for Web-based multimedia presentations.

In summary, experience from both the CD-ROM community and from the Web community suggests that it would be beneficial to adopt a declarative format for expressing media synchronization on the Web as an alternative and a complement to scripting languages. ■

About the Author

Philipp Hoschka
W3C/INRIA
B. P. 93 060902
Sophia-Antipolis, Cedex
France
hoschka@sophia.inria.fr

Philipp works on the integration of real-time data transmission (audio, video) into the Web. He organized a Birds of a Feather session on this subject at the WWW4 conference in December 1995.

Before joining the W3C in January 1996, Philipp was a member of the high speed networking research group at INRIA. This group is one of the leading research groups worldwide in the area of transmission of real-time data over the Internet. Philipp received a Ph.D. degree in Computer Science for his work on automatic code optimization of marshalling code. He also holds a Master's Degree in Computer Science from the University of Karlsruhe, Germany.

Though the profusion of programming language choices can seem like the most important aspect of automating the Web, a clearer understanding of Web architecture points to the choices that lie elsewhere. The decision is not whether to build a customer-tracking database in VBScript or JavaScript; it's how to do it: with a database gateway, a custom server, a handwritten HTTP Common Gateway Interface (CGI) script, an uploadable server extension ("servlet"), with interactive client-side forms, with customer-tracking cookies, or even with custom clients. This section of the World Wide Web Journal *describes the technology choices at each of these junctures, as far as automating the client, the server, and the back-end services.*

Starting from the user's perspective, client-side automation can range from simple animated glitz to task-specific browser customization. Nick Heinle's "JavaScript: When HTML Is Not Enough" describes a quick and popular solution for lightweight interactivity. Paul Lomax's "VBScript: Active Clients and Servers" explains how Visual Basic scripting can begin at this level, as well as reach back up the transaction toward the server. While both of these embeddable languages are expressive, they are completely distinct and alienated from their HTML hosts. MIT researchers present a radically different approach, merging scripts and documents, in "Curl: A Gentle Slope Language for the Web."

The next access point is within the Web server itself. Far and away the most popular way to extend servers today is to replace the "file" behind a URL with an executable script. Lincoln Stein's "Exploring CGI with Perl" describes the interface to these scripts and how they can be used with HTML FORMs and HTTP Cookies to export applications over the Web. Of course, on each platform and in each server, these hooks take a slightly different form. CGI itself originated on UNIX and mutated on other platforms, as Ron Petrusha justifies in "Why Win-CGI?" On the other hand, programmers can bypass the external interface entirely and transplant their code into the server, as in "The LWP Library," by Clint Wong.

Finally, Web automation can bridge the gap between Web servers and back-end information services. Shishir Gundavaram's "World Wide Web Gateways" constructs a Web-to-Netnews translator as a prototypical example. At the other end of the power-complexity tradeoff, Peter Lazar profiles how four commercial toolkits provide "Web Database Connectivity with Scripting Languages."

VBSCRIPT

ACTIVE CLIENTS AND SERVERS

Paul Lomax

Abstract

As the move towards a dynamic Web goes on, the distinction between desktop and Web are becoming ever more blurred. Web pages are no longer simply HTML and graphics; they now include scripted applications. In this article we explore VBScript, a subset of Visual Basic for Applications, which enhances the user's experience of a Web site; reduces wasteful use of bandwidth by allowing more processing at the client; allows pages to be dynamically created at the browser; and interfaces and manipulates ActiveX controls at the browser. But VBScript is more than just a client-side scripting language. This article also describes how it can be used at the server in conjunction with Active Server Pages to create applications every bit as powerful as desktop VB applications.

Active Scripting: The Dynamic Future of the Web?

In an incredibly short time, the Web has been transformed from a repository of purely textual documents to a cornucopia of sights, sounds, flashing lights, and fairground-like razzmatazz.

Probably because of the human races' need to develop, change and improve whatever it touches, the development of the Web has continued at an almost alarming and unerring pace, with both the business community and public alike caught up in the enthusiasm and drive to use, exploit, and change the Web.

Since the first `<A HREF>` tag was included in a Web page, the Web has been interactive. A user can click on a highlighted word or phrase (or graphic) and be instantly transported to another page—on another Web server on another continent—and thereby interact with the Web page. However, the page is still lifeless in itself: it cannot "do" anything. Even the interactive hyperlinking is not a function of the page, and any change requires downloading a new page from the Web server. Therefore, Web pages are interactive rather than dynamic.

Desktop applications, on the other hand, are dynamic—they change during execution depending upon the user's wishes. A desktop application reacts to the user's inputs and actions through events such as typing at the keyboard or moving a mouse. As application developers, we must concentrate on the user in order to create successful applications.

Computer users demand high standards (unless they've just gotten their hands on the latest Beta copy!), and vote quickly with a click of the mouse by abandoning one Web site in favor of another. With the vast numbers of places for Web users to explore, the competition to entice visitors is fierce. Enhancing a visitor's experience, however, doesn't necessarily mean having the "coolest" animated logos or the brightest color scheme that only a pair of Ray-Bans could tame. Often, a Web site's experience is enhanced by it's *usability.* [*] For instance:

- How quickly can the user become familiar with the layout?

- How easy is the site to navigate around?

---

[*] See Keith Instone's article entitled "Usability Engineering for the Web," in the Winter 1997 issue, *Advancing HTML: Style and Substance.*

- What features have been included to save the visitors precious time?

- How quickly can the visitor find the information they need?

With the relentless move toward a seamless desktop and Web, more time and thought will have to be put into user interface issues. Unlike with Windows applications, in which users have become accustomed to loading an application for the first time, understanding key elements of the interface, and knowing where to go for help, no such standards exist on Web pages. It is essential, therefore, that the user interface for the Web be easy to interpret and quick to learn.

An integral part of creating a smooth user interface—one that is functional, easy to maintain, and, above all, intuitive, is scripting. Scripts, whether they are run at the server or at the browser, allow you to change a lifeless HTML document into dynamic Web applications. And the newest scripting language (in many ways the oldest too) is Microsoft Visual Basic Scripting Edition (VBScript).

VBScript: The New Member of the VB Family

Visual Basic has become an important part of client-server programming all over the world. Mission-critical, enterprise-wide applications are written in VB: its speed and ease of development and maintenance allow corporations to prototype, develop, and deploy applications in a fraction of the time it once took. Visual Basic programmers, once looked upon as the hobbyists of the programming world, are now commanding top rates along with an increase in their stature (well I would say that wouldn't I?).

The advent of the COM interface and OLE, which allowed applications to interact with each other, opened the way for a light version of Visual Basic to be added in to applications such as Excel, thus enabling the experienced user or application developer to create custom applications. It was from this light version, called Visual Basic for Applications (VBA), that VBScript was created.

VBScript has inherited almost all the functionality of VBA, apart from anything that requires interfacing with either the computer or an application outside the host application.[*] Rather than starting from the ground up, VBScript was apparently stripped out of VBA in a very short space of time.

A recent upgrade to the original issue of VBScript, VBScript 2.0 adds further functionality to the language, some of which puts its object handling on a par with VB4, but only when run at the server.

Parallels can be drawn between how VBA and VBScript are used. First, both make use of Microsoft Forms 2.0 controls—an enhanced set of text boxes, combo boxes, list box es, option buttons, etc.—that have even more functionality than the forms controls within Visual Basic. Another similarity between VBA and VBScript is that the only interface is the host application: VBA operates through Excel, Project, and now Word '97 via the COM interfaces within the Document Object Model. Similarly, VBScript has no user interface (apart from the Message and Input dialogs); instead it uses the MSIE Object Model on the client side and the Active Server Object Model on the server side.

VBScript is a safe language, which means that, in itself, it cannot operate outside an Object Model (currently the MSIE Object Model and the Active Server Object Model). However, VBScript is also extensible through its ability to create instances of OLE Servers. When used at the browser, strict restrictions are placed upon it as to what type of object it can create. Currently, for example, client-side VBScript can use only the intrinsic **Err** object and the associative array **Dictionary** object. When run at the server, though, VB Script can create instances of any OLE/COM object—

---

[*] The host application in this case being Microsoft Internet Explorer—MSIE.

even those you have written yourself. On the server side, this gives VBScript the ability to interface with databases through ODBC and open, write, and read disk files.

VBScript versus JavaScript

As scripting languages go, there's really very little to choose from between VBScript and JavaScript (or, as Microsoft has called their implementation, JScript).* On the face of it, JavaScript has more going for it: more browsers—by a huge margin—support JavaScript. By definition this means that if you write a script in an HTML page using JavaScript, the vast majority of Web users will be able to take advantage of the functionality you've provided.

But—and this is a big "but"—how many JavaScript developers are there in the world? By *developers*, I mean people who can create fully functional applications, not just copy in some code that will create an annoying message scrolling along the status bar of the browser! I'd venture to say, very few. How many people have both the time and the motivation to sit down and really learn a whole new language? If people don't use a language in large numbers, applications don't get written, applications don't get seen by other people, and so it goes. In short, the language remains as nothing more than a promising alternative.

On the other hand, there are millions of Visual Basic developers around the world who, with very little effort, can simply adapt the skills they already possess to create complex Web applications using VBScript. VBScript is a subset of Visual Basic for Applications (VBA), and with the release of version 2, is starting to acquire its own functions (some of which would be nice to see climb up the VB tree to Visual Basic).

Remember, too, that many HTML authors are not programmers; creating a Web page may well be their first foray into anything that could be likened to a programming language. Learning the JavaScript language is a daunting task for this audience. In contrast, VBScript's easy-to-read style can be picked up much more quickly, allowing results to be achieved faster, and thereby adding to the developer's satisfaction and motivation. Don't get me wrong: programming languages are programming languages, and I smile when I read phrases such as "using this new language even the non-programmer can create" . . . etc. etc." Sure, an understanding of programming concepts is a prerequisite to creating complex applications, but VBScript throws very few surprises your way. The syntax is logical and readily understood. (A very minor point to interject here is that VBScript is case-*in*sensitive, whereas JavaScript is case-sensitive, a fact that is potentially frustrating for the developer.)

Another advantage of VBScript is its ease of integration with client-side controls, and a vast range of which are available. Quite literally, within minutes, you can create a form containing all the text boxes, drop-down lists, and options that you could wish for, link them all together with VBScript, and presto—an application that looks, feels, and operates like a Windows application.

Netscape's JavaScript (nee LiveScript) suffered in it's original incarnation from a whole host of memory and other "known issues" (bugs!). Most of these have now been addressed, but not without affecting confidence in JavaScript, and perhaps in client-side scripting in general. However, having used VBScript for about 12 months, many hours a day and almost every day, I can truly say that there are very few bugs in it (which, unfortunately, I can't say for the documentation which accompanies it).

At the risk of being flamed to a crisp, it's hard to ignore the fact that as scripting languages go, a major advantage is that VBScript is a Microsoft product. Of course only time will tell, but it

---

* See Nick Heinle's article entitled "JavaScript: When HTML Is Not Enough," in this issue of the *World Wide Web Journal*.

would be a very brave person that bets against Microsoft. While Microsoft doesn't always offer the best product to do the job, taken with the integration afforded by their wide range of products, it is very compelling for business managers to specify Microsoft products, rather than risk the inevitable incompatibilities that tend to creep in down the line.

The Importance of VBScript in Intranets

While Netscape dominates in terms of numbers on the Web, the combination of Microsoft NT4 and Internet Information Server (IIS) are becoming the major force in the corporate Intranet market. Because of cost and logistics, corporations must leverage the investment already made in their IT systems. For many corporations this means extending their Microsoft systems to build their Intranet; in fact, for most businesses currently using Windows NT4, with, say, SQL Server and Visual Basic, the act of creating an Intranet will be relatively easy and inexpensive. Given the ease with which the Office and Back Office suites dovetail together in the corporate Intranet, I can think of no motivation for a corporate IT manager to specify moving towards a Javascript/Java package, in preference to ActiveX[*] and VBScript.

Client-Side Scripting with VBScript

Let's first make a distinction between scripts designed to run within a browser (client-side) and those designed to run unseen at the server (server-side).

The former—which we explore here—is the "public" face of VBScript, the glitzy front end. It controls and interfaces with ActiveX controls, performs data validation, and creates dynamic Web applications. The latter, which we describe in the section "Server-Side Scripting," is never (or should never) be seen by anyone but the programmer. (The server-side scripts create dynamic pages at the server, and all that should ever be seen is the result of the script, not the script itself.)

Client-side scripting is still relatively new and still under-utilized. If Web designers still appear reluctant to "get on board" with client-side scripting, this is probably a symptom of a fear of alienating the majority of Netscape users by writing scripts in VBScript—which only MSIE can read without a plug-in—combined with a lack of time and/or motivation to learn JavaScript. Therefore, the easy option is to leave pages as they are, unscripted.

Another reason why many Web designers choose not to add scripting to their pages is the public perception of scripting. Only the other day I saw a message on a newsgroup headed, "Can I catch a virus from JavaScript?" Quite rightly, one of the preoccupations of many Web users has to do with their safety and security while traveling around the Web. For this reason, client-side scripting is restricted to operating within the browser. The one exception to this (although this, too, is under the control of the browser) is the ability to write a *cookies* file to the user's hard drive.[†] When used within the browser, therefore, VBScript cannot access the hard drive, and most of the latest object-related functionality is only available when run at the server.

Most people who have heard of VBScript (and who know roughly what it is) associate it inextricably with ActiveX controls. However, VBScript can lead a separate life on its own—well nearly on its own—it can also be used to interface with and even control the MSIE browser itself.

---

[*] See the section entitled "The ActiveX Glue," later in this article.
[†] See the Fall 1996 issue of the *World Wide Web Journal, Building an Industrial Strength Web*, for articles and specs describing cookies.

Interaction with the MSIE Scripting Object Hierarchy

For all but the simplest tasks, you will have to interact with the `Scripting Object` hierarchy in some way. As you become more familiar with client-side scripting, you will find that you start to think of the browser in terms of a series or collection of objects, rather than as a single entity. When you write normal HTML documents, your only real concern is with the document itself; from time to time you may have to specify a target for a hyperlink outside the current scope, like another frame, but that's about it.

Client-side scripting, on the other hand, is very different. Even accessing the value of a text box within a form on your page involves accessing the `Object` hierarchy in the correct sequence. However, once you understand the `Object` hierarchy, even the more complex tasks of, say, accessing a text box in another frame, become straightforward.

The Microsoft Internet Explorer browser is made up of several main objects, each of which you can interrogate to obtain property values, control using the objects methods, and react to by writing handlers for the object's events.

The browser objects in the following sections are shown in the order in which they appear in the hierarchy from the top down. The main rule to bear in mind when referencing the `Object` hierarchy is this: Always start your reference with the topmost object and reference all objects which appear between the top and the object you wish to reference. We'll look at this as we go through the `Object` hierarchy, and again at the end.

The Window object

The `Window` object is the main object from which all others are derived. This is the main browser application window itself. Unless you are referencing objects within a frame, the `Window` object reference is implicit. The following code snippet demonstrates the use of the `Alert` method of the `Window` object. Both lines of code produce identical results:

```
Window.Alert  Hello World
Alert  Hello World
```

The first call to the **Alert** method explicitly uses the **Window** object, while the second call, which is the more common way of referencing the Window objects, methods, and properties, makes use of the implicit **Window** object.

The most common **Window** object methods include the following:

Alert
Displays a simple message box with an "OK" click button.

Status
Displays a text string in the status bar at the bottom of the browser window.

Open
Creates a new window, and allows you to specify the appearance of that new window.

The **Window** object has one event, the **OnLoad** event, which allows you to create a script which will execute as soon as the page has completed downloading into the browser.

The Frame object

The **Frame** object is actually an array of **Frame** objects, whose immediate parent is the **Window** object. As such, there can be more than one **Frame** object, just as there can be more than one frame within a window. **Frame** object arrays can also be nested; that is, a frame within a frame. You access a **Frame** object by its name or by its ordinal number in the **Frame** object's array (which always starts at 0).

Referencing an object or control in another frame can cause a great deal of confusion unless you follow the rule of beginning your reference with the topmost object in the hierarchy. For example, let's say you have a FRAMESET document, which has two frames called **leftFrame** and **right-Frame**. The document in **rightFrame** contains a form called `frmForm1`, which in turn contains a text box called `txtText1`. The document in `leftFrame` contains a script, and you want to automatically change or set the value in the `txtText1` text box from this script.

If the form was within the same document as the script, you would access the `Value` property of the `txtText1` text box as follows:

```
Document.frmForm1.txtText1.Value =
    Some value
```

However, this form resides in a completely separate document, the only link to which is the browser itself. You must, therefore, start your reference with the browser window—which you refer to as `Top`, then reference the name of the frame. You can then carry on the reference to the text box in the normal way, like this:

```
Top.rightFrame.Document.frmForm1.
    txtText1.Value = Some Value
```

Naming your HTML objects is not only good programming practice, it will allow for more understandable, readable, and maintainable code. For example, the FRAMESET definition in the preceding example would look like this

```
<FRAMESET COLS 50%,50%>
  <FRAME SRC= somedoc.html
     NAME= leftFrame >
  <FRAME SRC= another.html
     NAME= rightFrame >
</FRAMESET>
```

If, however, you haven't named the frames, you will need to access them via their ordinal number in the `Frames` array, and your code would then look like this:

```
Top.Frames(1).Document.frmForm1.
    txtText1.Value = Some Value
```

Remember that the `Frames` array begins with 0, so the second frame is `Frames(1)`.

When a frame is present in a window, it inherits all the properties, methods, and events of the window.

The Document object

As its name suggests, the `Document` object refers to the actual HTML page itself. Each page or frame can contain only one `Document` object. The immediate parent of a `Document` object is either a frame object if the document has been loaded into a Frame, or a `Window` object where there are no frames.

Interacting with the `Document` object allows you to add variable text within an HTML document as it downloads to the browser, and even create complete new HTML documents directly from the browser.

The Form object

Just as there can be more than one form on an HTML document, there can be more than one `Form` object attached to a `Document` object. The `Form` object is therefore an array of objects. You can reference forms by name or by their ordinal number in the `Forms()` array. The `Forms()` array always starts at 0, and the position of a particular form in the array is determined by its position in the document. Therefore, the first form from the top of the document will be `Forms(0)`, the next `Forms(1)`, and so on.

Being able to access the `Forms` properties, methods, and events from VBScript allows you to dynamically change the `Action` property. So you can, for example, have the form point at a different server-side script depending upon user input. You can also programmatically submit the form, which allows you to validate form data prior to submission.

WARNING

A note about ActiveX controls and HTML forms. There's nothing to stop you from placing an ActiveX control, like a text box, within an HTML form. However, the HTML form knows nothing of ActiveX controls and ignores their data when the time comes to submit the form to the server. The only work-around to this is to programmatically copy the data from your ActiveX form controls into HTML hidden controls prior to submission.

The Element object

Although the `Element` object is so called, it is actually a loose collection of several different types of objects, or to be more precise, controls. These controls, which are associated with forms and data input include the text box, option buttons, and the like. With the exception of the `<SELECT>` control, the `Element` object (also known as Intrinsic HTML Controls) are defined using the `<INPUT>` tag.

The `Element` object is an array consisting of the various HTML controls that make up the form. As such, you can reference an element by its name or by its ordinal position within the array.

The immediate parent of the `Element` object is the `Form` object, so to reference an element, you must first reference the form, like this:

```
Document.frmForm1.text1.value
```

Although it's not documented, there is a `Count` property for the `Element` object, which returns the total number of `Element` objects in the `Element` array. Using this count as the upper limit of a For...Next loop, you can then iterate through the array like this:

```
For i = 0 to Document.frmForm1.
    Elements.Count - 1
    If Document.frmForm1.
    Elements(i).value = Hello
    World Then
Alert Found it
    End If
Next
```

Notice that because the array begins at 0 for the first `Element` object, the highest `Elements()` array index will be `Count -1`.

By far the simplest method of referencing the `Element` object is by their individual names. In fact, to create VB-style event handlers (code that executes in response to an event in the object)

you must use only the name of the element. For example, below is the event handler for the `OnClick` event on an HTML button control, called `myButton`:

```
Sub myButton_OnClick
    Alert  Hello World
End Sub
```

Additional objects

The following objects are shown out of the scope of the hierarchy, as they tend to cloud the way in which you would reference the objects in your code.

- The `Navigator` object is mainly for compatibility with other browsers: it exposes information about the application. The `Navigator` object's immediate parent is the `Window` object.

- The `History` object allows you to programmatically move back and forth within the browser's history list. While you can move to the *n*th item in the list, unfortunately you can't find out how many items are in the list!

- The `Location` object provides details on the current URL and also a method (`.href`) by which you can programatically move to a new URL.

When your application needs to interface with the document, forms, frames, and so on, you must use the MSIE Object Model. On the client side, therefore, VBScript and the MSIE Object Model are inextricably linked. Even without the inclusion of ActiveX Controls, you can use VBScript with the MSIE Object Model to create dynamic, powerful, and flexible Web pages, as we'll see in the next section.

Dynamic Web Pages

Here's a familiar scenario: A user enters data into an HTML form, and clicks "Submit." The data is transported across the Web to the server where a script or program springs into life. The data is validated by the script, but one of the required fields has not been input by the user. Another page is then constructed at the server to inform the user of the missing field, and sent back to the browser. The user reads the failure message, clicks the "Back" button, fills in the required field, and resubmits the form. Hopefully it will be accepted this time!

Here's another scenario: You want to give users a set of options, and based on the choice of the first set of options, present a second set of options. The only way to implement this multiple level of options in HTML is to ask the user to make a selection from the first set of options, submit this to the server, where a script then creates the page to present a new page of options based on the first.

HTML pages are interactive. A user can interact with an HTML page by clicking a hyperlink or entering data in a form. But when you need to inform the user of something, however trivial, (other than what was originally placed on the current HTML page), a new document must be sent from the server. HTML documents are *interactive* but not *dynamic*. All these transmissions back and forth across the Web waste the user's time, cause frustration, and above all, waste bandwidth. Furthermore, the user is presented with a "clunky" interface, which is poles apart from the smooth operation of the Windows interface they are used to.

Adding VBScript to a Web page can transform it into a dynamic Web application. You can interact with the browser, the document, and any controls placed within the page to create an environment that feels and acts like a Windows application. You can create new pages from the browser without having to waste time and bandwidth by going back to the server. You can also add variable content to an HTML page using VBScript as the page downloads into the browser. You can even launch a completely new browser window from your script, and have a certain amount of control over its size and appearance.

Here's a quick example of how to include some useful maintenance information at the bottom of each page:

```
<CENTER><FONT=1><B>
<SCRIPT LANGUAGE= vbscript >
    Document.Write  Last Modified:
            & Document.LastModified
</SCRIPT>
</B></FONT></CENTER>
```

Displaying the date and time that a document was last modified (as shown in Figure 1) is just as easy from the server, but what about displaying or obtaining date and time at the client? Let's say you want a slightly different feel to your Web site, depending upon the time of day. One way you could try and implement this is to somehow decide (based on the calling IP) where in the world the client is located, then based on the time difference (which you'd have to store in a database), work out what the time was at the client. A somewhat lengthy and complex process.

The easy way is to use a client-side script to determine the local time, and produce your customized page at the browser. Here's a snippet of VBScript Code which allows you to change the background and font colors based on the time of day.

```
<SCRIPT LANGUAGE= vbscript >
Dim sBGCol
Dim sFGCol

If Hour(Now()) < 19 And Hour(Now())
         > 6 Then
    sBGCol =  white
    sFGCol =  blue
Else
    sBGCol =  black
    sFGCol =  yellow
End If

Document.Write  <BODY BGCOLOR=  &
    sBGCol &   TEXT= & sFGCol &
    >
</SCRIPT>
```

Client-side scripting is about taking decisions or executing processes based on the user's input or from variables gleaned from the client machine

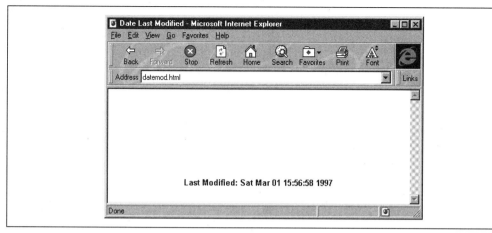

Figure 1

(or both), without having to waste time and bandwidth referring back to the server.

In this section we concentrated on how you can use just the MSIE Object Model to create dynamic Web applications. But VBScript goes much further—it is also the glue between the browser and ActiveX controls.

The ActiveX Glue

ActiveX controls can be split into two categories:

- Forms-type controls, which you group into a form for user input and the like. These controls have properties, methods, and events, all of which require VBScript code to interface them with the outside world.

- The complete self-contained application, an example of which is the Surround Video control that you can download from the Microsoft Web site.

In some respects, using VBScript with ActiveX controls is more straightforward than with HTML controls. This is because the ActiveX controls can be referenced directly. For example, to reference an HTML text box within a form you would code something like this:

```
sMyVal = Document.Form1.Text1.Value
```

Accessing the value of an ActiveX text box on the same page, however, is done like this:

```
sMyVal = Text1.Value
```

or like this:

```
sMyVal = Text1.Text
```

ActiveX controls do not form part of the HTML Object hierarchy and expose their properties, methods, and events on a global basis within the scope of the document.

Using ActiveX forms controls in preference to HTML controls lets you use a vast range of properties, methods, and events to create windows-like applications. All too often, when programming, things move along fine until you want to do that little bit extra, only to find that what you want to achieve isn't supported by the language or controls you're using. One of the most powerful things about the ActiveX controls is their ability to change dynamically.

To illustrate how to use ActiveX controls dynamically, Example 1 takes one of the scenarios that I used at the start of this section. You want to give the user several options; based on the result of these options, you will give the user a further set of options.

Example 1

```
<HTML>
<HEAD>
<TITLE>New Page</TITLE>

    <SCRIPT LANGUAGE="vbscript">
     this part of the script executes as the page is loading
     into the browser
     dimension three variables to hold the arrays
    Dim sOptionsOne
    Dim sOptionsTwo
    Dim sRegions
     populate the arrays
    sRegions = Array("Europe", "Middle East")
    sOptionsOne = Array("England", "France", "Germany", "Holland")
    sOptionsTwo = Array("Saudi Arabia","Bahrain","Dubai","Kuwait")
    Sub Window_OnLoad()
         this event handler executes immediately after the page
         has loaded
        Dim I
         populate the first combo box with values from the
         sRegions array
        For i = 0 to UBound(sRegions)
            ComboBox1.AddItem sRegions(i)
        Next
    End Sub
    Sub ComboBox1_Click()
         this event handler executes when the user selects a region
        Dim I
         clear out the countries combo
        Call ComboBox2.Clear()
         fill the countries combo with the relevant countries
        If ComboBox1.List(ComboBox1.ListIndex) = "Europe" Then
         For i = 0 to UBound(sOptionsOne)
                ComboBox2.AddItem sOptionsOne(i)
         Next
        Else
         For i = 0 to UBound(sOptionsTwo)
                ComboBox2.AddItem sOptionsTwo(i)
         Next
        End If

    End Sub
    </SCRIPT>

</HEAD>
<BODY BGCOLOR="white">
<FONT FACE="arial"><B>
<CENTER>
Select a Region
    <OBJECT ID="ComboBox1" WIDTH=137 HEIGHT=24
     CLASSID="CLSID:8BD21D30-EC42-11CE-9E0D-00AA006002F3">
        <PARAM NAME="VariousPropertyBits" VALUE="746604571">
        <PARAM NAME="DisplayStyle" VALUE="3">
```

Example 1 *(continued)*

```
            <PARAM NAME="Size" VALUE="3620;635">
            <PARAM NAME="MatchEntry" VALUE="1">
            <PARAM NAME="ShowDropButtonWhen" VALUE="2">
            <PARAM NAME="FontCharSet" VALUE="0">
            <PARAM NAME="FontPitchAndFamily" VALUE="2">
            <PARAM NAME="FontWeight" VALUE="0">
    </OBJECT>
<BR><BR>
Select a Country
    <OBJECT ID="ComboBox2" WIDTH=137 HEIGHT=24
     CLASSID="CLSID:8BD21D30-EC42-11CE-9E0D-00AA006002F3">
            <PARAM NAME="VariousPropertyBits" VALUE="746604571">
            <PARAM NAME="DisplayStyle" VALUE="3">
            <PARAM NAME="Size" VALUE="3620;635">
            <PARAM NAME="MatchEntry" VALUE="1">
            <PARAM NAME="ShowDropButtonWhen" VALUE="2">
            <PARAM NAME="FontCharSet" VALUE="0">
            <PARAM NAME="FontPitchAndFamily" VALUE="2">
            <PARAM NAME="FontWeight" VALUE="0">
    </OBJECT>
</BODY>
</HTML>
```

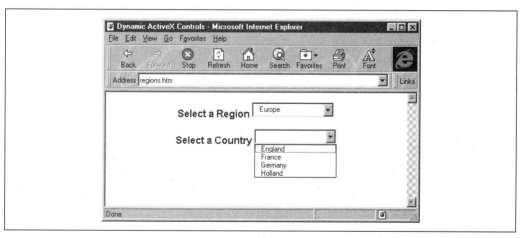

Figure 2

If the Object definition for the ActiveX controls in Example 1 looks a little daunting, don't worry. The ActiveX controls were placed on the page (see Figures 2 and 3) in minutes using the ActiveX Control Pad, described in the section entitled "Active Scripting Tools," later in this article.

Client-Side VBScript Examples

Example 2 is a data validation example, using HTML Intrinsic Controls. The code in Example 2 generated the page shown in Figure 4.

Example 2.1 makes use of the HTML Layout control to create an input form that will be much

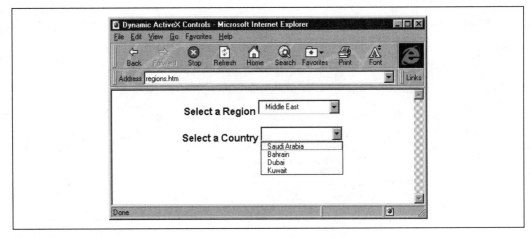

Figure 3

Example 2

```
<HTML>
<HEAD>
<TITLE>Data Validation</TITLE>
<SCRIPT LANGUAGE="vbscript">
  Sub cmdSubmit_OnClick

     If Not IsNumeric(Document.frmForm1.txtNumber.Value) Then
         MsgBox "Invalid Number Format",vbCritical + vbOKOnly,"Data Not
    Submitted"
         Exit Sub
     End If
     If InStr(Document.frmForm1.txtEMail.Value, "@")  = 0 Then
         MsgBox "Invalid EMail Address",vbCritical + vbOKOnly,"Data Not
    Submitted"
         Exit Sub
     End If
     If Not IsDate(Document.frmForm1.txtDOB.Value) Then
         MsgBox "Invalid Date of Birth",vbCritical + vbOKOnly,"Data Not
    Submitted"
         Exit Sub
     End If
     iResponse = MsgBox ("Data Validated, transmit to server?", _
                    vbYesNoCancel + vbQuestion, _
                    "About to transmit")
     If iResponse = vbYes Then
        Document.frmForm1.Submit
     Else
        Alert "Submit Cancelled"
     End If
  End Sub

</SCRIPT>
</HEAD>
```

Example 2 *(continued)*

```
<BODY BGCOLOR="white">
 <FONT="arial" SIZE=2><B>
 <CENTER>
  <FORM NAME="frmForm1" ACTION="anything.any" METHOD=POST>
    Enter a number
    <INPUT TYPE="text" NAME="txtNumber"><BR>
    Enter your Email Address
    <INPUT TYPE="text" NAME="txtEMail"><BR>
    Enter your Date of Birth
    <INPUT TYPE="text" NAME="txtDOB"><BR>
    <INPUT TYPE="button" NAME="cmdSubmit" VALUE="Submit">
  </FORM>
 </CENTER>
</BODY>
```

more familiar to Windows users. The following functionality has been included in the user interface of this simple form, all of which is impossible using standard HTML controls.

- As the user tabs into the text box, the background color of the particular text box changes color (in this case to a light blue—cyan—which, contrary to the VBScript documentation, is *not* a shade of red!).

- Again, as the user enters a text box the font style is changed to bold, allowing the current text to be easily distinguished.

- Note that the "Submit" button (see the form shown in Figure 5) has an accelerator defined as the "S"; therefore, the user can "click" the "Submit" button by using the Alt+S combination from the keyboard.

Snippets of the source code follow, starting with one of the scripts that makes up the `.alx HTML Layout` control file. An HTML `Layout` control is defined in a separate file that is then itself defined as an object to be included in the parent HTML document. The script in Example 2.1 attaches two event handlers to the control `TextBox3` in the `Layout` control. Almost identical scripts were also written for each of the other two text boxes in the `.alx Layout` control file.

Example 2.2 shows another part of the scripting that makes up the `.alx Layout` Control file. It shows the first few lines of definition code for the ActiveX controls from the HTML `Layout` file—I haven't included them all for fear of sending you to sleep!

Finally Example 2.3 shows the complete HTML code used for the HTML page that hosts the `.alx Layout` Control file.

As you can see, the HTML document simply houses the Layout Control; all the functionality for this form is held within the Layout Control itself. Changes can be made to the form without having to change the HTML page in any way.

Server-Side Scripting

An increasingly important role for VBScript is to be found at the server. As with client-side VBScript, server-side VBScript is the glue between controls and objects, only this time the controls and objects reside and run at the server.

Server-side scripting was around a long time before client-side scripting, and while a reluctance for Web designers to use client-side scripting is still evident, no such reluctance is seen for server-side scripting. In fact, languages such as Perl and PHP/FI (*http://www.vex.net/php/*) continue to gain popularity.

One reason why Web designers may choose server-side scripting is that the resultant HTML page can be viewed and used on any HTML Web

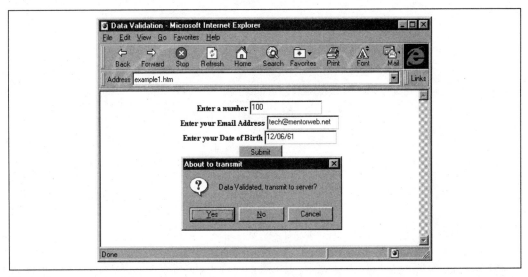

Figure 4

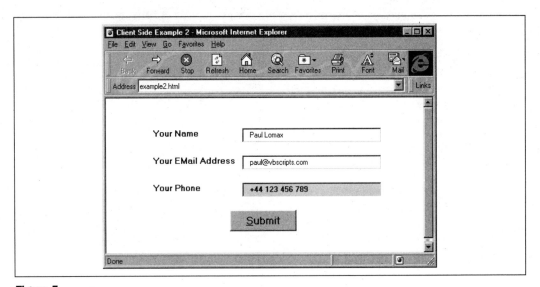

Figure 5

Example 2.1   The Enter and Exit Events for TextBox3

```
<SCRIPT LANGUAGE="VBScript">
<!--
Sub TextBox3_Enter()
    TextBox3.BackColor = vbCyan
    TextBox3.Font.Bold = True
End sub
```

Example 2.1   The Enter and Exit Events for TextBox3

```
Sub TextBox3_Exit(Cancel)
    TextBox3.BackColor = vbWhite
    TextBox3.Font.Bold = False
End Sub
-->
</SCRIPT>
```

Example 2.2   One of the ActiveX Text Boxes Defined in HTML

```
DIV BACKGROUND="#ffffff" ID="Layout2"
    STYLE="LAYOUT:FIXED;WIDTH:320pt;HEIGHT:169pt;">
    <OBJECT ID="TextBox1"
     CLASSID="CLSID:8BD21D10-EC42-11CE-9E0D-00AA006002F3"
    STYLE="TOP:25pt;LEFT:132pt;WIDTH:173pt;HEIGHT:17pt;TABINDEX:0;ZINDEX:0;">
        <PARAM NAME="VariousPropertyBits" VALUE="746604571">
        <PARAM NAME="Size" VALUE="6112;582">
        <PARAM NAME="FontCharSet" VALUE="0">
        <PARAM NAME="FontPitchAndFamily" VALUE="2">
        <PARAM NAME="FontWeight" VALUE="0">
    </OBJECT>
```

browser. Compatibility of the HTML page with the browser is not an issue.

As the development of the Web continues, as with all software, users and developers need to push the limits of the technology with more and more new and adventurous things. It is now not uncommon for databases to be accessed and queried during the creation of a page at the server, the resulting recordset being displayed as an HTML page and transmitted to the client. Small standalone programs written in C++, Java, and Visual Basic often run unseen to create customized pages based on user response.

In the next section we'll explore how VBScript fits into the creation of Web pages at the server as an integral part of a new Microsoft technology called Active Server Pages.

Example 2.3   The Host HTML Document

```
<HTML>
<HEAD>
<TITLE>Client Side Example 2</TITLE>
</HEAD>
<BODY BGCOLOR="white">
<CENTER>
<OBJECT CLASSID="CLSID:812AE312-8B8E-11CF-93C8-00AA00C08FDF"
ID="example2Layout_alx" STYLE="LEFT:0;TOP:0">
<PARAM NAME="ALXPATH" REF VALUE="example2Layout.alx">
 </OBJECT>
</BODY>
</HTML>
```

Active Server Pages (ASP)

Microsoft Active Server Pages (ASP) is a server-side environment used to create and compile Web applications.

So what's the difference between creating pages at the server from, say, Perl scripts, and creating pages at the server from the ASP environment? Well, there are a couple of subtle yet important distinctions that have to be made.

- First, you need to make the distinction between a bunch of HTML documents which are hyperlinked together and reside within the same Web page and an ASP application. Simply, ASP sees these documents as a complete application with a common root, which even allows common properties, objects, and a common session. When a user downloads a page from an ASP Web site for the first time, the application and a unique session is deemed to have started—it is even possible to program the ASP application to force a particular start page to be loaded regardless of the first page requested.

- Second, the technology of Active Server Pages allows controls and objects normally associated with the windows desktop environment to be executed at the server and the results transmitted as HTML. Windows Client-Server programming makes use of a technology called *remote automation.* Automation servers are small self contained programs which live on the server and spring into life when called, passing results and data back to the client program. There are thousands and thousands of these automation servers in use throughout the world. They now have a new name: *ActiveX Server Components.* Again, Microsoft has allowed developers to leverage their current knowledge and investment.

To illustrate this point, take a real scenario—I know this one to be factual—of trying to put a database online before the advent of Active Server Pages and its related technology. The company in question had an SQL Server database running on an NT platform with a Visual Basic client program. The plan was, because of the nature of the data, to open the database up to the public over the Web, allowing them to make queries on the database and view the results. At the time, the only platform capable of handling a high volume Web site was UNIX, which posed no real problems since a Sybase SQL server could be put in place. However, the server-side programming would have to be done using a combination of Perl and C++—a large undertaking that eventually put the whole project on hold until a more cost-effective solution could be found.

The solution, which was not available at the time, is with us now. The company has since upgraded to NT4, SQL Server 6.5, and has installed the Microsoft Internet Information Server (IIS) and ASP. This means that with only minor modifications, their current automation servers can be used, and the developers within the company can put their SQL Server and VB experience to good use creating the Web pages that obtain their data from the company's SQL Server database. The project will now take a fraction of the time at a fraction of the cost it might otherwise have taken.

So how does ASP work?

1. You create your active server page using scripts, object references (more about these later) and normal HTML, and save the file in an *.asp* file.

2. When the client browser requests an *.asp* file from the Web server, the Web server then calls ASP, which reads the file, interpreting the code and calling the various objects and ActiveX server components as necessary.

3. The output of all ActiveX server components and objects is ultimately HTML, and the HTML page that finally results from this processing is then sent to the browser in the usual way.

The client browser therefore sees a normal HTML page, the user sees the results of sophisticated server side processing, and apart from the unusual filename extension is unaware that this is anything other than a HTML page.

Active Server Pages operates on the following platforms:

- Microsoft Internet Information Server version 3.0 on Windows NT Server

- Microsoft Peer Web Services Version 3.0 on Windows NT Workstation

- Microsoft Personal Web Server on Windows 95

VBScript for ASP

Unlike MSIE, whose default langauge is JScript, ASP's default langauge is VBScript. And unlike client-side scripting, which requires you to use a <SCRIPT> tag to contain your script, server-side VBScript needs only a simple <% %> to be recognized.

The <% %> and <%= %> tags

ASP scripts are separated from the rest of the document by the <% and %> tags. Expressions to be output as part of the HTML page are delimited with the <%= and %> tags. The nice thing about these tags is that they can be used for multiple line scripts, statements and even single expressions. For example:

```
<%myVar= Hello World %>
```

assigns the string "Hello World" to a variable called myVar. Because VBScript uses a special data type called a variant, you don't have to predefine or dimension the myVar variable—you just start using it. Now let's print out the variable to the HTML page:

```
<H2>I d just like to say
    <%=myVar%></H2>
```

Within the <% %> tags, you can use the full range of VBScript language constructs, keywords, and functions, enabling you to write sophisticated scripts that run at the server. You can also write scripts and functions common to many pages within the ASP application, save them in an *.inc* file and include them in an HTML page with a single call.

Server-Side Includes

Server-side includes allow you to create a file for inclusion in the ASP page, which will be processed through the ASP engine as though it were an integral part of the *.asp* file.

To use server-side includes, you simply use the #INCLUDE preprocessor directive, like this:

```
<!--#INCLUDE FILE="myinclude.inc"-->
```

Prior to processing the page, ASP scans the *.asp* file from top to bottom, looking for any included files. If one is found, the content of the included file replaces the #INCLUDE tag. Any #INCLUDE directives in the included file are also handled at this stage. This means you can nest #INCLUDE tags, although you cannot create circular references—that is, you can't try and include the file that is including the INCLUDE file (clear as mud?) If file *A* contains an INCLUDE directive referencing file *B*, file *B* can't contain an INCLUDE directive referencing file *A*.

INCLUDE files allow you to easily create standard scripts, HTML menus, and other code common to several pages. A good example of this would be an INCLUDE file like the one below:

```
<BODY BACKGROUND= myback.gif
    TEXT= blue >
<FONT FACE= arial >
```

This may not appear to be startling as an INCLUDE file, but imagine being able to change the color scheme for an entire Web site by amending one file! Although it may never happen—your client may not like your choice of background—within a minute you can change it for the whole Web site.

Within a complex Web site of maybe 20 or 30 pages, all of which use a similar menu, the chances of an error on one of the menus is quite high (until it's fully debugged). However, if the menus were created using a combination of INCLUDE files and scripts, you may only need to specify the menu once, reducing the chance of an error to almost nil. (I suppose you could look at it another way, and say that if you have an error in the included file, every page will contain an error! . . . but at least it's consistent.)

Dynamically Creating Client-Side Scripts

One of the most exciting things about ASP is its ability to create variable client-side scripts. This opens up all sorts of possibilities: you can modify the variables and values within a script based on, say, the user's selection from the database.

Using server-side scripts to create or modify client-side scripts is easy: you simply interlace server-side scripts within your client-side script. When the page is generated by ASP, only the client-side script, complete with the result of the server-side script, is left. Here's a quick example:

```
<%
    If iSomething = 1 Then
        sControl =  cmdButton1
    Else
        sControl =  cmdButton2
    End if
%>
<SCRIPT LANGUAGE= vbscript >
 Sub <%=sControl%>_OnClick
    Alert  you clicked
    <%=sControl%>
 End Sub
</SCRIPT>
```

A server-side script is used first to decide if sControl should be cmdButton1 or cmdButton2. Next, two server-side output commands are used to fill in the variables in the client-side script. For instance, if the server-side variable iSomething equals 1, the HTML code that will reach the client will read like this:

```
<SCRIPT LANGUAGE= vbscript >
 Sub cmdButton1_OnClick
    Alert  you clicked cmdButton1
 End Sub
</SCRIPT>
```

Active Server Pages Built-In Objects

In very much the same way that client-side VBScript has access to the browsers' objects when used at the server, VBScript can access and manipulate the Active Server Pages framework through it's five built-in objects. Many of the objects, properties, and methods are designed to work with application scope, which means that all pages in the ASP application have access to the object or data. For this reason, a special page never seen by the user, called *Global.asa*, is included in the ASP application. When a user enters the application for the first time in a session, the *Global.asa* file is run, and any global settings are then made for this user's current session.

The five built-in objects are described in the sections that follow.

The Application object

An ASP application is the *.asp* file in a Web directory and its subdirectories. The Application object, which is instantiated in the *Global.asa* file, can be used to share data across the ASP application by allowing you to store values within the object as user-defined properties. Due to the fact that your ASP application may be used by many different users at the same time, the Application object allows you to lock and unlock the user-defined properties when you are updating them—an essential part of a multi-user environment.

Here's a simple example of how to store a value in the Application object. These values can then be accessed by all the files that make up the application.

```
<% Application( MyBackColor ) =
    green  %>
```

Then ,on each page of the application, you can create a uniform <BODY> tag like this:

```
<BODY
    BGCOLOR=<%=Application( MyBackCo
    lor )%> >
```

The Request object

The `Request` object contains the values passed to the server as part of an HTTP request. The values are held in the `Request` object in five collections:

- The `QueryString` collection contains the values passed to the server by a `Form` submission in a request using the GET method. The values are passed in the HTTP query string which follows the question mark (?) in the HTTP request.

- The `Form` collection contains the values passed to the server by a `Form` submission using a POST method.

- The `Cookies` contains the values of any cookies transmitted as part of the HTTP request.

- The `ClientCertificate` collection contains the values requested from the client browser by the server in an SSL protocol connection.

- The `ServerVariables` collection contains the environment variables such as `HTTP_USER_AGENT`.

Here's a quick `Request` example that shows how to use the `Form` collection. Let's say you have a `Form` on an HTML page with an `<INPUT>` text box called `EMailAddr`. To assign the value of `EMailAddr` to a variable called `sEMail` within the *.asp* file, which has been specified as the ACTION for the form, you would use the following code:

```
<% sEmail = Request.
   Form("EMailAddr")%>
```

Suppose also that on the same form you have a `<SELECT>` control called `SkillType`, which you allow the user to perform multiple selections on. When the data is transmitted to the server there will be multiple name-value pairs for the `SkillType` variable. When ASP encounters more than one name-value pair with the same name, it creates a collection or array for the name, and adds values to the collection as they arrive.

To access these values you can either use the `Count` property of the collection to obtain the number of values in the collection, or you can use the VBScript For Each...Next loop.

```
<%
  For i = 1 To Request.
    Form("SkillType").Count
    sSkillArray(i) = Request.
    Form( SkillType)(i)
  Next
%>
<%
  For Each item in Request.
    Form( SkillType )
    i = i  + 1
    sSkillArray(i) = item
  Next
%>
```

The Response object

The `Response` object is used to send information and output back to the client. This can be achieved in two ways:

- By sending `Cookies` back to the browser to be stored for use at a later time.

- By using the `Response` object's `Write` method, which places a string in the HTTP HTML output.

To illustrate how the `Response` object's `Write` method works, let's carry on the example that we started with the `Request` object above. This time, instead of assigning the incoming values to variables on the server, let's write them back to an HTML page as a confirmation of the user's data entry.

```
<% Response.Write Request.
   Form("EMailAddr")
   For Each item in Request.
   Form( SkillType )
       Response.Write item &  <BR>
   Next
%>
```

The Server object

The `Server` object allows you to interact with the server by exposing a property and several utility methods.

The `ScriptTimeout` property sets the time that a script is allowed to execute before it times out. For example:

```
<% Server.ScriptTimeout = 30 %>
```

Methods include the following:

- `CreateObject` is used to create an instance of a server component.

- `HTMLEncode` is used to apply HTML encoding to a specified string.

- `MapPath` is used to map a virtual path, for example the relative path to the current page, to physical path.

- `URLEncode` is used to apply URL encoding rules to a string.

The Session object

The `Session` Object stores information about a user session. A session is created when a particular user downloads a page from the ASP application for the first time; that is, the user does not have a current session in force. The session remains in force until there is no activity from the user for the given period (in minutes) set by the session timeout property. Using the `Abandon` method, you can also programatically end the current user session.

During the session, the values held within the `Session` object are available throughout the application. The `Session` object is only available to clients that support and accept cookies.

Properties include the following:

- `SessionID` returns the session identification for the current user.

- `Timeout` sets or returns the timeout period for this session, in minutes.

Methods include the following:

- `Abandon` destroys the current `Session` object and releases its resources.

Active Server Pages Components

ASP components are server-side ActiveX applications, which you call from within your ASP script by creating them as object instances. These applications automate and enable some neat extensions to the normal capabilities of ASP. These five components are described below.

Advertisement Rotator

The advertisement rotator allows you to specify a range of banner adverts, which will be shown randomly on your pages. There is also a facility to state what weighting or percentage of selections should be given to each advert in your list. A redirection can be built into the advert list to allow for logging of click-through rates.

Browser Capabilities

One of the nice things about creating variable pages at the server is that the HTML you create can be viewable by all flavors of browser (well, that's the theory anyway). We all know that unless you stoop to the lowest common denominator, someone, somewhere isn't going to see your page as it was intended. That's where the browser capabilities component comes in. During the creation of the page you can answer such questions as, "Does the browser support . . . Frames? Tables? VBScript? JavaScript? HTML?" Then you can create the optimal page for the calling browser. Combined with ASP's Server Side Include facility you can create an infinitely variable set of pages.

Content Linker

Earlier, I mentioned adding a common menu using the `Include` directive. To go one better than that you can use the content linker component. The content linker uses a textual list of the URLs within the current application, from which you can create your menus and navigational aids.

Database Access

This is arguably the most important Active Server component. Whether you are creating a small scale application to interface Access, run through the Personal Web Server on Windows 95, or a complex real-time Web application running on NT4 using SQL Server, the Database Access component will allow you to link into the database with the minimum of fuss and work. Your ASP script can send SQL queries to the database and display the results in as many formats as you can come up with using HTML and ActiveX client-side controls. Because the query is built and executed on the server, the speed of retrieval is very fast. You then simply reference the fields in the resultant recordset to create your Web page.

Database access is achieved using ODBC, and the OBDC data object is usually created in the *Global.asa* file as the current session commences. The benefits of this are twofold. First, the *Global.asa* file cannot be accessed from the client, so any password information that is held within the data object creation string is hidden. Second, the overhead in terms of processing time, which is associated with creating the link to the database, is experienced only once, at the beginning of the session; all subsequent processing is transacted through the now open data connection.

There is, however, one drawback to this method of opening the database: you can end up with many open connections to the database, each hogging valuable resources. The connections will not be dropped until the session has either timed out or been explicitly abandoned. The only way around this is to take advantage of the new Microsoft Transaction server, which allocates connections from a pool of open connections to the database. There are many other advantages to the Transaction Server, and if you are operating a database from a Web page I would strongly suggest you look into installing the Transaction server.

Text Stream

The text stream component allows you to create, open, read from, and write to an ASCII text file within the Web. I suppose if you take this to its logical conclusion, you could thus create INCLUDE files dynamically, which could be used to create new and variable client-side scripts, based on the user input earlier in the ASP application!

Active Server components add flexibility, power, and sophistication to any Web application, be it for commercial, private, or public viewing.

The concept of Active server components has the potential to do for ASP what VBX (and later OCX) custom controls did for Visual Basic. Hundreds, if not thousands, of third-party software houses will be producing neatly packaged extensions to ASP allowing more and more sophisticated ASP applications to be written—thus enhancing still further the experience for the Web user and functionality of the Web site. Program developers in VB, C++, and Java can all write Active Server components. The drive of commercial enterprises into Intranets will assure a ready and lucrative market for well written and useful Active Server components, which can only serve to add fuel to the fire.

A Server-Side Scripting Example

The following examples show how to update an SQL database from a Web page. These particular examples runs on my personal Web server on Windows 95 and uses an Access database. By changing only one line of code (the connection string), however, it could operate on an NT4 IIS Web server linking into SQL Server.

The examples follow from the earlier examples for the Request and Response methods. This time we ask the user for their name, email address, and a selection of their skills. The data is then captured into two referential database tables. The first table, "users," holds the user's

Example 3.1   The Global.asa File

```
<SCRIPT LANGUAGE=VBScript RUNAT=Server>
Sub Session_OnStart
    Session("DataConn_ConnectionString") = "DSN=MS Access 7.0 Database;" _
                                         & "DBQ=C:\W3C\w3c.mdb;" _
                                         & "DefaultDir=C:\W3C;" _
                                         & "DriverId=25;" _
                                         & "FIL=MS Access;" _
                                         & "MaxBufferSize=512;" _
                                         & "PageTimeout=5;"
    Session("DataConn_ConnectionTimeout") = 15
    Session("DataConn_CommandTimeout") = 30
    Session("DataConn_RuntimeUserName") = ""
    Session("DataConn_RuntimePassword") = ""
End Sub
</SCRIPT>
```

name and email address, and the second table, "skills," holds the user's name and skill. A one-to-many link on the user's name (not an ideal link in the real world) exists between the two tables.

Example 3.1 is the *Global.asa* file, which contains one event: the `Session_OnStart` event. When the user enters the Web site (application) for the first time, this event is executed. The code saves several variables needed for the data connection within the `Session` object. These session variables are guarded from possible viewing by prying eyes, and are gloablly available to all files in the application.

The first variable is the `ConnectionString`, which is used to link into the database using ODBC. As you will see, the connection is to an

access database on my local hard drive but could just as easily have been an SQL Server database.

Note that in Example 3.1, I have used the VBScript line continuation character (_) combined with the string concatentation operator (&) extensively in the `ConnectionString` line. I find this much easier to read and debug! However, you can write the string in one long line.

The first HTML the user will load is *default.htm*, shown in Example 3.2. This is a standard HTML document containing a simple HTML form. The form defines two text boxes and a Select control. The form's action property has been set to point at an *.asp* file called *process.asp* that lives in the same directory as *default.htm*.

Example 3.2   The default.htm file

```
<HTML>
<HEAD>
<TITLE>Sample Input Form</TITLE>
</HEAD>
<BODY BGCOLOR="white">
<CENTER>
<H2> Welcome to my web </H2>
<BR>
<FORM ACTION="process.asp" METHOD=POST>
Please enter your name
<INPUT TYPE="text" NAME="txtUserName">
<BR>
Please enter your Email Address
```

Example 3.2 *(continued)*   The default.htm file

```
<INPUT TYPE="text" NAME="txtEMail">
<BR>
Please select one or more skills
<SELECT NAME="sltSkills" SIZE=5 MULTIPLE>
<OPTION>Word for Windows
<OPTION>HTML
<OPTION>Visual Basic
<OPTION>Java
<OPTION>ActiveX
<OPTION>VBScript
<OPTION>JScript
</SELECT>
<BR>
<INPUT TYPE="submit" NAME="cmdSubmit" VALUE="Submit">
</FORM>
</CENTER>
</BODY>
</HTML>
```

Now for the good bit, *process.asp*, shown in Example 3.3. First of all, the scripting language is set for the document. This means that you don't need to keep specifying it if you have multiple scripts within the document.

Next comes the initial HTML code, to set up the document when it arrives at the browser.

The first line of script creates a **Connection** object, with the name of **DBConn**. The **DBConn** object variable will now be used to set the required properties and perform the database update. The timeout properties of the **Connection** object are set next, and the connection is then opened. Note the use of the global session variables. The first SQL string, which will update the "users" table, is constructed using the incoming form data. Again, purely for readability, I've used the line continuation and concatenation characters.

The record is added to the database table by calling the connection's **Execute** method. This is the most basic way of inserting a record (please note that I've not included any error handling in this example).

A "For Each...Next" loop then performs the required number of inserts into the skills table again using the information passed in from the form.

Finally, the data is echoed to the HTML page using the **Response** object's **Write** method, as shown previously.

Example 3.3   The process.asp File

```
<%@ LANGUAGE="VBSCRIPT" %>
<HTML>
<HEAD>
<TITLE>Sample Process</TITLE>
</HEAD>
<BODY BGCOLOR="white">
<CENTER>
Thank you.<BR>
<%
    Set DBConn = Server.CreateObject("ADODB.Connection")
```

Example 3.3 *(continued)*   The process.asp File

```
DBConn.ConnectionTimeout = Session("DataConn_ConnectionTimeout")
DBConn.CommandTimeout = Session("DataConn_CommandTimeout")
DBConn.Open Session("DataConn_ConnectionString"), _
            Session("DataConn_RuntimeUserName"), _
            Session("DataConn_RuntimePassword")
sSQL = "INSERT INTO users " _
    & "( UserName, EmailAddress ) " _
  & "VALUES (" _
  & "'" & Request.Form("txtUserName") & "'" _
  & ", " _
  & "'" & Request.Form("txtEmail") & "'" _
  & ")"
DBConn.Execute sSQL
For Each sSkill In Request.Form("sltSkills")
    sSQL = "INSERT INTO skills " _
          & "( UserName, Skill ) " _
      & "VALUES (" _
          & "'" & Request.Form("txtUserName") & "'"_
          & ", " _
          & "'" & sSkill & "'"_
          & ")"
    DBConn.Execute sSQL
Next
%>
<%

    Response.Write Request.Form("txtUserName") & "<BR>"
    Response.Write Request.Form("txtEmail") & "<BR>"

    For Each item in Request.Form("sltSkills")
        Response.Write item & "<BR>"
    Next
%>
</BODY>
</HTML>
```

The code above is VBScript, but with the exception of the "For Each...Next" loop (not the code within it), none of the above VBScript code is available to you when writing a client-side script. Although, VBScript has had one hand tied behind its back for client-side scripting, on the server, VBScript is every bit as powerful as Visual Basic.

Active Scripting Tools

When VBScript was launched, all you had to work with was a single run-time DLL, which operated via MSIE 3.0. Now there seems to be an ever-growing array of tools, most of them freely downloadable from the Microsoft Web site.

Notepad
(Don't laugh!) Outside the VB development environment, this is my most used app! The original multiscripting language development environment! (Old habits die hard.)

ActiveX Control Pad
Freely available from the Microsoft Web site, this tool is invaluable for inserting ActiveX controls into an HTML document, featuring an easy-to-use properties window that lets you specify how the control will appear on the page. When you've finished, the control pad will create the full Object definition and place it in the HTML page.

HTML Layout Control

The "run-time" is part of the full install of MSIE, but requires the ActiveX control pad to develop HTML layout control *.alx* files. The results are fast and easy, enabling the creation of windows-like forms, with enhanced events, properties, and methods.

Script Wizard

Works in conjunction with both the control pad and the layout control. With this wizard you create simple client-side scripts using point and click. The script wizard recognizes both ActiveX controls and HTML intrinsic controls.

Active Scripting Debugger

The Microsoft Scripting Debugger is currently available for free download from the Microsoft Web site. It's easy to install and use. It can be launched by selecting the View Source option in the File menu of MSIE, which would normally launch Notepad. The Scripting Debugger allows you to trace execution of a script. By stepping through the script line by line at run-time, you can determine the value of variable at run-time and even evaluate values. The Scripting Debugger can save hours of frustrating work trying to track down those illusive little gremlins.

Visual InterDev

Not free, Visual Interdev was formerly known as Internet Studio. All of Microsoft's Internet and Web developments over the past year or so come together in one singing and dancing development environment. Part of the new Development Studio range, Visual Interdev handles everything with ease and great style.

The Future of Active Scripting

Trying to predict how Active Scripting will progress in the near to medium future seems almost futile at the moment. One has a feeling that no matter how outlandish an idea of the future you may have, it's probably going to happen, and sooner than you think. Only twelve months ago, what is now reality was a dream.

For example, sitting in front of my Windows 95 machine just south of London, I can create Web pages, create new database tables in my SQL Server database, view the database graphically, create ASP applications that access the SQL Server database, and I can even administer my IIS and NT4 Server from the Web. Oh, and by the way, my SQL Server database and NT4/IIS server are situated in Wyoming! (A few miles west of here!)

There is no doubt that Microsoft is into Web servers and Web browsers for the long run, and while they are, active scripting will play a vital and ever-increasing role in gluing together the many and various technologies that allow us to create new and exciting applications. Before long, the browser and desktop will merge into one, and again the glue will be active scripting. Just around the corner is HTML, which is dynamic even after loading into the browser.

With the release of Visual Basic 5, VB is sure to come to the forefront of sophisticated ActiveX control and object creation. NT4 and IIS provide a formidable platform on top of which everything sits. Visual Interdev and ASP will change the way we create, manage, and maintain Web sites (sorry—applications!), and the vital link between all these technologies is VBScript. ■

About the Author

Paul Lomax
Shibui Highfield Road,
Biggin Hill
Westerham, Kent TN16 3UX
England
tech@mentorweb.net

Paul Lomax is Technical Director of Mentorweb (*http://www.mentorweb.net/*), a leading Web design and hosting company. He has been a programmer for over 12 years and has been a dedicated fan of Visual Basic since version 1.

Paul has written systems for Financial Derivatives forecasting, Satellite TV Broadcasting, the Life Assurance industry, and a major materials tracking system for the Oil and Gas industry, having worked for clients in the UK, Germany, Holland, Denmark, Saudi Arabia, and Bahrain. He is also responsible for the concept, design, and programming of the successful "Contact" series of national business databases. Over the past two years Paul has created and maintained over 60 commercial Web sites for Mentorweb's clients. Paul has also created a Web resource dedicated to VBScript at *http://www.vbscripts.com/*.

Paul and his family—wife Deborah and children Russel and Victoria—have recently returned to their home in England after several years spent living in the Arabian gulf.

JavaScript
When HTML Is Not Enough

Nick Heinle

Abstract

In one sentence, JavaScript can be described as a simple scripting language designed to work with and control HTML. A language that's growing in popularity, it's an important technology for any self-respecting Web developer. In this article, you will learn why JavaScript exists, see examples of how JavaScript is used on the Web, and be introduced to the fundamental concepts of programming with JavaScript. In addition, this article presents two examples of JavaScript in action and gives tutorials on how to implement those examples on your own sites.

In the beginning there was HTML, and it was good. HTML allowed us Web authors to create structured, laid out pages, with images, text, and the like. It was a great tool for displaying information in a comprehensible and often visually appealing way. But we soon realized that it was not enough. The Web grew in popularity, and needed interactivity, instant feedback; static HTML was not enough anymore.

A Brief History of JavaScript

The answer to the problem of static HTML would come in December 1995, co-developed by Netscape Communications and Sun Microsystems, and its name would be JavaScript (originally called LiveScript, but changed for marketing reasons). JavaScript was designed to be a simple, effective scripting language for the Web and tied closely with HTML. Unlike other programming languages of the time (e.g., Java, CGI scripts), JavaScript was built right into the browser and worked alongside HTML. To many, the name JavaScript implied that it was a simplified version of Java. Though much of JavaScript's syntax was inspired by Java, the two have very different purposes. Java was designed as a programming language for writing powerful applets (portable programs) that could be embedded into a small rectangular area on a Web page. JavaScript, on the other hand, was a much simpler scripting language designed to work with and control HTML.

To this day, many journalists still suggest that JavaScript is a simpler way of creating Java applets, thus contributing to a common misconception.

In this article, you will learn the fundamental concepts of programming with JavaScript and be introduced to some examples of the scripting language in actual Web sites.

Why Does JavaScript Exist?

HTML, by design, is a language whose sole purpose is to lay out and format text and images. The purpose of JavaScript is to add some interactivity to HTML, to allow for user interaction and feedback, and to link HTML to other technologies such as Java, plug-ins, etc. With event handlers, JavaScript can catch events that occur on a page, such as the clicking of a button or the mouse moving over a link. These event handlers can then execute code to respond to those actions. In the case of a button being clicked, perhaps a script could be written to validate a form. In the case of the mouse moving over a link, perhaps a script could display an explanation of the link in the browser's status bar. Essentially, HTML is JavaScript's interface.

In addition to interacting with HTML, JavaScript can control Java applets and even certain plug-ins, thus allowing Web developers to tie these different tools together in the creation of more dynamic Web sites.

The Web Takes Notice

Back in April of 1996 I launched a Web site called JavaScript Tip of the Week (*http://www. webreference.com/javascript/*) to help Web developers learn the language and provide useful applications for Web sites. Little did I know how popular the site would become and how interested Web developers would be in this new language and what it could accomplish. Clearly, Web developers recognized that HTML was not dynamic enough to create exciting, interactive Web sites, and they were all looking for something more. JavaScript is a big part of that answer.

In a sense, JavaScript is a language for the people. It doesn't require a computer science degree and allows designers as well as programmers to use the language in creating Web sites. A cursory survey of popular commercial Web sites shows that JavaScript is growing in popularity as developers realize its full potential. Remote controls, pop-up windows, rollover images, and more advanced applications like interactive games and client-side database programs are all within the reach of JavaScript, and the Web is taking notice. The fact that the majority of Web browsers (Navigator and Internet Explorer) support JavaScript (though to different extent, as you will learn later) is also a plus for those looking for across-the-board compatibility.

A popular example of JavaScript in use can be found in the official Star Wars Web site (see Figure 1), where Luke Skywalker is "animated" to pick up his laser saber. Target sites around the various planets (not shown) also appear to "lock on" as the mouse is moved over them. This is accomplished by using JavaScript to modify images directly on the page, which are commonly referred to as *dynamic images.*

Another example of dynamic images can be found in the menu at the top of IBM's Web site (see Figure 2). When the mouse is moved over one of the image links, the image becomes active and a tool tip–like description of the link is displayed right below it.

These glitzy examples illustrate ways JavaScript can be used to enhance the aesthetics of a Web site, but there are also more utilitarian applications. MSN's (Microsoft Network) CarPoint (see Figure 3) makes extensive use of JavaScript in its car finder database application. It allows you to choose a vehicle based on a number of specifications: vehicle type, price, safety features, horse-

Figure 1   Star War's Web site at http://www.starwars.com

Figure 2 IBM's Web site at http://www.ibm.com

power, and fuel economy. Having made your selections, the application displays a list of the vehicles that satisfy those criteria.

Over the past year, examples like these have become standard. More and more commercial Web sites are using JavaScript to weave a better Web.

As the Web evolves, so does JavaScript. Originally, JavaScript's primary function was to validate forms, control frames, and aide in database applications. But since the release of JavaScript 1.0 with Netscape Navigator 2.0, its ability to control Web pages has increased manyfold. Now, with JavaScript 1.2, released with Navigator 4.0, it is

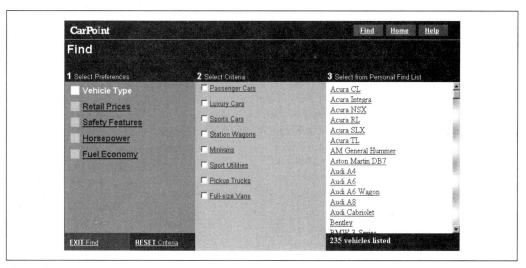

Figure 3 MSN's CarPoint Car Finder http://carpoint.msn.com/ie/Find/default.asp

possible to create full-fledged multimedia presentations using a combination of plug-ins, Java applets, and HTML, all tied together with JavaScript. No doubt JavaScript will continue to play a major role in development of a more interactive and dynamic World Wide Web.

Issues and Problems

Even though widely used, JavaScript has its fair share of problems. The fact that it keeps evolving in form and function from one browser to the next creates compatibility problems. For example, the dynamic images discussed earlier are not supported in the original version of JavaScript that came with Navigator 2.0 (and Internet Explorer). Therefore, the script has to be written around older browsers. Another issue is that scripts often behave differently in Internet Explorer than they do in Navigator; this is, of course, because Microsoft had to reverse engineer its implementation of JavaScript, called "JScript."

One of the first problems with JavaScript, back when Navigator 2.0 was released, dealt with security. Web developers were able to create hidden "mailto" forms that automatically submitted themselves to the server. The problem was that, in effect, people were unwittingly giving their e-mail addresses to Web sites. Netscape responded quickly by posting a version of the browser that fixed this problem.

From a programmer's point of view, JavaScript is lacking in certain areas. For example, there is no Switch/Case statement in all but the newest versions of JavaScript (1.2 and beyond). Another problem is that while JavaScript is object-based, it's not a true object-oriented programming language. There is no way to create a true class for objects in JavaScript as you would in C++ or Java, though you can create user-defined objects using constructor functions.

JavaScript is not alone in its ambition to become the Web's "standard" client-side scripting language. Its competitor, if you can call it that, is a scripting language introduced by Microsoft: VBScript.[*] VBScript, though based on the Visual Basic programming language, is very similar in function to JavaScript. The problem with VBScript is that it's not supported by Netscape Navigator, which leads one to question its practical use outside of the corporate Intranet (at least for the time being).

An Introduction to Programming with JavaScript

An Object-Oriented World

There are millions of "objects" in the real world: trees, telephones, people—almost everything we deal with is an object. One could say that we live in an object oriented world. Because of this, programming languages, such as Java and C++, are object-oriented as well. JavaScript is supposed to be an object-oriented language, but it "lacks" in many respects, as most programmers will tell you. Regardless, you should treat JavaScript as an object-oriented langauge.

In JavaScript, there are a large number of objects. For example, the page is an object: document. The (browser) window is an object as well: window. Before you understand how objects work in JavaScript, you have to relate them to real life. To do this, we are going to use a familiar object: your car. Let's be a little abstract and think of your car in terms of JavaScript. We can do this by creating and manipulating our own car object, which we will name mycar. This is purely hypothetical—there is obviously no car object in JavaScript—and is for purposes of learning only. We can begin by defining mycar as a new car object:

```
mycar = new Car();
```

---

[*] VBScript is described in Paul Lomax's article entitled "VBScript: Active Clients and Servers," also in this issue.

You've seen this syntax before; when we we created a `Date` object. Here, however, we are creating a car object and naming it `mycar`. Now you can begin to manipulate the car object and, in the process, learn a few things about object-oriented programming.

The property concept

A property is a concept that is used all the time in object-oriented programming. Your car has many different properties: color, brand, horsepower, and price, to name a few. What if you want to change the color property of your car object to red; in other words, paint your car red. In English, you would say, "I want the `color` of `mycar` to be `red`."

In JavaScript, the syntax is slightly different:

```
mycar.color = "red";
```

Your car object, `mycar`, is separated from its property, `color`, by a dot. This is the equivalent of saying, "the `color` of `mycar`". After you have referred to your car's `color` property in this way, you can then do something with that property. In this example, the `color` property of `mycar` is set to "red" using an equal sign. This is like finishing the sentence, "I want the `color` of `mycar` . . . to be `red`."

To apply this to JavaScript, why not use an object and a property that are commonly used: `window.location`. Just as color is a property *of* your car, the location bar is a property *of* the browser window. To change the currently displayed document in the browser window, use the same syntax as you did before, separating the window object from its location property with a dot and setting that combination equal to something:

```
window.location = "somefile.html";
```

The `status` property is part of the `window` object as color is part of your car. This analogy will help you to understand how objects work as you start getting more into the language.

The method concept

Methods, like functions, are used to preform the JavaScript equivalent of "actions." The difference is that methods are directly associated with an object. Think about it in terms of your car again: `mycar`. In addition to having properties, your car has actions that you can "do to it," such as accelerate, break, and honk. These actions, when associated with the car object, are referred to as methods. To accelerate your car object, you could run its `accelerate` method:

```
mycar.accelerate();
```

The syntax here is similar to when you are working with a property, such as `color`, but the telltale double parentheses denote that this is a method. A more useful `accelerate()` method would allow you to tell the car object how much you want to accelerate. Perhaps you could pass it the speed in mph:

```
mycar.accelerate(15);
```

This would accelerate the car by 15 mph.

A very common example of a method is the `write()` method of the `document` object: you've used it before, but now you should understand why it looks like it does:

```
document.write("Here's the text I'm
     passing to the write method.");
```

You always pass the `document.write()` method a value, as you did with `mycar.accelerate()`. The value that you pass `document.write()`, most likely some text or HTML, is displayed on the page. There are a multitude of objects in JavaScript, and therefore there are a multitude of methods as well. Even variables can have methods, as you will see later on.

The JavaScript Tree

When you think of JavaScript and how it interacts with the browser, think of a tree. In general, JavaScript organizes all of the parts of the browser window and all of the elements (e.g., forms, images) on a page like a tree. It begins with a main object (the trunk), objects off of the main object (branches), and methods and properties off of those objects (leaves). The main object, the trunk, is always the current browser window, referred to as `window`. There are many branches off of the browser window: the page currently displayed in the window, called `document`, the current location of the window, called `location`, and the history (all of the visited pages) of the window, `history`. Inside each of these branches, you'll find more objects. For example, the `docu-ment` object contains all of the elements on a given page: forms, images, applets, even plug-ins are reflected as objects. To illustrate this concept, Figure 4 is a small "slice" of the JavaScript tree for you to look at.

As you can see, the tree begins with the browser window and branches off from there (this is by no means the complete JavaScript tree, which would take up about 20 pages). So, whenever you want to access something in the JavaScript tree, you have to "climb" up to it. To better understand this, let's create our own example of "climbing the tree" using forms. Here's the HTML document that we will be working with:

```
<HTML>
<BODY>
<FORM NAME = "branch">
<INPUT TYPE = "text" NAME = "leaf">
```

```
</FORM>
</BODY>
</HTML>
```

The names of the form and text input as defined in their HTML tags correspond to the names used by JavaScript. If you want to get the `value` (the entered text) of the text input named `leaf` inside the form named `branch` inside the page (which is in the current browser window), you can access it as follows through JavaScript:

```
window.document.branch.leaf.value;
```

Using the famliar dot structure, you "climb" up from the window to the document to the form to the text input to the text input's value.

As a sidebar, the tree is designed to make sense, but the truth is that much of it is ambiguous, especially for the beginner. It takes quite a bit of practice before you can fully understand how it all fits together. For example, you could also access the text input's value like this:

```
window.document.forms[0].
    elements[0].value
```

Though it looks different, it says the same thing as the previous example. All of the forms in the document are stored in an array named `forms`. All of the controls (also called elements, not to be

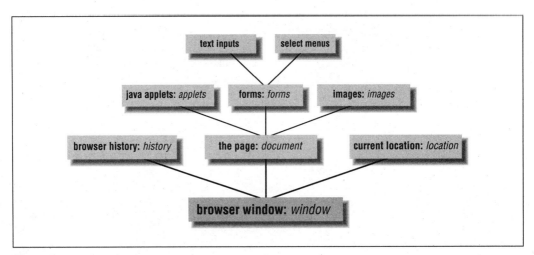

Figure 4   The JavaScript tree

Figure 5   Menu, inactive (http://www.prenhall.com)

confused with elements in an array) of the form, such as the text input, are stored in an array named `elements`, a property of the `forms` array. Accessing the first element in the `forms` array, `forms[0]`, gives you the first form on the page; since there's only one form on the page, you know that `branch` is the first form. (If `branch` were the second form, you would say `forms[1]`.) Once in the scope of the form, you can access the text input from the `elements` array. If the text input is the first control in the form, it can be referred to as `elements[0]`.

This often confusing naming system can be made simpler by sticking with one method of naming things. Everything in this article will be referred to by its given name (as was done in the previous example), not by its order in an array of objects.

Real Examples, Real Sites: Using JavaScript on the Web

Teach an Old Dog New Tricks: The Image Object

For some strange reason, visitors love images that change when the mouse is moved over them. Perhaps it's because the "rollover" image is remi-niscent of the many desktop applications and multimedia titles that they are accustomed to, or perhaps it signifies to them that, "Yes, you can click here." Whatever the reason, image rollovers are an interesting effect to add to your site.

One of the most compelling examples of the rollover is the combination of the static image and the animated image (an animated GIF). To illustrate this, let's take a look at Prentice Hall's Web site (see Figure 5), which does a great job of combining the two.

When you first enter the site, everything is static; there's no movement to be seen. When you roll over one of the image links, however, that quickly changes. If you move your mouse over the "Web Gallery" link, for example, the text of the image suddenly lights up and the cartoon computer next to it starts its screen saver. Move on over to the "Author Guide," and the typewriter next to it starts typing numbers and letters. The dog even wags its tail and blinks (now you're excited).

So how does this work? Let's analyze the setup. Each rollover in the menu is actually a separate image; it's not one giant image map. There are total of four rollovers, each of contisting of two

Figure 6   Menu, Active (http://www.prenhall.com)

image files. For example, the "Web Gallery" image has both an active and inactive image. In Figure 6, the active images text is a vibrant orange, whereas the text in the inactive image is a more suble gray. When you move your mouse over one of the rollovers, the the active image file is displayed. When the mouse is moved off, the inactive image is displayed.

Let's begin the rollover script by employing some browser detection. Since dynamic images only work in Netscape 3 and greater, we need to look out for those older browsers.

```
bName = navigator.appName;
bVer = parseInt(navigator.
    appVersion);
  if (bName == "Netscape" && bVer
  >= 3) version = "n3";
  else version = "n2";
```

Next we need to preload all of the images, active and inactive alike. This is accomplished by creating image objects for all of our images, as shown in Example 1.

Example 1

```
if (version == "n3") {
    img1on = new Image();          // Create four image objects for the
    img1on.src = "catalogon.gif";  // active images; the images displayed
    img2on = new Image();          // when the mouse moves over the
    img2on.src = "galleryon.gif";  // rollovers.
    img3on = new Image();
    img3on.src = "authoron.gif";
    img4on = new Image();
    img4on.src = "mailon.gif";

    img1off = new Image();          // Create four image objects for the
    img1off.src = "catalogoff.gif"; // inactive images; the images
    img2off = new Image();          // displayed when the mouse moves off
    img2off.src = "galleryoff.gif"; // the rollovers.
    img3off = new Image();
```

Example 1 *(continued)*

```
img3off.src = "authoroff.gif";
img4off = new Image();
img4off.src = "mailoff.gif";
}
```

The first set of image objects, beginning with img1on, preloads the image files that will be displayed when the mouse moves over a given rollover. Notice that all of these image objects have the same suffix: on. The actual image files that correspond to these image objects also have similar names, but they don't have to be similar (e.g., "catalogon.gif" with img1on). The second set of image objects, beginning with img1off, preload the image files that are displayed when the mouse is moved off a given rollover. Notice they share a similar suffix as well: off. The names of all the image objects (not the image files) should be left unchanged, unless of course you want to add more rollovers. For example, if you want five rollovers in the menu instead of four, add them using the same naming system with the on/off suffix, like so:

```
img5on = new Image();
img5on.src = "anotherimageon.gif";
img5off = new Image();
img5off.src = "anotherimageoff.gif";
```

Where "anotherimageon.gif" and "anotherimageoff.gif" are the names of your active and inactive image files, respectively. After you've preloaded all these images, you've got to create the images and their links on the page (the actual "rollover"):

```
<A
 HREF = "catalog.html"
 onMouseOver = "imgAct('img1')"
 onMouseOut = "imgInact('img1')">
<IMG NAME = "img1" BORDER = 0
    HEIGHT = 71 WIDTH = 500 SRC =
    "catalogoff.gif"></A>
```

This, for instance, is the first rollover in the menu, "Catalog", because its name is img1. Notice that inside the link, onMouseOver and onMouseOut event handlers pass two functions (we'll get to those in a minute) the name of the image. We need three more images (and links) to complete the menu, each named img2, img3, etc.

When the mouse is moved over a rollover, onMouseOver runs the imgAct() function.

```
function imgAct(imgName) {
    if (version == "n3") {
    document[imgName].src =
    eval(imgName + "on.src");
    }
}
```

This function takes the name of the image that you pass it, gives it to variable imgName, and adds the on suffix to it. For example, when the mouse is moved over the first rollover, "Catalog", imgAct() is passed the name img1. When the on suffix is added to that name, the result is img1on, the name of the active "Catalog" image's image object. Once the name of the image object is determined, the physical image (rollover) on the page, document.img1, is changed to that image file. Conversly, when the mouse is moved off the image, the function imgInact() is run.

```
function imgInact(imgName) {
    if (version == "n3") {
    document[imgName].src =
    eval(imgName + "off.src");
    }
}
```

Function imgInact(), shown in Example 2, does the same thing as imgAct(), except it adds the off suffix to the name that it's passed, thereby displaying the inactive image file.

A Remote for Your Site

Remotes are everywhere nowadays: TVs, stereos, garages, and even computers have them. With the coming of JavaScript the remote is now an easy and familiar solution to your navigational problems. A remote created in JavaScript works

Example 2

```
<HTML>
<HEAD><TITLE>Teach An Old Dog New Tricks: Image Rollovers</TITLE>
<SCRIPT LANGUAGE = "JavaScript">
<!--

// Detect if browser is Netscape 3 or greater.
bName = navigator.appName;
bVer = parseInt(navigator.appVersion);
    if (bName == "Netscape" && bVer >= 3) version = "n3";
    else version = "n2";

// Create image objects, preload all active and inactive images.
    if (version == "n3") {
    img1on = new Image();          // Create four image objects for the
    img1on.src = "catalogon.gif";  // active images; the images displayed
    img2on = new Image();          // when the mouse moves over the
    img2on.src = "galleryon.gif";  // rollovers.
    img3on = new Image();
    img3on.src = "authoron.gif";
    img4on = new Image();
    img4on.src = "mailon.gif";

    img1off = new Image();          // Create four image objects for the
    img1off.src = "catalogoff.gif"; // inactive images; the images
    img2off = new Image();          // displayed when the mouse moves off
    img2off.src = "galleryoff.gif"; // the rollovers.
    img3off = new Image();
    img3off.src = "authoroff.gif";
    img4off = new Image();
    img4off.src = "mailoff.gif";
    }

// Function to "activate" images.
function imgAct(imgName) {
    if (version == "n3") {
    document[imgName].src = eval(imgName + "on.src");
    }
}

// Function to "deactivate" images.
function imgInact(imgName) {
    if (version == "n3") {
    document[imgName].src = eval(imgName + "off.src");
    }
}

// -->
</SCRIPT>
</HEAD>
<BODY BGCOLOR = "#FFFFFF">

<A HREF = "catalog.html"
 onMouseOver = "imgAct('img1')"
```

Example 2 *(continued)*

```
    onMouseOut = "imgInact('img1')">
<IMG NAME= "img1" BORDER = 0 HEIGHT = 71 WIDTH = 500 SRC = "catalogoff.gif"></A>

<A HREF = "gallery.html"
 onMouseOver = "imgAct('img2')"
 onMouseOut = "imgInact('img2')">
<IMG NAME= "img2" BORDER = 0 HEIGHT = 71 WIDTH = 500 SRC = "galleryoff.gif"></A>

<A HREF = "author.html"
 onMouseOver = "imgAct('img3')"
 onMouseOut = "imgInact('img3')">
<IMG NAME= "img3" BORDER = 0 HEIGHT = 71 WIDTH = 500 SRC = "authoroff.gif"></A>

<A HREF = "mail.html"
 onMouseOver = "imgAct('img4')"
 onMouseOut = "imgInact('img4')">
<IMG NAME= "img4" BORDER = 0 HEIGHT = 71 WIDTH = 500 SRC = "mailoff.gif"></A>

</BODY>
</HTML>
```

like a real remote does: it stays handy and can be used to control something. A JavaScript remote controls your site, or more precisely, the browser in which your site is displayed. You can use it to jump around your site, perform a search on your site, and a plethora of other tasks. The advantage is that your visitors get a familiar metaphor (the remote) and that you save space on all of your pages (no need for navigation bars). Even if you keep your old navigation devices, the remote will compliment them nicely.

Web Review, a well-known Web publication, has a great looking remote (see Figure 7). It uses the

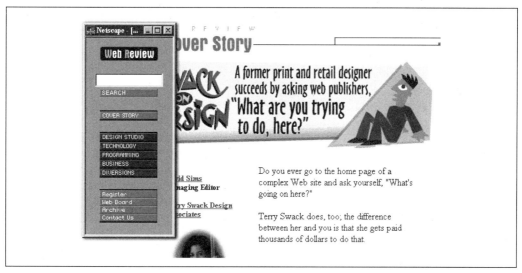

Figure 7   Web Review remote at http://www.webreview.com

metaphor to its fullest: it has the "big buttons" that you find on a TV remote, and it allows for a search of the site with the click of a button.

To begin, you have to create code to open the remote window.

```
function makeRemote() {
remote = window.open("","remote",
    "width=350, height=400");
remote.location.href = "http://www.
    domain.com/remote.html ";
    if (remote.opener == null)
    remote.opener = window;
}
```

The first line creates a new window named remote, 400 pixels in height and 350 in width. Because of a bug in Netscape 2 (for the Mac and UNIX), you have to set the location of the window after the window is initially opened. The location should be a full URL, not a relative one. Even though this will affect only a small percentage of your visitors, it's nice to be compatible with the widest range of browsers.

```
if (remote.opener == null) remote.
    opener = window;
```

This line is very important. In JavaScript, if a browser window creates (or opens) a new window, the original browser window is referred to as the new window's opener. opener is a property of the new window. If the new window (in this case, the remote) wants to manipulate the browser window that opened it, it can refer to that browser window as opener. As usual, this doesn't work quite right in Netscape 2, so this remote launching code automatically makes the browser window the remote's opener. From now on, when the remote window communicates with the original browser window, it will always refer to it as opener.

To launch the remote, you can use a link anywhere in the page:

```
<A HREF = "javascript:makeRemote()">
    Start Remote
</A>
```

or put the onLoad event handler in the BODY tag to display it automatically.

```
<BODY onLoad = "makeRemote()">
```

The page to which you direct the new window, "remote.html", is where the actual remote is located. The next step is to create the remote in "remote.html". Do this like you would any other page, with a few exceptions. For example, any link inside the remote must be redirected to the browser window, opener, that launched it. If you use ordinary links in your remote, the remote will change its own location, not the opener's. The function that you need to use to redirect your remote's links to the opener is very basic.

```
function go(url) { opener.location.
    href = url; }
```

All go() does is take the URL that you pass it and tell the main browser window, opener, to go to that URL.

```
The Amazing Remote <BR>
<A HREF = "javascript:go('index.
    html')">Front Page</A>
<A HREF = "javascript:go('map.
    html')">Site Map</A>
```

These links use the JavaScript pseudo-protocol (as I like to call it) you learned earlier to run go() and redirect the link whenever it is clicked. Include a URL of your choice, and the remote will work accordingly.

Now you may wonder, "How do I get the select menu, or any other navigational device, to work in the remote?" Think back to the select menu: to change the location of the window when a page is selected, the script uses a function called goPage(). Inside goPage() is line that uses window.location.href to change the location of the window. To make the select menu change the location of the opener instead of the window, you have to modify that line: in place of window, put opener. If you don't put opener in place of window, the select menu will change the remote's location.

```
function goPage(form) {
i = form.menu.selectedIndex;
    if (i != 0) {
```

```
        opener.location.href =
            urls[i + 1];
    }
  }
}
```

What this means is that you can treat the opener as you would any other window. Changing its location is just one of the many options that you have. Once you understand this basic concept, you can make your remote do a lot more than redirect links.

A feature that you see in many remotes, notably Yahoo!'s, is the ability to preform a search. Adding a search mechanism, or almost any type of form, can be done using a simple trick. Instead of targeting the search to the current window, which is done by default, target the search to the opener window. Aside from the modified target, the remote version of the search form can be identical to the original version.

The first step in creating a search mechanism for your remote is to add an extra line to the remote launching code.

```
function makeRemote() {
remote = window.open("","remote",
   "width=350,height=400");
remote.location.href = "http://
   webreference.com/javascript/
      970106/remote.html";
   if (remote.opener == null)
      remote.opener = window;
remote.opener.name = "opener";
  }
```

This new line uses the opener's name property, which is actually accessible in HTML, to name the opener window "opener". Just as you use TARGET to redirect links and forms to a frame, this line of code allows you to use it to redirect links

and forms (that are in the remote) to the opener. For example, a link in the remote can now be redirected to the opener by simply putting TARGET = opener inside a link.

This is just an HTML/JavaScript trick, don't get it confused with the JavaScript opener property. The opener property is a totally different animal, as was discussed earlier, and is only accessible through JavaScript.

Now place your form in the remote as you would in any other scenario. There is only one thing that needs to be changed: the form's target. Since the opener is now named "opener", make the form's target "opener". For this example, Web Review's search form is used.

```
<FORM TARGET = "opener" ACTION=
   "http://webreview.com/cgi-bin/
   AT-webreview_cleansearch.cgi"
   METHOD="post">
<INPUT TYPE="text" NAME="search"
   SIZE="13" MAXLENGTH="256">
<INPUT TYPE ="hidden" NAME="sp"
   VALUE="sp">
<INPUT TYPE="image" SRC="/universal/
   images/button-search.gif"
   BORDER="0" NAME="send" VALUE=
   "search">
</FORM>
```

The form will now function in the remote as it does in any other page. The difference is that the results of the form (in this example, the search results) will be displayed in the opener, not the remote. The great thing about this method is that it can be used easily with a wide range of forms, and not just for searches.

The page that the remote is launched from is shown in Example 3.

Example 3

```
<HTML>
<HEAD><TITLE>Remote Launching Page</TITLE>
<SCRIPT LANGUAGE = "JavaScript">
<!--

function makeRemote() {
remote = window.open("","remote","width=350,height=400");
```

Example 3 *(continued)*

```
remote.location.href = "http://webreference.com/javascript/970106/remote.html";
    if (remote.opener == null) remote.opener = window;
remote.opener.name = "opener";
}

//-->
</SCRIPT>
</HEAD>
<BODY>
Remote Launching Page
<BR>
<A HREF = "javascript:makeRemote()">Open Remote</A>
</BODY>
</HTML>
```

The remote control (this document should be named "remote.html") is shown in Example 4.

With the addition of the target tag, you can now include any form inside the remote.

```
    </BODY>
    </HTML>
```

Where JavaScript is Headed

Like any Internet technology, JavaScript's future is hard to predict. The language has evolved from a lowly forms validator to a more poweful (and appealing) multimedia scripting language. One of the newest additions to JavaScript's arsenal, Layers, allows pages to lose their static feel by adding movement, animation, and even transition effects to all elements of the page. (If you are interested in Layers, you may want to read *http://home.netscape.com/comprod/products/communicator/layers/layers_glossary.html* and *http://www.webreview.com/97/03/07/coder/index.html*.) But

Example 4

```
<HTML>
<HEAD><TITLE>Remote</TITLE>
<SCRIPT LANGUAGE = "JavaScript">
<!--

function go(url) {
opener.location.href = url;
}

//-->
</SCRIPT>
</HEAD>
<BODY>
The Remote
<P>
Links directed to the opener:
<BR>
<A HREF = "javascript:go('index.html')">Front Page</A>
<A HREF = "javascript:go('map.html')">Site Map</A>
```

one wonders if competing technologies, like Microsoft's dynamic HTML, will steal the hearts of Web developers and designers and leave JavaScript biting the dust. Only time will tell, but if the hopes of a startup in Mountain View, California, come true, JavaScript will have a long and prosperous future. ■

About the Author

Nick Heinle
27 Meadowbrook Rd.
Needham, MA 02192
carter@gis.net

Nick Heinle, a native of Chicago, currently resides in Needham, Massachusetts, with his Internet connection (and his family). He is writing a book on JavaScript for O'Reilly & Associates, designed to teach everyone from the novice HTML coder to the expert programmer how to script with the best of them.

Scripting the Web with Python[*]

Guido van Rossum

Abstract

Python is a versatile interpreted language that can be used for many different programming and script-
ing tasks on and off the Web. It has been used for everything from CGI scripts and HTTP servers, via
HTML generators, to a complete browser with support for applets written in Python. And all this software
is available for free on the Web! This article presents a smorgasbord of Python Web applications, culmi-
nating with a detailed example: a Python script to check links in a Web subtree.

Introduction

One of the many programming languages used on the World Wide Web is Python, named after the famed British comedy troupe (but otherwise unrelated to it).

I'd like to present a little background first. Python's development started around 1990. I combined earlier experiences in implementing an elegant, interpreted high-level teaching language called "ABC" with my desire for a scripting tool that was well integrated in the UNIX and C world, and found that object orientation was the key to extensibility. After about a year of internal use, primarily by the Amoeba group at CWI in Amsterdam [19], I posted the complete Python sources to the *comp.sources* newsgroup; since then it has been a very successful experiment in both distributed software engineering and online community building. Python has been ported to every platform under the sun—from VMS and IBM big metal to new systems like BeOS, to embedded systems like OS/9 and VxWorks, and to all common platforms: Mac, DOS/Windows (3.1, 95, NT), and UNIX.

Python is currently supported by the nonprofit Python Software Activity. The PSA has its own Web site [1], which is mirrored at half a dozen locations. All Python software can be downloaded and used for free, with no strings

attached. Two excellent online tutorials [2] [3] and two great in-depth books [4] [5] are available for those who wish to learn more about Python. The PSA Web site also has made nearly all Python documentation available online. The online Python community gathers in the *comp.lang. python* newsgroup as well as in several special interest mailing lists maintained by the PSA. The PSA also organizes Python workshops and conferences.

Python's attractiveness as a scripting language lies in its syntactic elegance combined with the power of its native data types, plus its extensibility through modules written in C or C++. A rich standard library and many free third-party packages complete the picture. There are several GUI options, both cross-platform and platform-specific.The standard GUI is based on Tk, and a rich Windows-specific GUI library is available for 32-bit Windows platforms. Another interesting third-party option is NumPy, a library for the efficient manipulation of large amounts of numerical data [6].

Python is often compared to other languages such as Java, Perl, or Tcl [7]. However, it occupies its own place in the spectrum of languages and does not compete with any of them. Python's place in this spectrum is roughly determined by ease of programming, ease of learning, and ease of program maintenance. For its excellence in

---

* The work reported in this article was supported in part by NSF grant number NCR-9302522 and DARPA grant number MDA-972-95-1-0003.

this area it may give up some performance when compared to other languages.

Server-Side Solutions

Python is used for numerous server-side activities. This section describes the following topics:

- A simple CGI script, the 101 of Web scripting

- How to use an HTTP server class written entirely in Python

- Embedding Python in the Apache and Netscape servers for more performance or flexibility

- A description of Digital Creation's "Bobo," which provides another way of integrating Python into a Web server

- Generating HTML. Several solutions are available, based on Python's powerful text processing capabilities as well as its object-oriented nature.

Basic CGI Scripting

Example 1 shows a simple CGI script written in Python. The script file is installed in the *cgi-bin* directory—follow the server instructions. The script starts off by defining a few string constants: `LOGFILE`, `Response`, and `Error`. The latter two show how multi-line HTML fragments can be embedded in Python source code between triple quotes (`"""`). They also show a convenient way to perform text substitutions: for example, following the statement

```
print Error % locals()
```

replaces the substring `%(email)s` with the string value of the local variable `email`, and so on.

The `main()` function of the script requires a little explanation. The first statement,

```
form = cgi.FieldStorage()
```

requests the `cgi` module to parse the `form` data sent by the client. This will retrieve the `form` data, no matter whether the form used `METHOD = GET` or `POST`. File uploads are also supported.

The `form` data is returned as a dictionary-like object, which can be accessed by `form` keys. The script looks for the keys `email` and `image`, where the latter is a file upload field (`<INPUT TYPE=file>` in HTML). If both entries are present, the uploaded file contents are saved to a temporary file, and the filename is written to a log file, presumably for later processing by another script.

Notice the use of reverse quotes (` `` `) when writing the log file: this converts any "funny" characters to octal escapes, so attempts to spoof the log file by sending `form` data containing control characters are useless. (Perhaps the only attack that could possibly cause some harm would be a request containing a massive amount of data—for instance, an email address of several megabytes. Python has no limitations on the size of most data types, so assuming this gets through the buffer limitations in the HTTP server, Python will happily append a megabytes-long line to the log file.)

Note that Python uses indentation to indicate statement grouping.

HTTP Server Class

For ultimate flexibility, it is possible to write the entire HTTP server in Python. The standard Python library makes this a breeze—a basic HTTP server can be implemented by the following little program:

```
import SimpleHTTPServer
SimpleHTTPServer.test()
```

I'm serious—those two lines are all you need!

This server provides access to all files in the current directory (and subdirectories). If you would like your server to support CGI requests as well, replace the module name with `CGIHTTPServer`. The server is a tad slow and not recommended for production use, but it may be sufficient if you need to run a basic personal server on your workstation. It is also a very easy way to prototype server changes that would otherwise require hacking highly complex C code. In addition, it is an ideal way to understand the HTTP protocol

Example 1

```
#! /usr/local/bin/python

import cgi, tempfile

LOGFILE = "/usr/tmp/images.log"

Response = """
<H1>Image saved as %(savefile)s</H1>
Email = %(email)s<BR>
Image = %(image)s
"""

Error = """
<H1>Error: email and image must be specified</H1>
Email = %(email)s<BR>
Image = %(image)s
"""

def main():
    form = cgi.FieldStorage()
    email = image = imagedata = None
    if form.has_key("email"):
        email = form["email"].value
    if form.has_key("image"):
        item = form["image"]
        if item.filename:
            image = item.filename
            imagedata = item.value
    if email and image:
        savefile = tempfile.mktemp()
        f = open(savefile, "wb")
        f.write(imagedata)
        f.close()
        logf = open(LOGFILE, "a")
        logf.write("%s: %s\n" % ('email', 'savefile'))
        logf.close()
        print Response % locals()
    else:
        print Error % locals()

try:
    print "Content-type: text/html\n\n"
    main()
except:
    cgi.print_exception()

# Here's a possible form for this script:
# <H1>Invitation</H1>
# <FORM ACTION="/cgi-bin/w3j2.py" METHOD=POST ENCTYPE="multipart/form-data">
# Email: <INPUT TYPE=text NAME=email><BR>
# Image: <INPUT TYPE=file NAME=image><BR>
# Click to submit: <INPUT TYPE=submit VALUE=" OK " NAME=submit>
# </FORM>
```

from the server's point of view. (Note that as distributed, this server doesn't have any security features.)

The two lines shown in the previous program don't, however, show the real power of Python's HTTP server classes. Using subclassing, you can add magic to your server. Example 2 shows how we add a simple request counter to our server.

The class MyRequestHandler is derived from the request handler class in the SimpleHTTPServer module; for brevity, we rename it to BaseClass here. The class extends two base class methods (do_GET and send_head) and adds a new method (send_counter).

Some notes:

- The do_GET method increments the global counter variable and then invokes the base class do_GET method.

- The send_head method checks if the path in the request is /counter.html. If so, it calls the new send_counter method; otherwise, it calls the base class send_head method.

- The send_counter method handles the response when the "magic" counter page is requested. It first sends the standard HTTP response headers (this code is duplicated from the base class send_head implementation), constructs the text of the counter page using the familiar % substitution operation (this time using a %d format to format an integer), and then returns a StringIO object created from the text.

The StringIO module in the standard Python library creates objects that behave like files for most practical purposes but whose data is stored in memory. In this case, the send_head method is supposed to return a readable file that is read by the base class do_GET method. The base class send_head method opens the real file corresponding to the path in the request, and we must return something compatible. Without the StringIO module, we would have had to write the text to a temporary file and open that; this would burden us with removing the temporary file after the request has been read.

Improvements such as saving the value of the counter on a file, keeping separate counters for each page, and constructing a GIF image from the counter value are left as exercises for the

Example 2

```
import StringIO
import SimpleHTTPServer

BaseClass = SimpleHTTPServer.SimpleHTTPRequestHandler

CounterTemplate = """
<H1>Server Statistics</H1>

This <A HREF=/index.html>server</A> has been accessed <b>%d</b> times.
"""

count = 0

class MyRequestHandler(BaseClass):

    def do_GET(self):
        global count
        count = count + 1
        BaseClass.do_GET(self)
```

Example 2 *(continued)*

```python
    def send_head(self):
        if self.path == "/counter.html":
            return self.send_counter()
        else:
            return BaseClass.send_head(self)

    def send_counter(self):
        self.send_response(200)
        self.send_header("Content-type", "text/html")
        self.end_headers()
        text = CounterTemplate % count
        return StringIO.StringIO(text)

def test():
    SimpleHTTPServer.test(MyRequestHandler)

test()
```

reader. (For the GIF image, you need the contributed *gd* (*gifdraw*) module [8].)

Server-Side Integration

If your needs are satisfied with a more traditional CGI-based approach, you may still want to speed up the running times of your CGI scripts. Of the number of possible approaches, perhaps the fastest solution is to embed the Python interpreter in your HTTP server. This generally requires source access to the server or a server with a plug-in architecture. As an example of the former, the next section describes how Python is embedded in the Apache server. The latter is exemplified in the following section by an embedding using the Netscape Server API. Finally, we'll examine Bobo, which provides yet another view of HTTP scripting with Python.

Python embedded in Apache

Apache is a free HTTP server for UNIX—its authors claim it is used more than any other server worldwide [9]. Much like Python, Apache is extensible with numerous modules that provide additional features. For example, the PyApache software by Lele Gaifax is an Apache

module that embeds the Python interpreter in the Apache server. (PyApache can be found on the Python Web site [1].) When a CGI script is requested by a client, the Python interpreter is ready for use, and the communication between Python and Apache is more efficient.

Normally, this design requires a UNIX process fork operation (compared to a fork+exec without embedding the interpreter). There's an experimental option that avoids even the process fork. However, the price paid for this added efficiency is a decrease in robustness. Changes to the Python interpreter's environment made by one CGI script can affect the execution of another (or a second invocation of the same script). This is fine as long as you write all CGI scripts yourself and are aware of the limitations. The source also warns about memory leaks when this option is used—undoubtedly, this will improve over time.[*]

Python embedded in the Netscape server

A more ambitious form of embedding is possible for the (commercial) Netscape Server. This approach is from Aaron Watters and is described in Chapter 12 of his book [4].

---

[*] A fix for this problem has been published in the Python newsgroup.

The Netscape Server can be instructed to load a shared library and to call a function in that library in response to a request for a specific data type. Watters describes how to create a shared library containing the entire Python interpreter (except for the `main()` function) plus two small "glue" files specific to the Netscape Server API.

The first glue file provides the entry points for the Netscape Server as follows:

- One entry point for server initialization

- One to handle a request

- One for server restart

The second glue file is a small Python extension module that allows Python code to call the entry points of the Netscape Server API (NSAPI).

The first glue file tries be as flexible as possible. All it does is register a Python object whose methods will be called back in response to later server requests. It is directed to load a Python module and call a function from that module through parameters in the NSAPI configuration file.

For example, the first glue file can be directed to add the directory */big/arw/public_html/book/embed* to Python's module search path, import the module `nsHOOKS`, and call the function `nsHOOKS.GO()`. The `GO()` function ends up importing NSAPI (the second glue file) and calling `nsapi.SetCallBack(callbackobject)` where `callbackobject` is an instance of a class that will receive subsequent requests from the server as method calls.

At this point, things get more than a bit ugly: the calling interface for the callback object is closely modeled after the NSAPI `callback` function—intended for C programmers—and proud of it!

(Refer to Watters' book for details.) The important message here is that we can get arbitrary Python code to run in response to specific service requests (recognized by filename extension), without going through CGI. And since the server extension remains loaded between requests, it's a cinch to create applications that maintain state between invocations. The server restart callback can be used to save the state to disk when the server is about to be taken off the air—although, of course, it would be wise to have some kind of backup mechanism to guard against crashes.

Bobo's Python Object Publisher

Bobo is the nickname for Digital Creation's answer to those who feel the need to go beyond CGI [10]. Among other things, Bobo contains an HTML generator that I'll discuss in a following section. But first of all, it introduces a level of abstraction between the code that implements an operation and the way it is invoked from the Web. This Bobo component is called the Python Object Publisher [11].

Using Bobo, you structure your application as one or more objects, whose methods will be invoked somehow by clients on the Web, like browsers. The way those invocations happen is completely transparent to your application. You can use CGI, ILU, FastCGI, PersistentCGI, or a Python HTTP server like the one described previously. For testing and debugging, a command-line interface is also provided.

When using CGI, the main advantages of using Bobo lie in its programming convenience, and the possibility of a future switch to a more efficient mechanism. Example 3 reimplements Example 1 using Bobo. Compare them side by side!

Example 3

```
import tempfile

LOGFILE = "/usr/tmp/images.log"
```

Example 3 *(continued)*

```
Response = """
<H1>Image saved as %(savefile)s</H1>
Email = %(email)s<BR>
Image = %(imagename)s
"""


Error = """
<H1>Error: email and image must be specified</H1>
Email = %(email)s<BR>
Image = %(imagename)s
"""


def response(email='', image=''):
    "Form response"
    imagename = image.filename
    if not (email and imagename):
        return Error % locals()
    imagedata = image.read()
    savefile = tempfile.mktemp()
    f = open(savefile, "wb")
    f.write(imagedata)
    f.close()
    logf = open(LOGFILE, "a")
    logf.write("%s: %s\n" % (`email`, `savefile`))
    logf.close()
    return Response % locals()

# Here's a function that sends a blank form.
# Its URL is http://<yourhost>/cgi-bin/sample/form"

Form = """
<H1>Invitation</H1>
<FORM ACTION="/cgi-bin/sample/response"
      METHOD=POST ENCTYPE="multipart/form-data">
Email: <INPUT TYPE=text NAME=email><BR>
Image: <INPUT TYPE=file NAME=image><BR>
Click to submit: <INPUT TYPE=submit VALUE=" OK " NAME=submit>
</FORM>
"""


def form():
    "Request form"
    return Form
```

Some notes:

- To activate the example, a small "bootstrap" script is copied from the Bobo directory to the directory containing the example module, and a symbolic link is created from the *cgi-bin* directory to the bootstrap script. The name of the symbolic link determines the module that is loaded by the bootstrap script. Thus, multiple modules can live in the same directory, sharing the bootstrap script, and get activated through separately named symbolic links to the bootstrap script.

- There is no "import Bobo" statement. The difference between the standard CGI approach and Bobo is rather like the difference between a window system in which you have to read and dispatch your own events, one at a time, versus a system in which you can specify a callback routine for a specific event that is invoked whenever the event occurs. (Bobo goes a step further and infers the mapping between events and callbacks from the source.)

- By default, Bobo allows only functions/methods with documentation strings to be called. You can also explicitly specify a list of public functions/methods, overriding the default.

- There is no need to define a class: for simple scripts, the module can serve as the object. (In fact, in order to maintain persistent state between invocations, some additional magic needs to be invoked; see the Bobo documentation.)

- Bobo takes care of generating the appropriate Content-type header and sending the HTML to the client (via the server); you need only return a string. Bobo even guesses whether the string is HTML or plain text; you can also return an object whose string representation is HTML text and Bobo will invoke the string conversion.

- A second function in the module exists to produce a blank form. Coding this into the original example would have been harder. In fact, it is very easy to chain forms in this manner—the <FORM> tag returned by the first form contains the URL (without hostname) of the second form as its ACTION attribute, and so on.

Generating HTML

Another popular server-side activity is to generate HTML on the fly. This is commonly done in CGI scripts but can be useful in almost any server-side activity. Of course, the simplest way to generate HTML is by using print statements, as shown in

Example 1. This quickly gets tedious and is error-prone, especially if the HTML generation is dependent on a lot of Python calculations—it is easy to lose track of matching string quotes, matching HTML tags, or matching parentheses.

In the sections that follow, I will discuss two radically different approaches:

- HTMLgen removes the need to write HTML as you know it, replacing all HTML constructs with Python class instances.

- Bobo Document Templates let you write nearly vanilla HTML with embedded directions for substitution of Python variables and expressions.

HTMLgen: Web weaving with Python

When you are generating HTML on the fly, you may want to try HTMLgen, written by Robin Friedrich [12] [13]. To quote the documentation for HTMLgen version 1.1:

HTMLgen is a class library for the generation of HTML documents with Python scripts. It's used when you want to create HTML pages containing information which changes from time to time. For example, you might want to have a page which provides an overall system summary of data collected nightly. Or maybe you have a catalog of data and images that you would like formed into a spiffy set of web pages for the world to browse. Python is a great scripting language for these tasks and with HTMLgen it's very straightforward to construct objects that are rendered out into consistently structured web pages. Of course, CGI scripts written in Python can take advantage of these classes as well.

Example 4 shows a simple application of HTMLgen. It starts off by instantiating the Minimal-Document class. (There's also a Document class, which is best used for large, multi-file documents.)

Example 4

```
import HTMLgen

def main():
    title = "Dealing with Python Attack"
    doc = HTMLgen.MinimalDocument(title=title)
    doc.append(HTMLgen.Center(HTMLgen.Heading(1, title)))
    doc.append(HTMLgen.HR(width="50%"))
    doc.append(HTMLgen.OrderedList([

        """Do not run away, the python can move faster than you can.""",

        """Lie flat on the ground on your back with your feet together,
        arms to your sides, head well down.""",

        """The python will attempt to push its head under you,
        experimenting at every possible point.  Keep calm; one wriggle
        and he will get under you, wrap his coils around you and crush
        you to death.""",

        """Eventually the python will get tired and decide to swallow
        you whole without the usual preliminaries.""",

        """He will probably start at your feet.  Keep calm.  You must
        let him swallow your foot.  It is quite painless and will take
        a long time.  If you lose your head and struggle, he will
        quickly whip his coils round you.""",

        """Keep calm and he will go on swallowing.  Wait patiently
        until he has swallowed about up to your knee.""",

        """Carefully take out your knife and insert it into the
        distended side of his mouth and with a quick rip, slit him
        up.""",

        ]))
    doc.append(HTMLgen.HR(width="50%"))
    doc.append(HTMLgen.Paragraph(
        """(The above instructions come from a book issued by the
        London Missionary Society in the 19th century for issue to
        missionaries coming to Africa.  One can only assume the writer
        had never dealt with a python before.)"""))
    doc.append(HTMLgen.HR(size=5))
    p = HTMLgen.Paragraph("This was originally sent by Eugene Griessel;\n")
    p.append(HTMLgen.Href(url="mailto:arw@somewhere",
                          text="Aaron Watters"))
    p.append("\nforwarded it to me.")
    doc.append(p)
    print doc

main()
```

The `MinimalDocument` class takes care of the boilerplate around the document such as `<HEAD>`, `<TITLE>`, and `<BODY>` tags and the corresponding end tags. The example then appends a number of items to the document instance—these will be rendered in the document's body. (All the rendering is actually done when the instance is printed, through string manipulations in its `__repr__` method for conversion to a string.)

The items appended are:

- A Heading element with level 1 (i.e., `<H1>`), nested inside a `<CENTER>` element.

- An `<HR>` element, with a specified width.

- An `<OL>` element with some string items; each item becomes a `<LI>` element. List items can also be other HTMLgen instances, or sublists. Lists can also be dynamically generated using the `append()` method.

- Another `<HR>`, followed by a text paragraph (embedded in `<P>` . . . `</P>`).

- Another `<HR>`, this time with a specified size (thickness).

- Another text paragraph, this time one built up out of several components, one of which contains a hyperlink.

HTMLgen contains classes to deal with virtually every legal HTML construct (even comments). It supports tables and forms, framesets, and images. The `Document` class has extensive support for navigation between documents using Next/Previous/Home buttons. There are also a bunch of utility functions—for example, for parsing URLs and pathnames and for manipulating image collections—and a collection of color names that are known to be renderable without dithering in Netscape's color cube.

Talk about a complete package. . . . And the price is right!

Bobo Document Templates

Digital Creation's Document Templates [14] are part of Bobo, mentioned earlier. The focus here is different from HTMLgen. Though Bobo doesn't help you get your `<H1>` . . . `</H1>` tags to match, it has a rich syntax for substituting Python values in the HTML. The idea is that the HTML can be created by a non-programmer who knows how to make good-looking Web pages, while the Python code is written by an experienced Python programmer. The substitutions require a minimal knowledge of Python.

For the Python programmer, there are two different classes, `HTML` and `String`, that use different substitution syntaxes, but otherwise have similar functionality. The `HTML` class uses HTML comments to specify substitutions, like this:

```
<!--#var total fmt=12.2f-->
```

The `String` class uses an extension of Python's `%(name)x` string formatting notation, like this:

```
%(date fmt=DayOfWeek upper)s
```

Some advanced features of Bobo Document Templates include:

- Application-defined formats

- Automatic invocation of Python functions and methods

- Nested templates

- Conditional insertion

- Iterative insertion, iterating over Python sequences. This supports "batch browsing" (e.g., "Your search returned 72583 results; click here for the next 10")

- Automatic summary statistics when iterating over sequences

In short, Python + Bobo = RPG for the Web!

Other Tools

Before I delve deeper into two client-side case studies, let me mention briefly that a wealth of other software for the Web is written in Python.

The Python Web site has a large collection of pointers to Python software available from other places on the Web, as well as a subsection devoted to Web software [15]. Another collection is available directly from the Python *ftp* site itself [16]. Among the offerings found on these pages are a shared workspace, more HTML generation tools, HTTPD server statistics tools, more servers, Netscape cookie support, and several collections of cool tricks and hacks.

Python can also be used for client-side scripting in Microsoft's Internet Explorer 3.0, through a nifty ActiveX scripting interface that puts Python at the same level as JavaScript or Visual Basic. Unfortunately, I'm not familiar enough with the Windows software to have come up with a working example; the Python Web site contains some pointers [17].

Grail®—A Web Browser written in Python*

One of the largest and most ambitious applications of Python on the Web is Grail, a full-featured Web browser written entirely in Python [18]. Grail, a free offering from the Corporation for National Research Initiatives (CNRI), is a testimonial to Python's ability to support the construction of large applications. It is the most complete browser available written in any interpreted language.

Grail's GUI component uses Ousterhout's Tk toolkit, which is available to Python users through the standard library module "Tkinter." Tkinter hides most details of using the Tcl language to control Tk and gives Python programmers a more object-oriented view on Tk's widget classes.

While Grail was developed almost exclusively on UNIX, it took only a small number of tweaks to remove or adapt the "UNIXisms" to make it run on Windows and Mac systems. The final 0.3 dis-

tribution will support all three platforms (with the exception of printing support for Mac and Windows).

I wrote Grail version 0.1 in less than two weeks, as a sort of demo; it consisted of under 2000 lines in 14 source files. It was released in August 1995. CNRI decided to develop it further based on very positive feedback. Grail 0.2 was a small group project and consisted of over 10,000 lines in about 50 files. It was released in November 1995.

After that, we became more ambitious. Grail 0.3 is bigger and better than ever, and two beta versions of it were released in early 1996. Version 0.3 beta 3 was released in March 1997, which we expect will soon be followed by a final release of version 0.3. Grail now comprises over 25,000 lines in more than 100 files.

Why Grail?

Throughout history, experimentalists have built their own tools to mold specialty items to suit their own purposes. This was the case with Grail. Having developed a browser that was written in a high level language and for which we had the sources, we decided to make these sources available for other experimentalists to use. It never was, nor is it now, intended to compete with commercially supplied browsers.

A free browser with full source available is of immense value to the research community: it can be ported to platforms that do not have commercial browser implementations, and it can be hacked to suit one's personal needs—or more likely, the needs of some research project. As an example of the latter, a French researcher, Vladimir Marangozov, modified Grail in an afternoon to add support for an experimental groupware protocol.

Some other applications of Grail wouldn't have been easy to accomplish with a commercial browser for the following reasons:

---

* Grail is a registered trademark of CNRI.

- Grail was originally written to demonstrate a form of document annotation; this involved implementing a new form of "fragment identifier" that consisted of a character range in the document (so that parts of a document could be addressed without having to modify the document to insert a label).

- Grail was the first browser to support CNRI's "handle" protocol. This is a URN (Uniform Resource Name) scheme that inserts an extra level of indirection between the identifier the user sees for a document and its actual URL.

- The handle support in Grail has also been used to demonstrate the fast retrieval of MEDLINE medical abstracts directly from a handle server.

- Grail has been extended to support ILU, Xerox PARC's Inter-Language Unification system (a CORBA-compatible distributed object system). Applets can access remote ILU objects or act as ILU object servers.

- Using the ILU support, an applet has been written that serves as a launcher for mobile agents.

- Grail is being used as a testbed for new HTML extensions.

- Grail is being used as a test client for the new HTTP 1.1 protocol.

Features

While Grail does not conform to any one particular user interface standard, it does have the familiar look of most Web browsers: a menu bar, a logo, a box to enter new URLs, and a page of multifont text with embedded graphics, forms, etc. The menu bar provides access to the usual collection of operations: Open File, Open URL, Print, Save, View Source, string search, as well as navigation control: Back, Forward, Reload, View History, and a fully featured bookmarking tool. There are several preference dialogs as well as a

small help menu. Grail's support for applets written in Python is described in the next section.

Grail currently supports most HTML 3.2 features, including tables, but excluding style sheets. Table support has some performance difficulties, due to the lack of interfaces for text measurement in Tk. (Tk 8.0 comes with the required functionality but is available only in alpha form at the time of writing.)

Grail does not support all the features of commercial browsers.. There are no background images or animations (except through Grail applets). There is less control over the alignment of embedded graphics.

Grail supports the three most popular protocols: HTTP, FTP, and MAILTO, as well as the "handle" protocol (mentioned previously) and some pseudo protocols for internal use ("doc:spam" points to a file named *spam* in the documentation tree at the Grail home site; "grail:spam" points to a file named *spam* in the Grail source tree). The exercise of adding other protocols is left to the reader.

There is a well-defined "plug-in" interface for adding protocols: you write a Python module with a given name (e.g., gopherAPI.py), which defines a class with a given name (e.g., `gopher_access`) that implements certain methods. Drop the module in the *protocols* subdirectory of either the Grail source directory or your personal Grail customization directory (*~/.grail* on UNIX), and you're all set.

Plug-in modules can be written to extend Grail along a number of other dimensions as well: new file types, new HTML tags, even new preference panels. (We are still thinking about a general mechanism to add new menus or new menu entries.)

Performance

Grail's performance is adequate on current hardware. The two main bottlenecks are the SGML/HTML parser, which is written in Python, and the speed with which formatted text can be spewed out to the display. The latter is dependent on the speed of the Tk text widget and further slowed down by Tkinter, the object-oriented Tk interface for Python (which is written in Python itself except for a small C module that invokes Tcl commands).

Applets

Grail's biggest boast is its support for applets—written in Python, of course. The advantages of writing applets in Python instead of in Java are that Python's higher level language and data types make programming much easier. Also, the Tk toolkit used for GUI programming in Grail applets is more powerful and easier to use than Java's AWT. This advantage is important for many Web applications, in which programming is often a part-time occupation for content and/or graphics experts who are generally creating Web pages. (This problem with Java has not escaped the browser vendors, who were quick to come up with JavaScript.[*] In my opinion, JavaScript

looks like a scaled-down Python with curly braces.)

A Grail applet is implemented as a Python class that is instantiated by the browser with optional parameters specified by the HTML <OBJECT> and <PARAM> tags. Apart from the fact that instantiation and the main event loop are implicit, the environment in which the applet runs does not differ significantly from that provided to normal Python programs; the Tkinter module is used in the same fashion, and the same collection of standard library modules is available. In fact, it is customary to include a few lines at the end of an applet module that will allow it to run with the standard Python interpreter, without interfering with its use as an applet.

Example 5 shows the source code for a simple applet that displays a continuously updated clock face. It is invoked by including the following in an HTML page:

```
<OBJECT CODEBASE=analogclock.py
        CLASSID=AnalogClock>***</OBJECT>
```

Example 5

```
from Tkinter import *
import time
from math import sin, cos, pi

class AnalogClock:

    def __init__(self, master, size=200):
        self.master = master
        bg = master['background']
        self.canvas = c = Canvas(master, width=size, height=size,
                              background=bg, highlightbackground=bg)
        c.pack()
        self.origin = (size*0.5, size*0.5)
        self.canvas.create_oval(11, 11, size-10, size-10, width=10,
                              fill='#a0a')
        self.little = self.create_hand(size*0.35, 7, 'blue')
        self.big = self.create_hand(size*0.4, 5)
        self.seconds = self.create_hand(size*0.41, 2, 'yellow')
        self.update()
```

---

[*] For more information on JavaScript, see Nick Heinle's article entitled "JavaScript: When HTML Is Not Enough," also in this issue.

Example 5 *(continued)*

```
    def create_hand(self, size, width, color='black'):
        ox, oy = self.origin
        item = self.canvas.create_line(ox, oy, ox+size, oy,
                                       width=width, fill=color)
        return item, size, width

    def update(self):
        try:
            t = time.time()
            year, month, day, hh, mm, ss, wday, yday, isdst = \
                time.localtime(t)
            self.update_hand(self.little, hh%12*5 + mm/12)
            self.update_hand(self.big, mm)
            self.update_hand(self.seconds, ss)
            self.master.after(int(1000*(1-t%1)), self.update)
        except TclError:
            # We may get here if the widget is deleted.
            pass

    def update_hand(self, (item, size, width), minutes):
        degrees = 6*minutes
        angle = degrees*pi*2/360
        ox, oy = self.origin
        x = ox + size*sin(angle)
        y = oy - size*cos(angle)
        self.canvas.coords(item, ox, oy, x, y)

if __name__ == '__main__':
    root = Tk(); frame = Frame(root); frame.pack()
    clock = AnalogClock(frame)
    root.mainloop()
```

The asterisks (***) can be any text to be shown by other browsers.

Applet Security

Applets are executed in Python's "restricted execution mode." In this mode, a few language features are removed, and others are changed so that the master program (in this case, Grail) has control over them. This facility is completely general and supports the creation of an unlimited number of distinct restricted environments (even nested ones).

Python's restricted execution mode is based on the observation that all access to external resources (i.e., the file system, processes, network, etc.) is provided to a Python program either through a "built-in" function (e.g., the open() function, which opens a file for reading and/or writing), or through a module that must first be imported. Consequently, restricted execution mode allows the master program to substitute an alternative collection of built-in functions and an alternative implementation of the import statement (which is, in fact, also invoked through a built-in function, even though it is syntactically a statement).

When some code executing in restricted mode invokes a function defined in the master program, that function executes in the environment and with the permissions of the master program. Thus, the master program can provide the restricted code with an "open" function that checks its arguments (for example, only opening files for reading and only in a designated directory) before calling the "real" open function.

Conversely, when the master program invokes some function defined in restricted mode, explicitly or implicitly, that function executes in restricted mode. Thus, the use of callback functions provides no security threat.

Grail restricts the use of "import" for applets to modules written in Python as well as a small number of extension modules written in C, deemed "safe" for use by applets, such as the math and regex modules. Grail also redefines the semantics of the import statement to support "network import" of modules living in the same directory (on a Web server) from which the applet module was loaded. Thus, applets can consist of multiple modules just like ordinary Python programs.

The language features taken away in restricted mode all fall in the category of "backdoors" or "loopholes" in the language. Most of these features are useful for writing debuggers, profilers, and similar "introspective" tools in Python. For example, in unrestricted mode, function objects have an attribute that allows access to their global variables; this provides a way for restricted code to gain access to the globals of the master program, so it is taken away. Thus, it is not possible to run the Python debugger or profiler in restricted mode. However, if this were desirable, the master program could provide a debugger or profiler for the restricted code it is managing.

Grail's Security Policies

Grail currently implements a rather "liberal" restricted environment to applets. First, it allows applets to read any file in the file system, file system permitting, whose name doesn't start with a period (subject to the access restrictions for the user who is running Grail). It allows writing of files only inside a *home* directory set aside specifically for the current applet. While the write restrictions are restrictive enough, the read restrictions are probably too liberal. For example,

one wouldn't want an applet to read the (publicly accessible) UNIX *password* file, since a rogue applet could easily communicate this information back to its home site, where a "crack" program tries to guess passwords.

Similarly, the network access restrictions for applets are too relaxed when considering firewalls and the like—applets can currently access any network address that is accessible to the user running Grail, and this may include company-internal Web servers that are inaccessible from outside the company's domain. This problem is the same as that with unrestricted access to the file system.

In addition there are some security holes that make it possible for an applet to modify Grail's user interface, perhaps tricking the user into invoking undesirable commands.

Finally, there is currently no protection against overuse of resources by applets. An applet could easily allocate all available disk space, virtual memory, stack space, or screen real estate, or enter an infinite loop without yielding to Grail's event loop. Such attacks, while annoying, generally do no more harm than that of a system crash, a risk we have all learned to cope with.

Stricter security policies are expected to be implemented in future versions of Grail. Stricter policies for file system and network access, while easy to add, will require new ways for the user to give applets access to selected files or network addresses. For example, a calendar applet may need access to the user's calendar file. Quota on disk space and screen real estate are also implementable. Tk 8.0 comes with a "virtual root window" feature that makes it possible to prevent all access from applets to the Grail user interface.

On the other hand, virtual memory quotas are hard to enforce. The Python expression $'x'*n$ tries to allocate n bytes of memory, and a malicious applet could easily try this for ever-increasing values of n. In such a case, the system would become unusable long before a `MemoryError` exception was raised. The only solution to catch this would be to implement quotas in the general memory allocator used by Python. Similarly, to prevent applets from monopolizing the CPU, multiple threads must be used (with a provision to control the scheduling of threads). However, this will have to wait until Tk is thread-safe.

Until then, the paranoid user can either turn applets off altogether or accept applets only from certain domain names. We are also thinking about a way to support "digitally signed" applets created by trusted parties. We hope that the lack of security won't keep people from trying Grail—after all, we're only at version 0.3!

Webchecker: Putting It All Together

For the finale, I'll show how easy it is to write a "web checker" in Python. This program will solve a common problem: how to find dangling links in a Web tree. A *Web tree* is defined as all (reachable) pages under a certain directory on a given Web server. A *dangling link* is defined as a link that yields an error when followed.

Two forms of links can be distinguished:

- "Internal" links that point within the same tree

- "External" links that point to some document outside the tree

The *webchecker* application must follow internal links to find all reachable documents in the tree; it needs to follow external links only to check that the linked-to document exists.

Let's assume that internal links can be recognized because they start with a given string (the "root" of the tree). For example, the Web tree rooted at *http://www.python.org/* consists of all pages we can find whose URL starts with this same string. Clearly, our program must be able to retrieve documents by URL and parse the HTML to find the links. It must also manage a data structure representing links we have already followed and links we still need to follow, since we can expect that there will be cycles in the "tree" (e.g., page *A* references page *B*, which references page *C*, which points back to page *A*). Fortunately, all these operations are easy to do with the standard Python library and Python's built-in data types.

Python's standard library contains modules that provide access to the details of the most important Web protocols such as FTP, Gopher, NNTP, and, of course, HTTP. (Modules for more protocols are available from their contributing authors.)

Example 6

```
import urllib

def geturl(url):
    "Return contents and Mime type of a URL"
    f = urllib.urlopen(url)
    data = f.read()
    headers = f.info()
    f.close()
    if headers.has_key("content-type"):
        mimetype = headers["content-type"]
    else:
        # No content-type header -- guess type based on extension
        if url[-5:] == ".html":
            mimetype = "text/html"
        else:
            # Don t know -- worst-case assumption
            mimetype = "application/octet-stream"
    return (data, mimetype)
```

The higher level module urllib hides most protocol details and lets you retrieve a file from anywhere on the Web by specifying its URL. There are also standard library modules that help in parsing HTML and in manipulating URLs.

The simplest operation in our program is retrieving a document given its URL. Example 6 shows the function geturl(), which returns a file's contents and its type, given its URL. It does this using the urllib module. The urllib.urlopen() function used here returns a file-like object that can be read to retrieve the contents of the given URL, but which also has a method info() returning a dictionary-like object containing the headers returned by the server. If the protocol used is not HTTP, it will return an empty dictionary. We're interested in the content-type header, which gives us the MIME type of the document (keys in the info dictionary are all lowercase). If there's no content-type header, we guess the content type based on the filename extension. (Obviously, one could do a better job here. In fact, the real *webchecker* application does do a better job, but showing that would be boring.

We'll come back to what happens when there is an error later.)

Next, let's see how we parse the HTML to extract the link info. Simplifying assumption: we're only interested in links expressed as HREF attributes on <A> tags. Other link forms, like <IMG> and <FORM>, are left as an exercise. Oddly enough, it's easier to use Python's SGML parser module instead of its HTML parser module.[*]

Example 7 shows the class LinkExtractor, which extract the links specified in the HREF attribute of the <A> tags. Note that the SGML parser does case folding of tag attribute names, while leaving the case of the attribute value unchanged—just the way we want it.

Some notes:

- The __init__ method is a constructor: it is automatically invoked when an instance of the LinkExtractor is created. It initializes the links instance variable to an empty list and then calls the base class constructor.

Example 7

```
from sgmllib import SGMLParser
import string

class LinkExtractor(SGMLParser):

    def __init__(self):
        self.links = []
        SGMLParser.__init__(self)

    def do_a(self, attributes):
        for (name, value) in attributes:
            if name == "href":
                value = cleanlink(value)
                if value:
                    self.links.append(value)

    def getlinks(self):
        return self.links
```

---

[*] Thanks to Fred Gansevles for this observation.

- The `do_a` method is invoked by the SGML parser when it encounters an `<A>` tag. The argument is a list of (name, value) pairs giving the tag's attributes.

Note that the SGML parser doesn't know anything about `<A>` tags in particular — whenever it encounters a `<FOO>` tag, it simply checks whether there is a corresponding `do_foo` method defined. This is the beauty of a dynamic language like Python. (Of course, Python's SGML parser doesn't know anything about SGML either—it is merely a scanner for the default reference representation of SGML. But this is good enough for parsing HTML!)

- Finally, the `getlinks()` method can be called by the user of the class to retrieve the list of links collected while parsing.

Example 8 shows the `cleanlink()` function, called in `do_a()`. It takes care of two nasty little details:

- It strips off "fragment identifiers," suffixes of the form `#whatever` that can occur in links but are not part of the URL syntax

- It removes all whitespace from the link

Example 9 shows the `getlinks()` function, which uses the LinkExtractor class. The `feed` and `close` methods are standard methods of the `SGMLParser` class; the former feeds the parser some data, the latter announces the end of the data.

Next, we need to interpret relative links. But there's a problem: it is common for HTML to link to other documents that live in the same directory, and the common idiom for this is to write something like the following:

```
See <A HREF="There.html">there</A>.
```

If the URL of the current file is *http://www.python. org/test/Here.html*, we want to translate this to *http://www.python.org/test/There.html*. You could also write `<A HREF = "../test/There.html">`

Example 8

```
def cleanlink(link):
    i = string.find(link,  # )
    if i >= 0:
        link = link[:i]              # Remove #fragment
    words = string.split(link)       # Split in whitespace delimited words
    return string.join(words, "")    # Join words without whitespace
```

Example 9

```
def getlinks(url):
    (data, mimetype) = geturl(url)
    if mimetype == "text/html":
        parser = LinkExtractor()
        parser.feed(data)
        parser.close()
        links = parser.getlinks()
    else:
        links = []      # Non-HTML data has no links
    return links
```

Example 10

```
import urlparse

def getfulllinks(url):
    links = getlinks(url)
    fulllinks = []
    for link in links:
        full = urlparse.urljoin(url, link)
        fulllinks.append(full)
    return fulllinks
```

or <A HREF = "/test/There.html">, all with the same result; in fact, there is an entire RFC devoted to this subject (RFC 1808). Fortunately, there's a standard library module, urlparse, exporting a routine, urljoin, that does the right thing just about every time. Example 10 shows the function getfulllinks(), which uses this to map the links returned by getlinks().

Now we're about ready to put together our complete *webchecker* application. We'll keep two lists, one of "done" links, and one of "todo" links. Every new link we find is compared to each list; if it occurs in neither, we put it on our todo list. Oh, and unless we want to check the entire World Wide Web, we need to skip links that aren't within the tree of interest. The expression

link[:len(root)] == root conveniently checks that the link has an initial substring equal to the root.

Another detail: we need to catch errors. Since the urllib.urlopen() routine will raise an IOError exception for just about anything that can go wrong, this is the only exception we need to catch. For the time being, we simply print the bad URL and continue our checking loop.

Example 11 shows the driver routine for our small *webchecker* program. This routine will traverse our entire subtree, printing "Checking <URL>" for each URL it is checking, and "*** Error for <URL> ***" for each failing URL—these are the bad links.

Example 11

```
def webchecker(root):
    todo = [root]
    done = []
    while todo:
        url = todo[0]
        done.append(url)
        del todo[0]
        print "Checking", url
        try:
            newlinks = getfulllinks(url)
        except IOError, msg:
            print "*** Error for", url, "***", msg
            continue
        for link in newlinks:
            if (link[:len(root)] == root and
                link not in done and link not in todo):
                todo.append(link)
```

There's one final little ugly detail that we need to take care of. As distributed, the urllib module fails to raise an IOError exception when an HTTP server returns an error; instead, it will return the HTML that the server returns with the error to display for the user. Without explaining why this works (it's another virtue of Python's dynamic nature), we execute the following statement:

```
del urllib.FancyURLopener.\
    http_error_default
```

This patches the urllib module so that it will raise an IOError after all. We can now point our *webchecker* to your favorite Web site:

```
webchecker("http://www.python.org/")
```

(Actually, don't use this example. The Python Web site is busy enough without being used as a guinea pig. Try your own Web site instead, and find its weaknesses!)

The program as shown still has several deficiencies. The biggest problem, perhaps, is while it tells you which URLs are bad, it doesn't tell you where those URLs were referenced from. This requires keeping some additional data with each link.

Example 12 shows a modified version of the driver that does this. Only the lines in boldface had to be added; no lines had to be changed.

Example 13 shows the entire program that we have developed so far.

Example 12

```
def webchecker(root):
    todo = [root]
    done = []
    refs = {root: ["<ROOT>"]}
    while todo:
        url = todo[0]
        done.append(url)
        del todo[0]
        print "Checking", url
        try:
            newlinks = getfulllinks(url)
        except IOError, msg:
            print "*** Error for", url, "***", msg
            print "*** Referenced from:"
            for ref in refs[url]:
                print "\t" + ref
            continue
        for link in newlinks:
            if not refs.has_key(link):
                refs[link] = [url]
            else:
                refs[link].append(url)
            if (link[:len(root)] == root and
                link not in done and link not in todo):
                todo.append(link)
```

Example 13

```python
import urllib

def geturl(url):
    "Return contents and Mime type of a URL"
    f = urllib.urlopen(url)
    data = f.read()
    headers = f.info()
    f.close()
    if headers.has_key("content-type"):
        mimetype = headers["content-type"]
    else:
        # No content-type header -- guess type based on extension
        if url[-5:] == ".html":
            mimetype = "text/html"
        else:
            # Don't know -- worst-case assumption
            mimetype = "application/octet-stream"
    return (data, mimetype)

from sgmllib import SGMLParser
import string

class LinkExtractor(SGMLParser):

    def __init__(self):
        self.links = []
        SGMLParser.__init__ (self)

    def do_a(self, attributes):
        for (name, value) in attributes:
            if name == "href":
                value = cleanlink(value)
                if value:
                    self.links.append(value)

    def getlinks(self):
        return self.links

def cleanlink(link):
    i = string.find(link, '#')
    if i >= 0:
        link = link[:i]            # Remove #fragment
    words = string.split(link)     # Split in whitespace delimited words
    return string.join(words, "")  # Join words without whitespace

def getlinks(url):
    (data, mimetype) = geturl(url)
    if mimetype == "text/html":
        parser = LinkExtractor()
        parser.feed(data)
        parser.close()
        links = parser.getlinks()
```

Example 13 *(continued)*

```
    else:
        links = []      # Non-HTML data has no links
    return links

import urlparse

def getfulllinks(url):
    links = getlinks(url)
    fulllinks = []
    for link in links:
        full = urlparse.urljoin(url, link)
        fulllinks.append(full)
    return fulllinks

def webchecker(root):
    todo = [root]
    done = []
    refs = {root: ["<ROOT>"]}
    while todo:
        url = todo[0]
        done.append(url)
        del todo[0]
        print "Checking", url
        try:
            newlinks = getfulllinks(url)
        except IOError, msg:
            print "*** Error for", url, "***", msg
            print "*** Referenced from:
            for ref in refs[url]:
                print "\t" + ref
            continue
        for link in newlinks:
            if not refs.has_key(link):
                refs[link] = [url]
            else:
                refs[link].append(url)
            if (link[:len(root)] == root and
                link not in done and link not in todo):
                todo.append(link)

del urllib.FancyURLopener.http_error_default

import sys
webchecker(sys.argv[1])
```

Okay, one more thing: it is relatively easy to turn the *webchecker* into a *webmirror* program—a program that makes a local copy of a Web tree. Here's one way to do it.

Modify the `geturl()` routine to call

```
    savedata(url, data)
```

(Put this just before the return statement.) Modify the driver to store the root URL as a global variable—for example, insert the following at the top:

```
    global gRoot
    gRoot = root
```

Example 14

```
import os

def savedata(url, data):
    if url[:len(gRoot)] != gRoot:          # Sanity check
        return
    relurl = url[len(gRoot):]              # Strip root
    while relurl and relurl[0] == /:       # Strip leading slashes
        relurl = relurl[1:]
    if not relurl or relurl[-1] == /:      # Special case directories
        relurl = relurl + "index.html"
    comps = string.split(relurl, /)
    path = os.curdir
    for c in comps:
        if not os.path.isdir(path):
            os.mkdir(path)
        path = os.path.join(path, c)
    # Now save the data
    print "Saving", url, "as", path
    f = open(path, "wb")
    f.write(data)
    f.close()
```

Now add the **savedata()** function, shown in Example 14, to the program, and voila—a *web-mirror* program!

Actually, this example is only scratching the surface of the possibilities. A more robust *web-checker* program, developed along the same lines, is available from the Python Web site. ■

References

8. Python Language home page, *http://www.python. org*

9. Guido van Rossum. "Python Tutorial," *http://www. python.org/doc/tut/tut.html*

10. Aaron Watters. "The What, Why, Who, and Where of Python," *UnixWorld Online, http://www.wcmb. com/uworld/archives/95/tutorial/005.html*

11. Aaron Watters, Guido van Rossum, and Jim Ahlstrom. *Internet Programming with Python*, MIS Press/Henry Holt publishers.

12. Mark Lutz. *Programming Python*, O'Reilly & Associates.

13. Jim Hugunin. Matrix SIG home page, *http://www. python.org/sigs/matrix-sig/*

14. "Python Compared to Other Languages," *http:// www.python.org/python/Comparisons.html*

15. Richard Jones. "GD module for Python," *http:// www.rdt.monash.edu.au/~richard/gdmodule/*

16. "Apache HTTP Server Project," *http://www.apache. org*

17. Digital Creations. Bobo, *http://www.digicool.com/ releases/bobo/*

18. Paul Everitt. "Using the Python Object Publisher," *http://www.digicool.com/releases/bobo/PythonObjectPublisher.html*

19. Robin Friedrich. HTMLgen 1.1 Online Documentation, *http://www.python.org/sigs/web-sig/HTMLgen/ html/main.html*

20. Robin Friedrich. Web SIG home page, *http://www. python.org/sigs/web-sig/*

21. Rob Page and Scott Cropper. "DocumentTemplate," *http://www.digicool.com/releases/bobo/DocumentTemplate-paper.html*

22. Pointers to Web-related contributed Python software, *http://www.python.org/python/Contributed. html#netweb*

23. Network-related contributed Python software, *ftp:// ftp.python.org/pub/python/contrib/Network/*

24. Mark Hammond. "Python and ActiveX Scripting," *http://www.python.org/ftp/python/pythonwin/html/ ActiveXScripting.html*

25. Grail home page, *http://grail.cnri.reston.va.us/ grail/*

26. Centrum voor Wiskunde en Informatica, translated as Center for Mathematics and Computer Science, is a government-funded research lab in Amsterdam. See *http://www.cwi.nl/* for more information.

27. RFC 1808, "Relative Uniform Resource Locators," by Roy T. Fielding, is available in print in vol. 1, no. 2 of the *World Wide Web Journal*, Key Specifications of the World Wide Web, and online at *ftp://ds.internic.net/rfc/rfc/1808.txt*.

About the Author

Guido van Rossum

Corporation for National Research Initiatives (CNRI)

1895 Preston White Drive

Reston, VA 20191

guido@cnri.reston.va.us, guido@python.org

http://www.python.org/~guido/

Guido van Rossum is the creator of the Python programming language. In 1982 he started work at CWI in Amsterdam, as a programmer and researcher. He first worked on the ABC programming language (Python's most influential predecessor), then on the Amoeba distributed operating system, and finally on a variety of multimedia applications. During this last period, the Python language gradually began taking over his life, culminating in 1995 in his departure to the U.S. to work for CNRI. At CNRI, Guido divides his time between further development of Python and the development of a number of Python-based applications, such as Grail.

CURL

A GENTLE SLOPE LANGUAGE FOR THE WEB

M. Hostetter, D. Kranz, C. Seed, C. Terman, S. Ward

Abstract

The work described in this paper explores the design of Curl, a single, coherent linguistic basis for expression of Web content at levels ranging from simple formatted text to contemporary object-oriented programming. Curl is part of a research effort aimed at eliminating discontinuities from the function/ sophistication curve. This yields an environment in which (1) incremental functionality requires incremental skill acquisition, and (2) a consistent semantics avoids communication obstacles between separately encapsulated fragments of content. We characterize Curl as a "gentle slop esystem" because it makes it easy to transition from one point to another in the function/sophistication spectrum.

Introduction

Curl is a new language for creating Web documents with almost any sort of content, from simple formatted text to complex interactive applets.

- *Text formatting.* Curl provides a rich set of formatting operations similar to those implemented by HTML tags. Unlike HTML, the Curl formatter can be extended by users to provide additional functionality, from simple macros (to provide a convenient way to switch to a particular font, size, and color) to direct control over the positioning of subcomponents (as in a TeX-like equation formatter). Several packages of useful formatting extensions are currently under development.

- *Scripting simple interactions.* Using a TK-like interface toolkit of interactive components, Curl makes it easy to build simple interactive Web pages. One can view interactive objects like buttons or editable fields as extensions to the basic formatting operations provided above—one uses the same easy-to-learn syntax to create interactive documents as to create regular text documents. There's no need to learn a separate scripting language!

- *Programming complex operations.* Other components of an interactive document may require more sophisticated mechanisms than are provided by the interface toolkit. These components can also be developed using Curl since, at its heart, Curl is really an object-oriented programming language. Curl expressions, class definitions, and procedure definitions embedded in the Web document are securely compiled to native code by the built-in, on-the-fly compiler and then executed without the need for any sort of interpreter. Curl provides many of the features of a modern object-oriented programming language: multiple inheritance, extensible syntax, a strong type system that includes a dynamic "any" type, safe execution through encapsulation of user code, and extensive checking performed both at compile and run time. Almost all of the Curl system and compiler are written in Curl.

Curl is intended to be a *gentle slope system*, accessible to content creators at all skill levels, ranging from authors new to the Web to experienced programmers. By using a simple, uniform language syntax and semantics, Curl avoids the discontinuities experienced by current Web users who have to juggle HTML, JavaScript, Java, Perl, etc. to create today's exciting sites. Our hope is that the single environment provided by Curl will be an attractive alternative for Web developers.

Gentle Slope Systems

Is a new language for specifying the content of Web documents really necessary? We think the answer is "yes" because of the following:

- The changing role of the Web

- The wide range of skills present in the community of Web authors

The World Wide Web is evolving from the constrained goal of hypertext presentation to a much more demanding role in networked computing: it is becoming the standard user interface to a wide and potentially unbounded class of computational services. This evolution naturally strains the capabilities of the simple markup language on which most Web content has been based. In order to accommodate new user-interaction models and functionality, the simple formatting functions of HTML [6,7,8] are commonly augmented by applets and scripts based on more powerful linguistic tools such as JavaScript [1], Java [2,3], or C++ [16]. Curl is designed to have the positive features of markup languages, scripting languages, and statically typed object-oriented programming languages.

This complex of independently conceived content production tools confronts potential Web authors with annoying—and potentially crippling—semantic and performance discontinuities. The enhancement of a Web page to include, say, an animation or interactive simulation requires escape from the simple markup language to an unrelated programming language within which the new functionality may be encapsulated. Such discontinuities are undesirable for at least two reasons:

1. They represent technological barriers that require substantial new skills to overcome: they tend to partition the content creators into nearly disjoint sets of *authors* versus *programmers*.

2. They present serious interface constraints among separately encapsulated functions. It

is difficult, for example, to reference some result of an encapsulated computation from external hypertext. It is also difficult to share structured data between different language levels because they usually use different representations.

Curl avoids these problems by using a consistent syntax and semantics for the expression of Web content at levels ranging from simple formatted text to contemporary object-oriented programming.

Thus, authors with simple tasks can write straightforward code and add more details when more complicated functionality or performance is required. We characterize Curl as a "gentle slope system" because it makes it easy to transition from one point to another in the function/sophistication spectrum.

Technical challenges confronted in the design of such a language stem largely from tensions between the ease-of-use characteristics we demand of formatting and scripting languages, and the performance and expressiveness goals we expect of contemporary system programming languages. Strong compile-time typing, for example, is inhumane in the former but essential in the latter. Storage allocation, object orientation, and the handling of English textual content are further examples where the tension between ease-of-use and performance/expressiveness present interesting conundrums for the language designer. In most cases where compromise was necessary, the scripting language aspects were treated as most important.

More generally, we are anxious to capture in Curl the easy approachability to which the Web owes much of its popularity. To a great extent this approachability derives from careful design decisions that allow (or even require) *under-specification* of function (e.g., output format), in contrast to conventional programming language semantics geared to the complete specification of behavior. Curl's design is explicitly aimed at reconciling the spirit of under-specification with the requirement that it scale to the sophisticated end of the programming spectrum.

Curl Overview

The name *Curl* derives from the principal syntactic feature of the language: Curl source files are arbitrary text, punctuated by expressions enclosed by curly brackets ({}). Like HTML, plain text is valid source; unlike HTML, the escapes extend to a real programming language. (See Figure 1.)

Interpreting the Curl source in Figure 1 requires definitions for the `bold` and + operators. In Curl, the meaning of {`operator` ...} is determined by first locating a definition for `operator` in the current environment and then calling upon that function to parse and interpret the remaining text "..." of the expression. Note that this mechanism allows the "..." text to have any desired structure since the parsing rules are dynamically defined.

In this example, the `bold` operator treats its arguments as a sequence of `Graphic` objects (in this case simple characters) to be displayed with the `bold` property set to true, while the + operator parses the remaining text as a sequence of sub-expressions to be evaluated and then summed. Every Curl object can be converted to a Graphic object (the conversion process is controlled by a method defined by the object's type) which, in turn, can be assembled into a formatted display by the Curl browser. An interesting side-effect of being able to view all Curl objects is that we can use the browser metaphor to good effect when building debuggers, inspectors, etc.

Curl comes with a large (and growing) repertoire of predefined operators which provide formatting operations and a TK-like toolkit of user-interface components. The widespread adoption of TCL/TK and, to a lesser extent, JavaScript/HTML, demonstrates that simple applications of these operators are often sufficient to fulfill many, if not most, of the needs of interactive documents. Figure 2 assembles a few of these components into a simple order form.

Since the values for `color` and `quantity` are `Dynamic` objects, the last line of the display changes automatically as the user manipulates the color and quantity controls. A `Dynamic` object incorporates a simple mechanism for propagating changes in its value to other dynamic objects that depend on first object's value. More sophisticated propagation rules could be supplied by the user by creating a new class of objects derived from `Dynamic` objects that have a different "propagate" method.

The screen shot in Figure 2 reflects the fact the user has selected something besides the default color (red) and quantity (0). Note that the "text-as-program paradigm" means that the `value` operator must be wrapped around variable names inside of paragraphs. Otherwise, the name of the variable as a text string will be displayed instead of its value. This example illustrates several Curl features:

- *Formatting model.* A TeX-like hierarchical "box-and-glue" formatting model that makes it easy to construct layouts.

Curl Source	*What User Sees*
The following characters are displayed using a {bold bold-faced font}. There are {+ 10 4} bold characters altogether.	The following characters are displayed using a **bold-faced font**. There are 14 bold characters altogether.

Figure 1

```
{let color:Dynamic='red
     count=0        | "quantity" can't depend on itself
     quantity:Dynamic=count
{vbox
   {title Beach Balls}
   {hbox "Color:"
        {radiobuttons foo 'red 'white 'blue
          action={color.set-value foo}}}
   {hbox "Quantity:"
        {button "Take another"
          action={quantity.set-value
                    {set count {+ count 1}}}}
        {button "Give one back"
          action={when {> count 0}
                    {quantity.set-value
                       {set count {- count 1}}}}}}
   {paragraph You've ordered {value quantity}
              {value color} beach balls!}}}
```

Beach Balls

Color: ⌄red   ⌃white   ⌄blue

Quantity: Take another   Give one back

You've ordered 3 white beach balls!

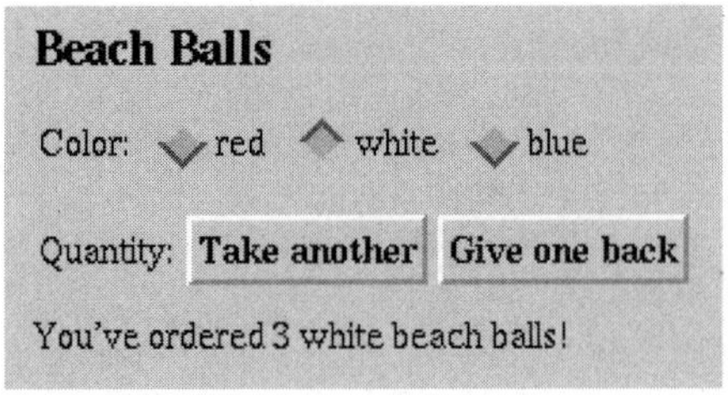

Figure 2

- *Naming environment.* A lexically-scoped naming environment which allows one to construct modular documents with interchangeable components. Languages with "flat" name spaces, like TCL, can make it difficult to reuse components since naming conflicts need to be resolved as code fragments are moved from document to document.

- *Object-oriented programming.* The use of objected-oriented programming to extend the behavior of the Curl system in an easily-accessible way. In this example the creator of the `Dynamic` class has encapsulated the knowledge of how a change in the value of a `Dynamic` object results ultimately in the updating of the display. Of course the current user doesn't have to understand how the underlying mechanism works in order to put it to effective use. This sort of extensibility is beyond the ken of most simple scripting languages.

Now suppose one wanted to compute the sales price too.

The Curl source in Figure 3 starts by reading in another Curl document into an environment named "Ballco." Environments completely encapsulate a document, making it easy to implement various security, storage management, and cleanup policies. Environments are themselves objects with instance variables and methods derived from the top-level definitions in the source documents. Thus `ballco.get-price` is a reference to the `get-price` procedure defined in Ballco's *prices.curl* file.

This example also illustrates the use of additional *threads of control* to create independent tasks that run in parallel with the user's main computation. In this case a separate thread is given the task of periodically querying the Ballco database for the latest beach ball price which is then used (with a suitable markup!) to update the price in the example document. Curl threads are preemptive and not specific to any particular platform; a simple `lock` object with `acquire` and `release` methods is used as the lowest-level synchronization primitive. The combination of threads and dynamic values makes it simple to incorporate information gleaned from the Web into a document. It also shows how procedure and variable

---

Curl Source

```
| grab Ballco's pricing server interface
{require ballco "http://www.ballco.com/prices.curl"}

| our current price for a beach ball
{define-variable ball-price:Dynamic={new Dynamic 10}}

{define {compute-overhead price}
  {return {* 1.6 price}}}

| update our beach ball price every 10 seconds using
| a simple overhead calculation
{create-thread
  {loop
    {ball-price.set-value
      {compute-overhead {ballco.get-price 'beach-ball}}}
    {sleep 10}}}           | update interval = 10 sec

{let ...
  {vbox
    ...
    {paragraph You've ordered {value quantity} {value color} beach balls
               which comes to a total of ${* ball-price quantity}}}}
```

What User Sees

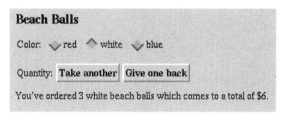

Figure 3

definitions are simply part of the document, though not displayed.

It is easy to see how a document can grow in incremental steps from a simple text file to include ever more sophisticated interface and information-gathering components. To make this transition a natural one, Curl provides a whole spectrum of operators. Of course, users are likely to want operations we haven't thought of (or had time to implement) so it makes sense to provide a way for new operators to be added to the Curl environment. The Curl graphical interface supports the usual things that Web users expect such as tables, hyperlinks, and images.

Example 1 shows a simple drag-and-drop interface and how a more sophisticated programmer can extend the functions available to technically naive authors. It is a Web page, designed by a Curl neophyte, that uses a `portfolio` object to track investments.

Example 1

```
{require portfolio "http://www.portfolios-galore.com/portfolio.curl"}

This is a simple demo of {bold Curl}, developed by the
{anchor url="http://cag-www.lcs.mit.edu" MIT Laboratory for Computer Science}.
```

Example 1 *(continued)*

```
It shows the graceful integration of programming with hypertext
Web content.  {anchor url="Documentation/overview.curl" Click here} for
documentation.

Our example concerns stocks, for example:
{portfolio.stock "NWIR" shares=500 cost=16.125}
{portfolio.stock "AAPL" shares=500 cost=23.5}
{portfolio.stock "HWP" shares=500 cost=48.25}

A small listing of popular stocks can be found {anchor url="topstocks.curl" here}.

Securities can be maintained in a {bold portfolio} using a drag-and-drop
user interface.

{let p={new portfolio.PortfolioBox
          {portfolio.stock "NSCP" units=100  cost=60.5}
          {portfolio.stock "MSFT" units=100 cost=101}
          }
  {vbox p.graphic
      {paragraph
      The total value of my portfolio is ${value p.value}.  As of this
      moment, I ve made a net profit of ${- p.value p.cost}.}}}
```

Figure 4 shows the document/program in
Example 1 viewed through the Curl browser.

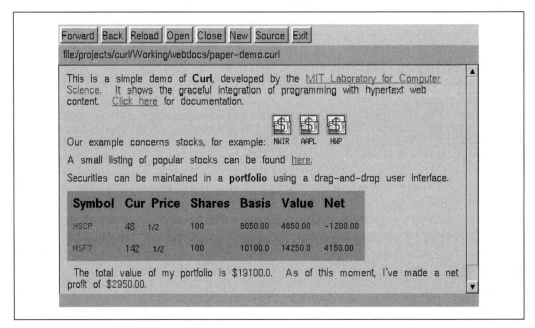

Figure 4

PortfolioBox and stock have been imported from the portfolio URL and offer some sophisticated features. The PortfolioBox displays as a table and accesses a quote server to maintain up-to-date prices. It provides direct-access editing features for portfolio manipulation, including a simple drop method that allows the shown stock objects to be dragged onto the portfolio window to automatically extend the set of securities tracked. The stock object has a simple drag method. In Figure 3, the value and cost fields of the portfolio are Dynamic, and the last paragraph will be automatically updated as the quantities of stock or their values change.

Curl as a Programming Language

Curl is both a language and an authoring environment, where the authoring environment was implemented as user extensions to Curl. The language can be used as an HTML replacement for the presentation of formatted text, whose capabilities include those of scripting languages as well as compiled, strongly-typed, object-oriented system programming.

Obvious influences on Curl's design include LISP [4,13,14,15], C++, Tcl/Tk [5], TeX [9], and HTML. Language design decisions directly reflect the goal of reconciling its simple accessibility to naive users with the power and efficiency demanded by sophisticated programming tasks. Salient features of Curl include the following:

Programs as documents

Execution of every Curl program results in a document containing a set of objects that may be displayed or otherwise manipulated. Curl includes an extensible GUI which provides for simple, structured arrangement of displayable objects. The debugging and development environment is integrated and accessible. Curl objects, along with the type information that describes them, may be browsed along with other Web content. Objects seen on the screen may be identified and inspected.

Syntax and Semantics

Extensibility. Arbitrary sublanguages can be embedded as new {. . .} forms and can be processed correctly by Curl, by simple extension of the environment. For example, the following Curl form:

```
{circuit-simulation-netlist
  M1 out in gnd gnd nmos w=4u l=1u
  M2 out in vdd vdd pmos w=8u l=1u
  VDD vdd gnd 5v
  VIN in gnd pwl(0 0 0.1 5)
  .tran .1n 10n
  .plot v(in) v(out)}
```

might be found in a document for an engineering course where the instructor wished to insert an interactive simulation for the student to explore.

Strong typing. Every variable and value may be declared and type-checked at compile time. Strong typing not only allows many programming errors to be caught at compile time but gives the Curl compiler the extra information it needs to produce efficient native code implementations.

Ambiguous types. In the absence of declarations, variables default to type any. A datum of type any is represented as a pair of words containing the run-time type of the datum and its value. The semantics of a Curl program are unchanged if all type declarations are eliminated, although its performance will suffer. This is the flip side of strong typing: providing types for each argument or variable can be a time consuming process which may not be worthwhile while prototyping new ideas or when efficiency is not of concern to the author.

Lexically scoped environment. Curl provides a structured name space whose bindings include variables, constants, types, and compilation hooks for arbitrary syntactic forms. The name space is instantiated as an *environment* which spans compile and run times, and which completely dictates the semantics that will be associated with source code during compilation. By carefully selecting which functions are made available in environments used to execute imported code, a considerable degree of safety can be achieved.

Procedural semantics. Procedures are first-class data, implemented using closures as necessary. Positional and keyword arguments are supported.

Objects. Types include classes, with multiple inheritance, arrays, and primitive types such as integers.

First-class types [11]. Types, including classes, are first-class objects: they are bound in the environment and obey consistent scoping rules; they may be arguments to or results from arbitrary computation both at compile and run-times. Having type information available at run time allows programs to examine and manipulate arbitrary objects without any pre-knowledge of their structure. This is particularly useful for applications like object inspectors or for building general purpose mechanism for transporting objects from machine to machine.

Portability, Performance, and Safety

Efficient native representations. Representation conventions for values with declared types are tag-less, consistent with C and C++, yielding similar code efficiency.

Incremental compilation. Local compilation of source code to native code is the basis of Curl portability, safety, program encapsulation, and performance. Code that has been compiled may be cached locally in memory or on disk.

Other Features

Threads. Curl supports a simple platform-independent thread model. Threads are particularly useful in the "real-time" environment of the Web where the use of blocking input/output can lead to extremely frustrating delays when accessing foreign data.

Garbage Collection. By default, Curl objects are garbage collected when they are no longer used.

Types

Efficient implementation on contemporary processors, as well as easy interfacing to foreign software environments, dictates the use of conventional C/C++ representations of data. To provide typeless simplicity for simple scripting-level programming, Curl provides the ambiguous type **any** which may require the run-time representation of type information. Thus,

```
{let a:any=5
  {define {f x:int}:int {return {+x
  3}}}
    {f a}}
```

will be compiled so that the ambiguously declared variable a carries a run-time type, while the formal parameter x to the integer procedure f does not. Passing a to f requires a cast, which involves a run-time type check after which the value portion of a is passed as an integer. To perform such casts efficiently, type information (when present) is separated from the representation of values. Because the storage for a value of type **any** is allocated by the compiler, casting a value to the ambiguous type never causes dynamic storage allocation.

Note that the omission of a type declaration for a variable means something different than in, for example, ML [12]. In ML the variable has a static type that the compiler must determine. In Curl, an omitted type is an under-specification and the actual type may change during program execution.

Since run-time representations are required for our extensible system of types, it is convenient to represent them as Curl objects and to expose them in the programming model. Thus, Curl types are simply values: they are named, passed, stored, and accessed identically to other Curl data. This treatment of types provides a natural and consistent semantics for type extension, for type portability (which reduces to the problem of object portability), and for extended type semantics. For example, in the following:

```
{let t1:type={array int}
     t2:type={list-of t1}
     x:t2
     ...}
```

`array` and `list-of` are procedures that generate types. This emancipation of types, while semantically appealing, presents certain challenges. It requires that compilation order be somewhat lazy, to accommodate circularities. Moreover, the expressibility of mutable type variables admits constructs whose efficient translation, or even whose meaning, is questionable. We currently forbid such constructs, requiring that types used in declarations be evaluable to compile-time constants.

Ambiguous types, as well as the object class hierarchy, yield a type lattice in which a value may have arbitrarily many types, only some of which are compile-time constants. The run-time type of a value v may be explored using $\{typeof\ v\}$, which returns the most specific type object appropriate to v, using run-time tags if necessary. Similarly, $\{isa\ t\ v\}$ tests the membership of v in type t, again using the fully-disambiguated run-time type of v.

Objects

Modern programming practice demands support for objects, and their advantages are particularly compelling in the context of an extensible Web programming environment. Objects provide a natural implementation for the hierarchy of displayed images on a Web page, and they support incremental extension of previously defined behavior. In its pure form, however, an object-oriented programming model fails to meet the "gentle-slope" goal: the naive user cannot simply add a variable to his otherwise textual Web page, for example. A consequent subgoal of Curl is the graceful integration of object semantics into a lexically-scoped procedural programming model.

Most Curl types are classes. In the abstract, a Curl class provides a namespace whose scope includes objects of that class. Within a class, names can be bound to values, both variable and constant; the latter includes methods specific to the class. Instances of a class have a run-time representation containing slots for the values of variable data, as well as dispatch tables for efficiently invoking methods of the class. Our current implementation uses representations similar to those of C++.

Graphic Objects

Curl's object-oriented graphical user interface combines both high-level interfaces with the usual repertoire of low-level primitives. A graphic image is represented as a hierarchical tree of `Graphic` objects. Leaves of the tree are primitive `Graphic` objects that know how to draw themselves, usually after looking up the values of various properties (see below). Primitive `Graphic` objects include:

- *Lines and curves.* Properties control the color, width, dash style, and end treatment (e.g., none, arrowhead, ball, . . .).

- *Rectangles, polygons, ellipses.* Properties control the width and color of the border, and the stipple and color of the fill. Various 3D effects are also provided for the borders of rectangles.

- *Text.* Properties control the color, size, and font family as well as indicating whether the text should be bold or italic.

- *Multiline text.* Similar to text, but can display itself across multiple lines.

- *Color bitmaps.* Curl supports the usual collection of image formats (GIF, JPEG, etc.).

- *Glue.* Glue has no visible representation but provides some parameterized dimensional flexibility that is useful in the formatting operations provided by Boxes (see below).

The basic graphic building block is the Box, which serves as the parent to a collection of primitive `Graphic` objects and instances of other Boxes. The displayable hierarchy consists of a tree (or graph) of such objects.

In addition to providing the abstraction mechanism for building complex images, various types of Boxes also control the positioning of their children using dimension information the children supply. Current formatting templates include:

- *Hboxes and vboxes.* These are one-dimensional formatters that create simple horizontal or vertical arrangements of their children, lining up their baselines or margins. As in TeX, the relative allocation of whitespace is controlled by the elasticity of any glue objects that have been added as children.

- *Tables.* A two-dimensional formatter that aligns the margins and baselines of its children on a Cartesian grid. The row and column of each child is specified as it is added to the table template; a child can span multiple rows and/or columns.

- *Paragraphs.* Children are positioned left-to-right, top-to-bottom. Children on the same line have their baselines aligned and the interline spacing is chosen to accommodate the tallest child on a line.

- *Canvases.* No explicit formatting is provided; each child is given a position as it's added to the canvas template.

This set of formatting primitives is sufficient to duplicate the effects of most text formatters and browsers with little effort on the part of the Curl user.

Much of the flexibility of Boxes comes from the use of properties to control the rendering of primitive objects. A property is a (name,value) binding and each `Graphic` object has an associated list of properties. When the value of a prop-erty is required, an upward search of the template/instance tree is performed, starting with the current object. Thus, properties can be viewed as a dynamically bound environment implemented using a deep binding mechanism. So, as in HTML, many of the rendering choices—color, font, etc.—are not made by individual templates but are instead inherited from their parents through their property bindings.

Notification of a change in a property's value is propagated through the tree which may, in turn, cause various reformatting operations to take place. If some `Graphic` object determines that its image has changed, it can request that it be re-rendered. Since there is sharing of objects within the tree, a re-render request may in fact cause more than one location on the output device to be redrawn. Curl uses the invalidate/repaint protocol used by many GUI frameworks, but users need not concern themselves with this machinery unless they want to.

As in Java, the dispatching of events (mouse motion, keystrokes, and so on) is controlled by the tree where the event handler for the visually topmost `Graphic` object that encloses the event location is invoked to deal with the event. Handlers can pass the event up the tree if they don't wish to handle the event themselves.

Naming and Environments

The resolution of names outside of classes, and its graceful integration with names within the class hierarchy, again involves the exposure of compilation machinery to potentially introspective Curl programs. Our goal was to provide a simple, structured, lexically-scoped environment for binding variables, types, constants, and language extensions.

Classes are bound within the environment, neatly embedding the hierarchy of class names as subtrees of the namespace. Name resolution is kept simple and unambiguous by requiring the syntax `obj.x` to access `x` from an object's class; the unqualified name `x` always references the innermost lexical binding. Thus, as shown in Example 2, the reference x within the method m gets 3, while self.x gets 4.

Note that types may be generated anonymously via class. Names of types derive solely from bindings in the environment, where c is the name of a type in the example. The define-class form builds a class and enters it into the current (lexically enclosing) environment.

Safety, Storage, and Encapsulation

The ability to import code from untrusted sources demands mechanisms for circumscribing the behavior of imported programs at various levels, providing "safe" execution relative to some criterion. The appropriate choice of safety criteria may vary depending on its purpose or source, or on the priorities of the user. A performance-critical JPEG decoder from a cryptographically-secured source, for example, might be executed unencumbered by run-time overhead; an applet from a strange Web page, however, might warrant carefully encapsulated execution. This variation engenders important subproblems:

- Policy issues which dictate the safety criterion

- Enforcement mechanisms sufficiently flexible to realize various performance/safety tradeoffs

We view the first as a subject for continuing research, supported in Curl by its attention to the second.

Curl, as a language, has a type system sufficiently high-level that Curl semantic guarantees can be maintained despite buggy or malignant code via a combination of compile-time and run-time type checks. This is exactly how Java provides this guarantee. These guarantees are the default for normal execution of untrusted code, but entail performance costs and functional restrictions that may be undesirable in high-performance code. For example, stack allocation or allocation in areas that are then reused may provide significant performance advantages. These unsafe mechanisms are also part of the Curl language but are not available in the environment used by untrusted code.

Since the compilation of Curl forms involves invoking compilation machinery attached to those forms in the compilation environment, the semantics of a Curl program are entirely derived from the environment in which it is compiled. A program compiled in an environment with no bindings for set or open-file, for example, has no access to these primitives. As all imported code is locally compiled, the tailoring of compilation environments provides an airtight mechanism for enforcement of an arbitrary variety of safety policies.

An untrusted applet from an interesting Web page might, for example, offer the user a desktop playpen in which a local simulation environment can be configured. In order to provide for the storage of the applet's state between visits to that page, local file system access is necessary; however, unconstrained access to the local file system presents a security flaw. Such needs can be safely accommodated, however, by providing a limited-access primitive which allows an applet to save

Example 2

```
{let x:int=3              | Initialize local variable
    c:type={class {}      | Define local class c
        x:int
        {define {m}:int {return {+ x self.x}}}}
    y:c={new c}           | Allocate an instance of c
    {set y.x 4}           | Assign to instance variable
    {y.m}}                | invoke method & return value
```

its state in a particular file from a user-mediated path, and to subsequently restore it transparently. An untrusted program might request a `savelet` object which supports such limited access to a single applet-specific file, and be prevented (by the restricted compilation environment) from arbitrary file accesses.

The low-level requirement for any security policy is freedom from stray memory accesses (minimally, from stray writes) and stray system calls. For a safe subset of Curl, one that does not allow stack allocation and other unsafe operations, this guarantee is provided by the above mentioned compilation machinery. For arbitrary Curl programs, an alternative to simply trusting that some code is correct is to use "sandboxing" [17]. In sandboxing, the compiler inserts a few extra instructions around writes and procedure calls to make sure that writes only occur to areas in memory that the compiler knows are okay, and that calls are only made to procedures under the compiler's control. A system environment that provided sandboxing would be an attractive target for Curl.

Comparison With Other Languages

Along with formatting and markup languages (like TeX and HTML), Curl shares the property that its input defaults to a textual document, and that its explicit output is itself a viewable image of that document. Markup languages like HTML don't address general purpose programming; to the extent that TeX does, it addresses it poorly.

Through the `object` tag, HTML allows an arbitrary external computation to be invoked from an HTML document and its result to be embedded in the document. Of course, the rest of the document cannot interact with the computation. In Curl, by contrast, the markups are expressions in the underlying language and can have arbitrary interactions with the document.

Tcl/Tk provides a scripting language and widget set that allows user interfaces to be constructed easily and integrated with a program. Curl procedures with types defaulting to **any** also provide this functionality but offer several advantages. First, Tcl is very inefficient because it represents everything as a string at the semantic level, while Curl's representations are based on objects and can be compiled to efficient code. Second, in order to provide new widgets in Tcl/Tk, one has to write code in C. Curl provides a uniform interface between code at all levels.

Syntactically, Curl resembles LISP and its dialects. We rely on the syntactic extensibility of prefix notation provided by LISP and extend it to include extensible text formatting as part of the language. Curl also differs from LISP in that it is, at its foundation, a statically-typed object-oriented language with non-tagged basic data representations. The part of Curl that is used like a conventional programming language most resembles Dylan [10], before it was changed to use C-like syntax.

The object semantics of Curl are similar to those of Java and C++. Unlike Java, Curl embeds objects within a lexically-scoped procedural programming model, it supports multiple inheritance, and it allows trusted code to exploit the semantic and efficiency advantages of unsafe operations. Unlike C++, Curl supports type safety.

Curl Implementations

Our Curl implementation contains the following components, all written in Curl:

- Platform-independent GUI.

- An incremental compiler that produces native code for x86 and Sparc. Work is underway on producing code for the Java Virtual Machine.

- An object inspector and symbolic debugger for code.

- A browser for viewing Curl programs.

The basic infrastructure code, such as the incremental compiler, are built into a static program image using a bootstrap compiler that compiles the non-formatting portion of Curl into C. This generated C code is linked with some hand-written C code that supports bootstrapping the Curl type system and kernel. Currently supported platforms are:

- PC running Windows NT, Windows 95, or Linux

- Sparc-based machines running SunOS or Solaris

Curl is available as a stand-alone executable for these platforms with plans for a compatible subset of Curl on the Java Virtual Machine in the near future. Interested readers are referred to the Curl Web site (*http://cag-www.lcs.mit.edu/curl*) for up-to-date information status and availability of the various Curl implementations.

Client versus Server-Side Processing

Because Curl is a general purpose, efficient programming language, it can be used to perform both client-side and server-side processing. In fact, when both the client and server are Curl programs, functionality can be adjusted dynamically between the client and server. We currently use a Curl program on our server to distribute Curl documents by translating them, on the fly, to HTML. This mechanism allows the browsing of Curl documentation without downloading the Curl display engine and compiler. Of course, many things that can be expressed in Curl cannot be translated into HTML, but could be translated into code for the Java virtual machine. Such code would run much less efficiently than our native Curl implementation but would allow a Curl author/programmer to rely on the fact that even the most naive user would be able to look at at her document.

Summary

One of the weak points of the Web today is that there is a dichotomy between programs and documents, and also between programmers and authors. This dichotomy is a result of the lack of

a linguistic tool with sufficient generality. Increasing the active content of a document should be as simple as making additional regions in the document show the result of a computation, and supplying code to compute what should be displayed in those regions. It should also not be necessary to rewrite parts of a document in a different language because it turned out that some part of the code ran too slowly. The Curl language and implementation show that it is possible to meet these goals.

The goal of integrating an authoring/programming language and environment with a gentle slope is a challenging one. There are many places where the most natural or useful syntax and semantics are in conflict. We have tried to resolve these conflicts in a tasteful way. We also had to choose a set of object semantics, a subject about which there is great controversy. The object semantics we have implemented have little impact on the overall system except that we insisted on efficient representations and low dispatch overhead.

Producing an interactive program/document is much easier when the appropriate level of abstraction can be used for all components without having to cross language and representation barriers. It is a challenge to provide high-performance and flexibility but our initial results are encouraging. ■

References

1. See *http://home.netscape.com/comprod/products/navigator/version_3.0/building_blocks/jscript/index.html.*

2. Gosling, Joy, Steele. *The Java Language Specification*, Addison-Wesley. August 1996.

3. Java white papers at *http://java.sun.com/nav/read/whitepapers.html.*

4. Clinger, William, and Jonathan Rees (editors). *The Revised Report on the Algorithmic Language Scheme*, Lisp Pointer IV(3): 1-55, July–September 1991.

5. Ousterhout, John K. *Tcl and the Tk Toolkit*, Addison-Wesley, 1993.

6. World Wide Web Consortium. *http://w3.org/.*

7. Berners-Lee, T., and D. Connolly. *Hypertext Markup Language: A Representation of Textual Information and Metainformation for Retrieval and Interchange*, CERN and Atrium Technology Inc. July 1993.

8. Berners-Lee, T., and D. Connolly. RFC 1866: Hypertext Markup Language—2.0, Nov 3, 1995.

9. Knuth, Donald E. *The Texbook: A Complete Guide to Computer Typesetting With TeX*, Addison-Wesley. April 1, 1988.

10. Apple Computer, *Dylan Reference Manual*, Apple Computer Inc., Cupertino, California, September 29, 1995. See also *http://www.cambridge.apple.com*.

11. Cardelli, L. *A Polymorphic Lambda Calculus with Type:Type*, Digital Equipment Corp., Systems Research Center, 1986.

12. Milner, Robin, Mads Tofte, and Robert Harper. *The Definition of Standard ML*, MIT Press, Cambridge, 1990.

13. Guy Steele, Jr. *Common Lisp,* Second Edition, Digital Press 1990.

14. Moon, David, et al, *LISP Machine Manual,* Fifth Edition, MIT Artificial Intelligense Laboratory, January 1983.

15. Bobrow, Daniel, et al. *A Common Lisp Object System Specification, Lisp and Symbolic Computation I*, January 1989.

16. Stroustrup, Bjarne. *The C++ Programming Language*, Addison Wesley, 1991.

17. Wahbe, Robert, Steven Lucco, Thomas E. Anderson, Susan L. Graham. "Efficient Software-Based Fault Isolation," *Proceedings of the Fourteenth ACM Symposium on Operating Systems Principles.* December, 1993.

Acknowledgments

The Curl project is supported by the Information Technology Office of the Defense Advanced Research Projects Agency as part of its Intelligent Collaboration and Visualization program.

About the Authors

All the authors can be contacted at:

MIT Laboratory for Computer Science
545 Technology Square
Cambridge, MA, 02139

General questions and comments can be sent to *curl@lcs.mit.edu*; email addresses for each author are given below.

Mat Hostetter (*mat@lcs.mit.edu*) is an M.Eng candidate in the Department of Electrical Engineering and Computer Science at the Massachusetts Institute of Technology. His current research interests include run-time code generation, CPU emulation, and high-performance compilers.

David Kranz (*kranz@lcs.mit.edu*) is a Principal Research Scientist at the MIT Laboratory for Computer Science. His research interests are in programming language design and implementation for parallel computing. Kranz received a B.A. from Swarthmore. While earning a Ph.D. at Yale, he worked on high-performance compilers for Scheme and applicative languages.

Cotton Seed (*cottons@lcs.mit.edu*) is a member of the research staff at the MIT Laboratory for Computer Science.

Chris Terman (*cjt@mit.edu*) is a Research Scientist at the MIT Laboratory for Computer Science. Chris has worked in both academic and industrial settings on a variety of projects including VLSI architectures and design methodologies, computer-aided design tools, language and compiler technology, and Web-based educational tools. He received a B.A. in Physics from Wesleyan University and S.M., E.E., and Ph.D. degrees in Computer Science from MIT.

Stephen Ward (*ward@mit.edu*) is a Professor in the Electrical Engineering and Computer Science Department at the Massachusetts Institute of Technology.

Exploring CGI with Perl

Lincoln Stein

Abstract

Despite rapid advances in the technology for creating Web pages with active content (Java, ActiveX, LiveWire, NSAPI, and WSAPI to name just a few), the vast majority of active Web pages are still using that old workhorse, the Common Gateway Interface. If you've ever worked with CGI, you might have thought its rules arbitrary, quixotic, byzantine. Well, you're quite right: it's all of those things and more. In this article, originally published in three installments of the Perl Journal (http://tpj.com), Lincoln Stein uses CGI.pm, a Perl module that hides the messy details of the CGI interface, to explore CGI scripting, maintaining state in CGI transactions, and CGI scripts and cookies.

The Elements of CGI Scripting

CGI stands for Common Gateway Interface; it's the standard way to attach a piece of software to a URL. The majority of URLs refer to static files. When a remote user requests the file's URL, the Web server translates the request into a physica-land returns it. However, URLs can also refer to executable files known as *CGI scripts*, the subject of our first topic as we explore the `CGI.pm` module. When the server accesses this type of URL, it executives the script, sending the script's output to the browser. This mechanism lets you create dynamic pages, questionnaires, database query screens, order forms, and other interactive documents. It's not limited to text: CGI scripts can generate on-the-fly pictures, sounds, animations, applets, or anything else.

The basic CGI script is simple:

```
#!/usr/bin/perl
print "Content-type: text/html\r\n";
print "\r\n"; chomp($time = `date`);
print <<EOF;
<HTML><HEAD>
<TITLE>Virtual Clock</TITLE>
</HEAD>
<BODY>
<H1>Virtual Clock</H1>
At the tone, the time will be
<STRONG>$time</STRONG>.
</BODY></HTML>
EOF
```

This script begins by printing out an HTTP header. HTTP headers consist of a series of email-style header fields separated by carriage-return/newline pairs-in Perl, `\r\n`.

After the last field, the header is terminated by a blank line-another `\r\n` sequence. Although HTTP recognizes many different field names, the only one you usually need is "Content-type", which tells the browser the document's MIME (Multipurpose Internet Mail Extension) type, determining how it will be displayed. You'll often want to specify `text/html` for the value of this field, but any MIME type, including graphics and audio, is acceptable.

Next, the script uses the UNIX *date* command to place the current time in the Perl variable `$time`. It then proceeds to print a short HTML document, incorporating the timestamp directly into the text.

The output on a browser will look something like that in Figure 1. Each time you reload the script in Figure 1, you'll see a different time and date.

Things get trickier when you need to process information passed to your script from the remote user. If you've spent any time on the Web, URLs invoking CGI scripts will look familiar. CGI scripts can be invoked without any parameters:

```
http://some.site/cgi-bin/hello_
    world.pl.
```

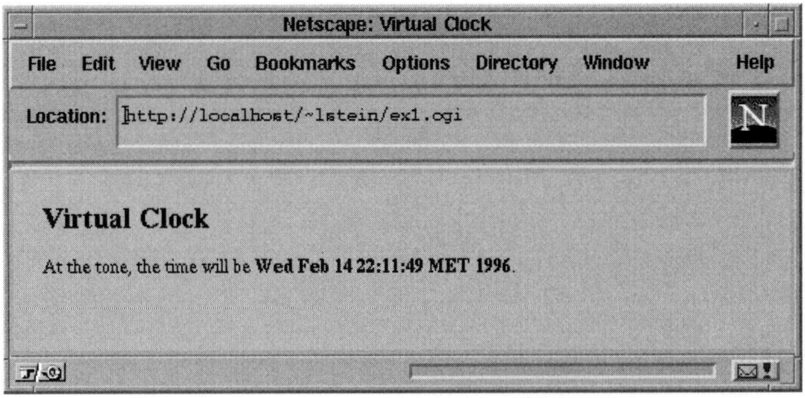

Figure 1

To send parameters to a script, add a question mark to the script name, followed by whatever parameters you want to send:

```
http://some.site/cgi-bin/index_
    search.pl?CGI+perl
http://some.site/cgi-bin/order.
    pl?cat_no=3921&quantity=2
```

These examples show the two most commonly used styles for parameter passing. The first shows the *keyword list* style, in which the parameters are a series of keywords separated by plus (+) signs. This style is traditionally used for various types of index searches. The second shows a *named parameter list*: a series of **parameter=value** pairs with ampersands (&) in between. This style is used internally by browsers to transmit the contents of a fill-out form.

Both the script's URL and its parameters are subject to URL escaping rules. Whitespace, control characters, and most punctuation characters are replaced by a percent sign (%) and the hexadecimal code for the character. For example, the space between the words "John Doe" should be passed to a CGI script like this:

```
http://some.site/cgi-bin/find_
    address.pl?name=John%20Doe
```

since spaces are ASCII 32, and 32 is hexadecimal 20.

The problem with processing script parameters is that, for various historical reasons, the rules for fetching and translating the parameters are annoyingly complex. Sometimes the script parameters are found in an environment variable. But they can also be accessed via the command line (*@ARGV*) array. Or, they can be passed via standard input. Usually you'll have to recognize the URL escape sequences and translate them, but in some circumstances the server will do that for you. Which rules apply depend on whether your script was generated by a GET or POST request (the former is usually generated when a user selects a hypertext link; the latter when a browser submits the contents of a fill-out form), whether the parameters are formatted using the keyword list or named parameter styles, and whether the browser takes advantage of the Netscape 2.0 file upload feature.

Fortunately CGI.pm knows the rules. It takes care of the details so that you can concentrate on your application.

CGI.pm combines several functions:

- It parses and decodes CGI parameter lists.

- It provides access to HTTP header information provided by the browser and server.

- It provides an easy way of generating HTTP header responses.

- It acts as a shortcut HTML generator for creating fill-out forms, and produces HTML that helps maintain the state of a form from page to page.

CGI.pm requires Perl 5.001 or higher. Its home base is:

```
http://www-genome.wi.mit.edu/ftp/
    pub/software/WWW/cgi_docs.html
```

It's also widely distributed via the CPAN.[*] It installs like any other Perl module. You can either copy it directly to your Perl library directory, or you can use the Perl5 *MakeMaker* program to locate the library directory and install CGI.pm for you.

Using CGI.pm, we can enhance the simple virtual clock script to allow the remote user some control over the time format. The script in Example 1 allows the user to control whether the time, day, month, and year are displayed, and toggle between displaying the time in 12-hour or 24-hour format.

Example 1

```perl
#!/usr/bin/perl

use CGI;

$q = new CGI; if ($q->param) {
    if ($q->param('time')) {
        $format = ($q->param('type') eq '12-hour') ? '%r ' : '%T ';
    }
    $format .= '%A ' if $q->param('day');
    $format .= '%B ' if $q->param('month');
    $format .= '%d ' if $q->param('day-of-month');
    $format .= '%Y ' if $q->param('year');
} else { $format = '%r %A %B %d %Y' }

chomp($time = `date '+$format'`);

# print the HTTP header and the HTML document
print $q->header;
print $q->start_html('Virtual Clock');

print "<H1>Virtual Clock</H1>At the tone, the time will be <STRONG>$time</STRONG>.
    ";
print "<HR><H2>Set Clock Format</H2>";

# create the clock settings form
print $q->start_form, "Show: ";
print $q->checkbox(-name=>'time', -checked=>1), $q->checkbox(-name=>'day',-
    checked=>1);
print $q->checkbox(-name=>'month',-checked=>1), $q->checkbox(-name=>'day-of-
    month',-checked=>1);
print $q->checkbox(-name=>'year', -checked=>1), "<P>";
print "Time style: ", $q->radio_group(-name=>'type',-values=>['12-hour','24-
    hour']),"<P>";
```

---

[*] The current list of the Comprehensive Perl Archive Network (CPAN) sites can be found at *http://perl.com/CPAN.*

Example 1 *(continued)*

```
print $q->reset(-name => 'Reset'), $q->submit(-name => 'Set');
print $q->end_form;
print $q->end_html;
```

The output of the script in Example 1 is shown in Figure 2.

Let's walk through this script step by step:

1. We load the CGI module and send a **new()** message to the CGI class. This creates a new CGI object, which we store in the Perl variable $q. Parameter parsing takes place during the **new()** call, so you don't have do it explicitly.

2. Next, using specifications determined by the script parameters, we create a format string to pass to the UNIX *date* command. The key to accessing script parameters is the CGI **param()** call, which is designed for the named parameter list style of script arguments (another method call, **keywords()**, is used to access keyword lists). Called without arguments, **param()** returns an array of all the named parameters. Called with the name of a parameter, **param()** returns its value, or an array of values if the parameter appears more than once in the script parameter list. In this case, we look for parameters named time, day, month, day-of-month, year, and style. Using their values, we build up a time format specifier to pass to the *date* command (see its manual page for details). If no parameters are present—for instance, if the script is being called for the very first time—we create a default format specifier. Then we call the *date* command and save its value in $time as before.

3. We create the HTTP header using the CGI **header()** method. This method returns a string containing a fully formed HTTP header, which the program immediately prints out. Called without any parameters, **header()** returns a string declaring that the document is of the content type text/html.

To create documents of other MIME types, you can call **header()** with the MIME type of your choice, for example:

```
print $q->header('image/gif');
```

You can also use the named-parameter style of calling to produce headers containing any of the fields defined in the HTTP protocol:

```
print $q->header
            (-Status => 200,
               -Type => 'image/gif',
             -Pragma => 'no cache',
    '-Content-length' => 8457);
```

You don't have to remember to write that blank line after the HTTP header. **header()** does it for you.

4. We start the HTML document by printing out the string returned by **start_html()**. Called with just one argument, this method returns an HTML <HEAD> section and the opening tag for the HTML <BODY>. The argument becomes the title of the document. As in **header()** you can call **start_html()** with named parameters to specify such things as the author's email address, or the background color (a Netscape extension):

```
print $q->start_html(
    -Title => 'Virtual Document',
   -Author => 'andy@putamen.com',
   -BGCOLOR => '#00A0A0');
```

5. The program then spits out a few lines of HTML, including the formatted time string.

6. This is followed by a horizontal line and a fill-out form that allows the user to adjust the format of the displayed time. CGI.pm has a whole series of HTML shortcuts for generating fill-out form elements. We start the form by printing out the <FORM> string returned by the **start_form()** method, and then create a series of checkboxes (using the

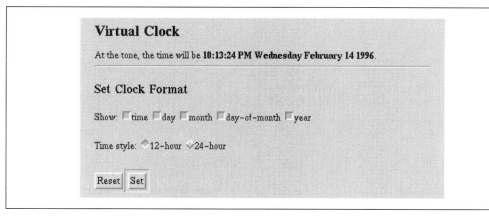

Figure 2

checkbox() method), a pair of radio buttons (using the radio_group() method), and the standard Reset and Submit buttons (using the reset() and submit() methods).

There are similar methods for creating text input fields, pop-up menus, scrolling lists, and clickable image maps. One of the features of these methods is that if a named parameter is defined from an earlier invocation of the script, its value is "sticky": a checkbox that was previously turned on will remain on. This feature makes it possible to keep track of a series of user interactions in order to create multipart questionnaires, shopping-cart scripts, and progressively more complex database queries.

Each of these methods accepts optional arguments that adjust the appearance and behavior; for example, you can adjust the height of a scrolling list with the -size parameter. After we finish the form, we close it with a call to end_form().

7. We end the virtual document by printing the string returned by end_html(), which returns the </BODY> and </HTML> tags.

In addition to its basic parameter-parsing, HTTP header-creating, and HTML shortcut-generating abilities, CGI.pm contains functions for saving and restoring the script's state to files and pipes, generating browser redirection instructions, and accessing useful information about the transaction, such as the type of browser, the machine it's running on, and the list of MIME types it can accept.

Saving State with CGI.pm

In this section, I'll discuss how to handle errors generated by CGI scripts and additional techniques for maintaining state using CGI.pm in CGI transactions.

We live in a stateful world. Just to be certain of that fact, I collected a few examples this morning:

- Today I'm in a certain frantic state of mind because this paper is due: I'll be this way for at least the rest of the afternoon or until the paper is finished, whichever comes first. This is an example of a *short-term state*.

- The federal budget is in a dreadful state of affairs, and there's no hope of it being cleared up until the last state has voted in the general election. This is an example of a *long-term state*.

- The weather is truly lovely today with balmy spring weather and bright sunshine. Because this is New England, however, it will stay nice only until sometime tonight, when the weather report predicts a snowstorm followed by an iron frost. This is typical of an *unstable state*.

If the world has state, why doesn't the World Wide Web? It would seem reasonable for the Web to have some memory. After all, people do tend to hang around a site for a while, exploring here and there. It would seem only polite for a Web site to remember the user who's been rattling around inside it for the past hour. But the HTTP protocol is stateless. Each request for a document is a new transaction; after the document is delivered, the Web server wipes its hands of the whole affair and starts fresh.

The HTTP protocol was designed that way because a stateless model is appropriate for the bulk of a Web server's job: to listen for requests for HTML documents and deliver them without fuss, frills, or idle chitchat. The fact that the implementors of the protocol saw fit to build this stateless protocol on top of the connection-oriented TCP network communications protocol, thereby ensuring that the Web is hobbled by the performance limitations of TCP without reaping any of its benefits, is a small irony that we won't discuss further.

CGI scripts, however, often fit the stateless model poorly. Many CGI scripts are search engines of some sort. People pose a question, the CGI script does a search, and returns an answer. The user looks at the results, refines or modifies his question, and asks again. Unfortunately, by the time the user has refined his query and wants to build on previous results, the original CGI script has terminated, and the search has to start all over again.

Or consider the important class of CGI scripts called "shopping carts." A user browses around an online catalog for a while. Whenever something takes his fancy, he presses a button that adds it to his shopping cart. When he's ready, he reviews the contents of the cart and (the vendor

hopes) presses a button that performs an online order.

In the absence of any stateful behavior in HTTP itself, CGI script writers have to keep track of state themselves. There are several techniques for doing this, as shown in the following list. Most of them rely on tricking or cajoling the browser into keeping track of the state for you.

- *Maintain state variables in the CGI parameters.* The simplest trick is to store all the data you want to keep track of in the query string passed from the browser to the CGI script. You can store the data directly in the URL used in a GET request or as settings in a fill-out form. As shown in the previous section, this is relatively easy to do with `CGI.pm`, because it was designed to create "sticky" state-maintaining forms. This paradigm breaks down, however, when there's a lot of data to keep track of or when it's important to maintain a chronologically accurate record of the user's actions even when the user hits the Back and Forward buttons.

- *Maintain the state on the server side with a specially spawned HTTP server.* You can defeat the limitation on HTTP by creating your own state-aware Web server. When a remote user starts a session, you spawn a new HTTP server that's dedicated to maintaining the state of that session, and you redirect the user to the new server's URL. This is how the state-maintaining miniserver module works.

- *Save the session's state to a disk file and use a session key to keep track of the files.* This technique, which we focus on here, works even when there's large amounts of state data and requires minimal data to be stored on the browser side of the connection.

Example 2 is a sample state-maintaining CGI script called `remember.cgi`. (The output of the script in Example 2 is shown in Figure 3.) When invoked, the script displays a form containing a single text input field and two buttons labeled

ADD and CLEAR (see Figure 3 for a screen shot). The user may type a short phrase into the text field and press ADD. This adds the phrase to the bottom of a growing list of phrases displayed at the bottom of the page. When the user presses CLEAR, the list is emptied. You can try it out for yourself at *http://www.genome.wi.mit.edu/WWW/ examples/ch9/remember.cgi.*

Example 2

```perl
01 #!/usr/bin/perl
02 # Collect the user's responses in a file and echo them back to him when
     requested.
03
04 $STATE_DIR = "./STATES";                          # must be writable by
                                                      # 'nobody'
05
06 use CGI;
07
08 $q = new CGI;
09 $session_key = $q->path_info();
10 $session_key =~ s|^/||;                           # get rid of the initial
                                                      # slash
11
12 unless (&valid($session_key)) {                   # If no valid session key
                                                      # has been provided,
13     $session_key = &generate_session_key($q);      # then we generate one,
                                                      # tack it on to the end of
                                                      # our URL
14     print $q->redirect($q->url() . "/$session_key");# as additional path
                                                      # information, and
                                                      # redirect the user
15     exit 0;                                        # to this new location.
16 }
17
18 $old_state = &fetch_old_state($session_key);
19
20 if ($q->param('action') eq 'ADD') {               # Add the new item(s) to
                                                      # the old list of items
21     @new_items = $q->param('item');
22     @old_items = $old_state->param('item');
23     $old_state->param('item',@old_items,@new_items);
24 } elsif ($q->param('action') eq 'CLEAR') {
25     $old_state->delete('item');
26 }
27
28 &save_state($old_state,$session_key);             # Save the new list to disk
29
30 print $q->header;                                 # Now, at last, generate
                                                      # something for the user
                                                      # to look at.
31 print $q->start_html("The growing list");
32 print <<END;
33 <h1>The Growing List</h1>
34 Type a short phrase into the text field below.  When you press <i>ADD</i>, it
   will be added to a history of the phrases
```

Example 2 *(continued)*

```
35 that you've typed.  The list is maintained on disk at the server end, so it
     won't get out of order if you press the "back"
36 button.  Press <i>CLEAR</i> to clear the list and start fresh.
37 END
38
39 print $q->start_form;
40 print $q->textfield(-name=>'item',-default=>'',-size=>50,-override=>1),"<p>";
41 print $q->submit(-name=>'action',-value=>'CLEAR');
42 print $q->submit(-name=>'action',-value=>'ADD');
43 print $q->end_form;
44 print "<hr><h2>Current list</h2>";
45
46 if ($old_state->param('item')) {
47     print "<ol>";
48     foreach $item ($old_state->param('item')) {
49         print "<li>",$q->escapeHTML($item);
50     }
51     print "</ol>";
52 } else { print "<i>Empty</i>" }
53
54 print <<END;
55 <hr><address>Lincoln D. Stein, lstein\@genome.wi.mit.edu<br>
56 <a href="/">Whitehead Institute/MIT Center for Genome Research</a></address>
57 END
58 print $q->end_html;
59
60 sub generate_session_key {               # Silly technique: we generate
                                            # a session key from the
61     my $q = shift;                        # remote IP address plus our
                                            # PID. More sophisticated
62     my($remote) = $q->remote_addr;        # scripts should use a better
                                            # technique.
63     return "$remote.$$";
64 }
65
66 sub valid {                               # Make sure the session ID
                                            # passed to us is valid
67     my $key = shift;                       # by looking for pattern ##.##.
                                            # ##.##.##
68     return $key=~/^\d+\.\d+\.\d+\.\d+.\d+$/;
69 }
70
71 sub fetch_old_state {                     # Open the existing file, if
                                            # any, and read the current
                                            # state.
72     my $session_key = shift;               # We use the CGI object here,
                                            # because it's
                                            # straightforward to do.
73     open(SAVEDSTATE,"$STATE_DIR/$session_key"); # We don't check for success
                                            # of the open(), because if
                                            # there is
```

Example 2 *(continued)*

```
74      my $state = new CGI(SAVEDSTATE);              # no file yet, the new
                                                      # CGI(FILEHANDLE) call will
                                                      # return an empty
75      close SAVEDSTATE;                             # parameter list, which is
                                                      # exactly what we want.
76      return $state;
77 }
78
79 sub save_state {
80      my($state,$session_key) = @_;
81      open(SAVEDSTATE, ">$STATE_DIR/$session_key") ||
82      die "Failed opening session state file: $!";
83      $state->save(SAVEDSTATE);
84      close SAVEDSTATE;
85 }
```

The script in Example 2 works by maintaining each session's state in a separate file. The files are kept in a subdirectory that is readable and writable by the Web server daemon. We keep track of the correspondence between files and browser sessions by generating a unique session key when the remote user first accesses the script. After the session key is generated, we arrange for the browser to pass the key back to us on each subsequent access to the script.

The technique this script uses to maintain the session key is to store it in the "additional path information" part of the URL. This is the part of the URL between the name of the script and the beginning of the query string. For example, in the following URL:

```
http://toto.com/cgi-bin/remember.
    cgi/202.2.13.1.117?item=
    hi%20there
```

the text /202.2.13.1.117 is the additional path information. Although the additional path information syntax was designed for passing file information to CGI scripts, there's no reason it can't be used for other purposes, and it's often easier to keep the session key here than mixing it up with the other script parameters.

Notes:

Lines 8-16 are responsible for generating a unique session key. After creating a new CGI object, the script fetches the additional path information and strips off the initial slash (**lines 9-10**). The session key is next passed to the subroutine valid() (**lines 66-69**). This subroutine performs a pattern match on the session key to ensure that it is a key generated by our program rather than something that the user happened to type in. Importantly, the valid() subroutine also returns false if the session key is an empty string, which happens the first time our script is called.

If the session key is blank or invalid, we generate a new key (**lines 12-16**) using the subroutine generate_session_key(). This subroutine, located at **lines 60-64**, is responsible for generating something that won't conflict with other concurrent sessions. In this example, we use the simple but imperfect expedient of concatenating the remote machine's IP address with the CGI script's process ID.

After creating a new session key, we generate a redirect directive to the browser, incorporating the session key into the new URL. If our script's URL is *http://toto.com/cgi-bin/remember.cgi* and the newly generated session key is *202.2.13.1.117*, we redirect the browser to *http://toto.com/cgi-bin/remember.cgi/202.2.13.1.117*.

The scripts exists after printing the redirect. It will be reinvoked almost immediately by the browser

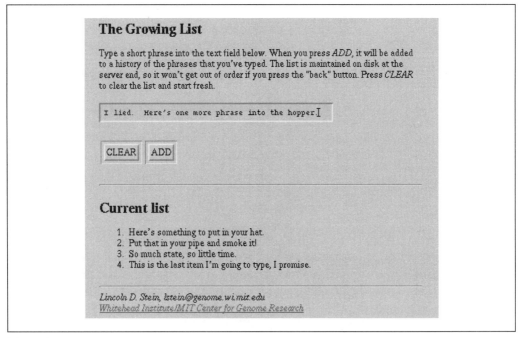

The Growing List

Type a short phrase into the text field below. When you press *ADD*, it will be added to a history of the phrases that you've typed. The list is maintained on disk at the server end, so it won't get out of order if you press the "back" button. Press *CLEAR* to clear the list and start fresh.

I lied. Here's one more phrase into the hopper.

CLEAR   ADD

Current list

1. Here's something to put in your hat.
2. Put that in your pipe and smoke it!
3. So much state, so little time.
4. This is the last item I'm going to type, I promise.

Lincoln D. Stein, lstein@genome.wi.mit.edu
Whitehead Institute/MIT Center for Genome Research

Figure 3

when it retrieves the new URL/session key combination.

The remainder of the script, from **line 18 onward**, contains the code that is invoked when the browser provides a valid session key. Line 18 calls `fetch_old_state()` to retrieve the current list of text lines. This subroutine, defined in lines 71-77, opens up a file that contains the saved state by using the session key directly as the name of the file. More sophisticated scripts will want to use the session key in more clever ways, such as the key to a record in a DBM file or a handle into a relational database session.

`fetch_old_state()` opens the file indicated by the session key, ignoring any "file not found" errors and passes the file handle to the CGI `new()` method. This creates a new CGI object with parameters initialized from data stored in the file. We create a new CGI object here solely because its `param()` method offers a convenient way to store multiple named parameters and

because of its ability to save and restore these named parameters to a file. We don't check first whether the file exists. If the file doesn't exist already, the CGI `new()` method returns an empty parameter list, which is exactly what we want. We close the file and return the new CGI object.

We now have two CGI objects:

- The first object, stored in the variable $q, was initialized from the current query and contains the contents of the text field and information about which button the user pressed when he submitted the fill-out form.

- The second object, stored in the variable $old_state, is the CGI object initialized from the saved file and contains cumulative information about the user's previous actions.

Lines 20–26 manipulate the saved state depending on the user's request. We find out which button the user pressed by examining the CGI query's "action" parameter (**line 20**). If equal to "ADD", we recover the contents of the text field from the query parameter "item" and add it to the cumulative list (**line 23**). If the "action" parameter is "CLEAR", we clear the list completely (**line 25**). Otherwise, no button was pressed, and we continue onward.

Next we save the updated list back to disk with `save_state()`, which reverses the process by opening up the file indicated by the session key and using the CGI `save()` method to dump out the contents of `$old_state`.

So far no text at all has been transmitted to the browser. It's a good idea to do all the back end work first, because network delays can make your CGI script hang during output. If the user presses the Stop button during this period, your CGI script will be terminated, potentially leaving things in an inconsistent state.

Lines 30-58 generate the HTML document. The script generates the HTTP header followed by the HTML preliminaries and some explanatory text (**lines 30-37**). Next it creates the fill-out form, using the `start_form()`, `end_form()`, and `form` element generating subroutines discussed previously. The only trick in this section is the use of the `-override` parameter in the call to `textfield()`. We want the contents of this field to be blank each time the page is displayed. For this purpose we set the contents to an empty string and use `-override` to have `CGI.pm` suppress the usual sticky behavior of fields.

After closing the form, we print out the current list of phrases in **lines 44-52**. Because there's no control over what the user types into the text field, it's important to escape any special HTML characters (such as angle brackets and ampersands) before incorporating it into our own document. Otherwise, the script might create a page that doesn't display properly. The `escapeHTML()` method accomplishes this.

Last, we end the page with `end_html()` and exit.

The script in Example 2 doesn't save a vast amount of state information: only one parameter, and a short one at that. However, the same techniques can be used to store and manipulate the contents of hundreds of parameters. In order to turn this from an example into a real world script, you'll need to make a few refinements.

You might want to change the way session keys are chosen. Although this script chooses its keys in a way that minimizes the chances of conflict between two sessions, it isn't suitable for security-sensitive applications. Such scripts should make sure that the remote user is entitled to use the provided session key in order to prevent one user from "stealing" another user's state. Checking the IP address for consistency is a one way to do this; password-protecting the script and incorporating the encrypted password into the session key would be an even better technique.

In order to make the script in Example 2 useful in the real world, you'll also need to remove state files when they've gone out of date. Otherwise, the scripts' PIDs will eventually roll over and start using ancient state files that are no longer valid. (There's also the risk of proliferating state files filling up your disk!) The easiest way to handle this on a UNIX system is with a *cron* job that runs at regular intervals looking for old state files and deleting them.

Another thing you might want to change is the way the session key is maintained. Netscape browsers support a "magic cookie" field that is guaranteed to be maintained for the entire length of a browser/server session. You can set the browser's magic cookie when the script first accesses the script, using `CGI.pm`'s `set_cookie()` method, and retrieve it on subsequent invocations of the script using `get_cookie()`. Unfortunately, only Netscape browsers support the magic cookie field, so it isn't useful for other browsers.

CGI Scripts and Cookies

Next up on our explanation of `CGI.pm`, we look at cookies. What's a cookie? The folks at Netscape came up with the idea for Navigator 1. 1. It's just a `name=value` pair, much like the named parameters used in the CGI query string. When a Web server or CGI script wants to save some state information, it creates a cookie or two and sends them to the browser inside the HTTP header. The browser keeps track of all the cookies sent to it by a particular server and stores them in an on-disk database so that the cookies persist even when the browser is closed and reopened later. The next time the browser connects to a Web site, it searches its database for all cookies that belong to that server and transmits them back to the server within the HTTP header.

Cookies can be permanent or set to expire after a number of hours or days. They can be made site-wide, so that the cookie is available to every URL on your site, or restricted to a partial URL path. You can also set a flag in the cookie so that it's transmitted over the Internet only when the browser and server are communicating by a secure protocol such as SSL. You can even create promiscuous cookies that are sent to every server in a particular Internet domain.

The idea is simple but powerful. If a CGI script needs to save a small amount of state information, such as the user's preferred background color, it can be stored directly in a cookie. If lots of information needs to be stored, you can keep the information in a database on the server's side and use the cookie to record a session key or user ID. Other browsers have begun to adopt cookies (notably Microsoft in its Internet Explorer), and cookies are on their way to becoming a part of the HTTP standard.

So how do you create a cookie? If you use the `CGI.pm` library it's a piece of cake:

```
0   #!/usr/bin/perl
1
2   use CGI qw(:standard);
3
```

```
4   $cookie1 = cookie
        (-name  => 'regular',
5        -value => 'chocolate chip');
6   $cookie2 = cookie
        (-name  => 'high fiber',
7        -value => 'oatmeal raisin');
8   print header(-cookie => [$cookie1,
        $cookie2]);
```

Line 2 loads the CGI library and imports the `:standard` set of function calls using a syntax that's new in library versions 2.21 and higher. This syntax allows you to call all of the CGI object's methods without explicitly creating a CGI instance—a default CGI object is created for you behind the scenes. **Lines 4-7** create two new cookies using the CGI `cookie()` method. The last step is to incorporate the cookies into the document's HTTP header. We do this in **line 8** by printing out the results of the `header()` method, passing it the `-cookie` parameter along with an array reference containing the two cookies.

When we run this script from the command line, the result is:

```
Set-cookie: regular=chocolate%20chip
Set-cookie:
    high%20fiber=oatmeal%20raisin
Content-type: text/html
```

As you can see, `CGI.pm` translates spaces into %20s, because the Netscape cookie specification prohibits whitespace and certain other characters, such as the semicolon. (It also places an upper limit of a few kilobytes on the size of a cookie, so don't try to store the text of Hamlet in one.) When the browser sees these two cookies it squirrels them away and returns them to your script the next time it needs a document from your server.

To retrieve the value of a cookie sent to you by the browser, use `cookie()` without a `-value` parameter:

```
0   #!/usr/bin/perl
1
2   use CGI qw(:standard);
3
4   $regular    = cookie('regular');
5   $high_fiber = cookie('high fiber');
```

```
6
7  print header(-type => 'text/plain'),
8      "The regular cookie is $regular.
       \n",
9      "The high fiber cookie is $high_
       fiber.";
```

In this example, **lines 4 and 5** retrieve the two cookies by name. **Lines 7-9** print out an HTTP header (containing no cookie this time), and two lines of text. The output of this script, when viewed in a browser, would be

```
The regular cookie is chocolate chip.
The high fiber cookie is oatmeal raisin.
```

The cookie() method is fairly flexible. You can save entire arrays as cookies by giving the -value parameter an array reference:

```
$c = cookie(-name => 'specials',
            -value=>['oatmeal',
                     'chocolate
                      chip','alfalfa']);
```

Or you can save and restore whole associative arrays:

```
$c = cookie(-name => 'prices',
            -value=> {   'oatmeal'   =>
                         '$0.50',
                  'chocolate_chip'=>
                         '$1.25',
                      'alfalfa'   =>
                         'free'});
```

Later you can recover the two cookies this way:

```
@specials = cookie('specials');
%prices   = cookie('prices');
```

By default, browsers will remember cookies that only until they exit, and will only send the cookie out to scripts with a URL path that's similar to the script that generated it. If you want them to remember the cookie for a longer period of time, pass an -expires parameter to cookie() containing the cookie's shelf life. To change the URL path over which the cookie is valid, pass its value in -path:

```
$c = cookie(-name  => 'regular',
            -value => 'oatmeal raisin',
             -path => '/cgi-bin/bakery',
          -expires => '+3d');
```

This cookie will expire in three days' time (`+3d`). Other cookie() parameters allow you to adjust the domain names and URL paths that trigger the browser to send a cookie, and to turn on cookie secure mode. The -path parameter shown here tells the browser to send the cookie to every program in /cgi-bin/bakery.

Example 3 shows how a CGI script called configure.cgi. When you call this script's URL you're presented with the fill-out form shown above. You can change the page's background color, the text size and color, and even customize it with your name. The next time you visit this page (even if you've closed the browser and come back to the page weeks later), it remembers all of these values and builds a page based on them.

Example 3

```
00  #!/usr/bin/perl
01
02  use CGI qw(:standard :html3);
03
04  # Some constants to use in our form.
05  @colors = qw/aqua black blue fuchsia gray green lime maroon navy olive purple
    red silver teal white yellow/;
06  @sizes = ("<default>", 1..7);
07
08  # recover the "preferences" cookie.
09  %preferences = cookie('preferences');
10
```

Example 3 *(continued)*

```perl
11  # If the user wants to change the background color or her name, they will
    appear among our CGI parameters.
12  foreach ('text', 'background', 'name', 'size') {
13      $preferences{$_} = param($_) || $preferences{$_};
14  }
15
16  # Set some defaults
17  $preferences{background} = $preferences{background} || 'silver';
18  $preferences{text} = $preferences{text} || 'black';
19
20  # Refresh the cookie so that it doesn't expire.
21  $the_cookie = cookie( -name => 'preferences',
22                        -value=> \%preferences,
23                        -path => '/',
24                     -expires => '+30d');
25  print header(-cookie => $the_cookie);
26
27  # Adjust the title to incorporate the user's name, if provided.
28  $title = $preferences{name} ? "Welcome back, $preferences{name}!" :
    "Customizable Page";
29
30  # Create the HTML page.  We use several of the HTML 3.2 extended tags to
    control the background color
31  # and the font size. It's safe to use these features because cookies don't
    work anywhere else anyway.
32  print start_html(-title => $title,
33                  -bgcolor => $preferences{background},
34                    -text => $preferences{text});
35
36  print basefont({SIZE=>$preferences{size}}) if $preferences{size} > 0;
37
38  print h1($title),<<END;
39  You can change the appearance of this page by submitting
40  the fill-out form below.  If you return to this page any time
41  within 30 days, your preferences will be restored.
42  END
43  ;
44  # Create the form
45  print hr,
46      start_form,
47
48      "Your first name: ",
49      textfield(-name    => 'name',
50               -default => $preferences{name},
51               -size    => 30), br,
52      table(
53        TR(
54          td("Preferred"),
55          td("Page color:"),
56          td(popup_menu(   -name => 'background',
57                         -values => \@colors,
58                         -default => $preferences{background}))
59            )
```

Example 3 *(continued)*

```
60              ),
61          TR(
62              td(''),
63              td("Text color:"),
64              td(popup_menu(   -name => 'text',
65                              -values => \@colors,
66                          -default => $preferences{text})
67              )
68          ),
69          TR(
70              td(''),
71              td("Font size:"),
72              td(popup_menu(   -name => 'size',
73                              -values => \@sizes,
74                          -default => $preferences{size})
75              )
76          )
77      ),
78      submit(-label => 'Set preferences'),
79      end_form,
80      hr;
81
82  print a({HREF=>"/"}, 'Go to the home page');
```

The script in Example 3 recognizes four CGI parameters used to change the configuration:

background
> Set the background color

text
> Set the text color

size
> Set the size to the indicated value (1–7)

name
> Set the username

Usually these parameters are sent to the script via the fill out form that it generates, but you could set them from within a URL this way:

```
/cgi-bin/configure.pl?background=silver&
    text=blue&name=Stein
```

Notes:

Let's walk through the code. **Line 2** imports the CGI library, bringing in both the standard method calls and a number of methods that generate HTML3-specific tags. Next we define a set of background colors and sizes. The choice of col-

ors may seem capricious, but it's not. These are the background colors defined by the newly released HTML3.2 standard, and they're based on the original colors used by the IBM VGA graphics display.

Line 9 is where we recover the user's previous preferences, if any. We use the **cookie()** method to fetch a cookie named "preferences" and store its value in a like-named associative array.

In **lines 12-14**, we fetch the CGI parameters named **text**, **background**, **name**, and **size**. If any of them are set, it indicates that the user wants to change the corresponding value saved in the browser's cookie. We store changed parameters in the **%preferences** associative array, replacing the original values.

Lines 17 and 18 set the text and background colors to reasonable defaults if they can't be found in either the cookie or the CGI script parameters.

Lines 21-25 generate the page's HTTP header. First we use the **cookie()** method to create the cookie containing the user's preferences. We set the expiration date for the cookie for 30 days in the future so that the cookie will be removed from the browser's database if the user doesn't return to this page within that time. We also set the optional -path parameter to /. This makes the cookie valid over our entire site so that it's available to every URL the browser fetches. Although we don't take advantage of this yet, it's useful if we later decide that these preferences should have a site-wide effect. Lastly we emit the HTTP header with the -cookie parameter set.

In **lines 30-36** we begin the HTML page. True to the intent of making it personalizable, we base the page title on the user's name. If it's set, the title and level 1 header both become "Welcome back <name>!" Otherwise, the title becomes an impersonal "Customizable page."

Line 32 calls the start_html() method to create the top part of the HTML page. It sets the title, the background color, and the text color based on the values in the %preferences array. **Line 36** sets the text size by calling the basefont() method. This simply generates a <BASEFONT> HTML tag with an appropriate SIZE attribute.

Lines 38 and up generate the content of the page. There's a brief introduction to the page, followed by the fill-out form used to change the settings. All the HTML is generated using CGI.pm "short-cuts," in which tags are generated by like-named method calls. For example, the hr() method generates the HTML tag <HR>. As shown in the first column in this series, we start the fill-out form with a call to start_form(), create the various form elements with calls to textfield(), popup_menu(), and submit(), and close the form with end_form().

When I first wrote the script in Example 2, the pop-up menus and popup menus in the form didn't line up well. Because all the elements were slightly different widths, everything was crooked. To fix this problem, I used the common trick of

placing the form elements inside an invisible HTML3 table. Assigning each element to its own cell forces the fields to line up. You can see how I did this in **lines 52-77**, where I define a table using a set of CGI.pm shortcuts. An outer call to table() generates the surrounding <TABLE> and </TABLE> tags. Within this are a series of TR() methods, each of which generates a <TR> tag. (In order to avoid conflict with Perl's built-in tr/// operator, this is one instance in which CGI.pm uses uppercase rather than lowercase shortcut names.) Within each TR() call, in turn, there are several td() calls that generate the <TD> ("table data") cells of the HTML table.

Fortunately my text editor auto-indents nicely, making it easy to see the HTML structure.

On a real site, of course, you'd want the user's preferences to affect all pages, not just one. This isn't a major undertaking; many modern Web servers now allow you to designate a script that preprocesses all files of a certain type. You can create a variation on the script shown here that takes an HTML document and inserts the appropriate <BASEFONT> and <BODY> tags based on the cookie preferences. Now just configure the server to pass all HTML documents through this script and you're set.

Cringe, Microsoft, cringe!

About the Author

Lincoln Stein
Whitehead Institute
MIT Center for Genome Research
One Kendall Square, Bldg. 300
Cambridge, MA 02139

On the surface, Lincoln Stein is the M.D./Ph.D. who directs informatics at the Whitehead Institute/MIT Center for Genome Research. In his heart, he's an irremediable Perl hacker. He can be contacted at *lstein@genome.wi.mit.edu.*

WHY WIN-CGI?

Ron Petrusha

Abstract

For most of the history of the Web, the Common Gateway Interface (CGI) and the Common Gateway Interface for Windows (Win-CGI) were responsible for providing most or all of the Web's active content. Recently, though, the hype surrounding the introduction of a wide range of new competing technologies—including server API applications, Java applets, client-side scripts, server-side scripts—has removed much of the luster of Win-CGI programming. This article assesses the role of Win-CGI in future Web development and argues that if the focus shifts away from emphasizing each technology's strongest feature to choosing the right tool for the job, Win-CGI remains a viable technology for Web development.

The Common Gateway Interface, along with server-side includes, have always been the sole means available for providing active content on the Web. That, however, is no longer the case. Over the last two years, a number of competing methods for developing interactive Web applications have appeared, broadening the number of technologies available for providing active content on the Web. These include:

- *Web Server APIs*, like ISAPI (for Microsoft Internet Information Server, Microsoft's Personal Web Servers, and O'Reilly's WebSite), WSAPI (for O'Reilly's WebSite), and NSAPI (for Netscape servers).

- *Client-side scripts*, like those written in VBScript or JavaScript.

- *Server-side includes*, which allows special markers to be inserted into an HTML page. When the page is sent to the browser, these markers are replaced with dynamic data.

- *Server-side scripts.*

In comparison to these, Win-CGI, with its reliance on temporary files and its use of a temporary private initialization file to transmit data from the Web server to the CGI application, seems rather hokey and hopelessly outdated. In this article, we'll take a step backward from showing you how to use Win-CGI to examine where and how

it fits in as a technique for developing Internet applications.

Assessing Available Technologies

Often, the way that we assess competing technologies is molded by the marketing departments of software companies. We are told that we should use a particular technology, which just happens to have been developed by that company, because it offers x. Typically, x is a single advantage, like "superior performance," "greater ease of development," "robustness," or even more vaguely, "a state of the art solution." Sometimes, x turns out to be more imaginary than real. But despite our better judgment, our thinking about competing technologies is more often than not profoundly molded by these marketing claims.

The marketing hype, of course, aims at getting us to adopt a particular technology at the expense of other, competing technologies. But from the viewpoint of a Web developer or content provider, what is most important about a particular technology is not that it offer a state-of-the-art solution or that it provide better performance than competing technologies. Instead, what is important is that:

- It provides a set of features that adequately address the needs of the application to be developed.

- Those features are reasonably accessible given the level of skill or expertise of the developer or content provider.

In the remainder of this section, we'll review the major alternatives for developing active content and attempt to assess the strengths and weaknesses of each. Along with a sample "Hello, World" application that gives you a sense of how to code using a particular technology, we'll evaluate it based on the following criteria:

- *Flexibility and power.* The extent to which an application developed using a particular technology can accommodate diverse and complex requirements.

- *Developer expertise.* The level of expertise required to learn and master the technology.

- *Development and testing time.* The length of time required to create a fully tested, robust Web application.

- *Adaptability to change.* The ease with which an existing application can be modified to reflect changing needs.

- *Life-cycle cost.* The cost of creating, maintaining, and modifying a Web application throughout its lifetime. An application's life-cycle cost varies directly with the developer expertise required to create it, the development and testing time needed to deploy it, and its adaptability to change.

- *Operational risk.* The extent to which application errors are capable of compromising the server and the entire Web site.

- *CPU overhead.* The degree to which applications developed using a particular technology consume more computer resources than applications developed with competing technologies.

- *Compatibility.* The extent to which applications developed for use on a particular server can be run on servers from other vendors that were developed for the same platform.

Web Server APIs

A major objection to both generic CGI and Win-CGI applications is that, for a variety of reasons, they result in poor performance. No less an authority than Microsoft's Dr. GUI, in the July/August 1996 issue of Microsoft's *Developer Network News*, [1] briefly discussed how to use Visual Basic to develop Win-CGI applications but then rejected it as a viable solution for Internet application development. His objection to Win-CGI was based on the overhead it entails in three areas:

- *Server overhead.* Since the Win-CGI application is an executable, every URL that invokes the application launches a separate process.

- *File I/O.* Since it uses a system of files as a bridge between the Web server and the CGI application, the Win-CGI interface maximizes its use of relatively slow files instead of fast memory.

- *String processing.* Win-CGI requires that the server spend a good deal of time parsing the information that it writes to or reads from its temporary files.

Of these three, the major objection to Win-CGI is that it runs out-of-process; that is, every invocation of the Win-CGI application generates a separate instance of the application. On a particularly busy server, this means that multiple instances of the application will be resident in memory at the same time and can result in severe performance bottlenecks. This situation worsens even more if the Win-CGI application uses OLE automation to invoke out-of-process OLE servers; in this case, multiple instances of the OLE server are resident in memory as well.

In contrast, Dr. GUI recommended ISAPI, the Internet Server Application Programming Interface. Other Web servers also have their own APIs—WebSite supports the WebSite API

(WSAPI),[*] and Netscape servers support the Netscape Server API (NSAPI)—for creating Web server extensions. The server APIs aim at solving the same set of problems as CGI and Win-CGI but do so more efficiently and without depleting the server's resources; in short, they offer a high-performance alternative to Win-CGI. Applications developed using any of the server APIs take the form of Windows dynamic link libraries (DLLs). Because they are dynamic link libraries, applications developed using the server APIs run in the same process as the server itself. And like all Windows DLLs, they support multiple threads of execution. If a DLL is invoked by multiple threads, each thread typically has its own data area. However, only a single copy of the DLL's code resides in memory.

Clearly, the fact that they run in the same process as the server gives the server APIs a clear advantage over CGI and Win-CGI. We'll assess this advantage more fully when we discuss the strengths and weaknesses of Win-CGI. In the meantime, let's begin our assessment of the server APIs by taking a look at a simple "Hello, World!" application developed using ISAPI, which is shown in Example 1.

Example 1

```
#include <windows.h>
#include <httpext.h>

// prototypes
BOOL WriteHTML(LPCTSTR str, EXTENSION_CONTROL_BLOCK *pECB) ;
VOID DecodeURL(char *str) ;


// DLL entry point
BOOL WINAPI DllMain (HINSTANCE hinstDLL, DWORD dwReason, LPVOID lpv)
    {
    // nothing to do
    return (TRUE);
    }


// GetExtensionVersion
//
// Global entry point that provides version of specification
BOOL WINAPI GetExtensionVersion( HSE_VERSION_INFO  *pVer )
    {
    pVer->dwExtensionVersion = MAKELONG(HSE_VERSION_MINOR,
                                    HSE_VERSION_MAJOR);
    lstrcpyn(pVer->lpszExtensionDesc,
            "ISAPI Version of Hello, World!",
            HSE_MAX_EXT_DLL_NAME_LEN );
    return TRUE;
    }

// HttpExtensionProc
//
// Per-instance entry point
```

---

[*] WebSite also supports ISAPI.

Example 1 *(continued)*

```
DWORD WINAPI HttpExtensionProc (EXTENSION_CONTROL_BLOCK *pECB)
   {
   char lpServerName[64] ;          // buffer for name of server
   char szString[256] ;             // output string
   char *lpUserName ;               // pointer to name of user in buffer
// char szContent[] = "Content-type: text/html\r\n\r\n\0" ;
   char szContent[] = "Content-type: text/html\r\n\r\n\0" ;
   HANDLE hHeap ;                    // memory handle
   LPBYTE lpFormData ;              // buffer for form data
   DWORD dwBufferSize ;            // size of buffer variable
   DWORD dwBytesRead ;

   // Get name of server
   dwBufferSize = sizeof(lpServerName) ;
   pECB->GetServerVariable(pECB->ConnID, TEXT("SERVER_NAME"),
                           lpServerName, &dwBufferSize) ;
   // Get user name
   hHeap = GetProcessHeap() ;
   lpFormData = HeapAlloc(hHeap, HEAP_ZERO_MEMORY,
                          pECB->cbTotalBytes + 1) ;
   // All submitted data in lpbData
   if (pECB->cbTotalBytes == pECB->cbAvailable)
      lstrcpy(lpFormData, pECB->lpbData) ;
   // poll buffer
   else
      {
      lpUserName = lpFormData ;
      dwBytesRead = 0 ;
      while (dwBytesRead < pECB->cbTotalBytes)
         {
         dwBufferSize = sizeof(lpFormData) ;
         pECB->ReadClient(pECB->ConnID, (LPVOID) lpUserName, &dwBufferSize) ;
         dwBytesRead = dwBytesRead + dwBufferSize ;
         lpUserName = lpUserName + dwBytesRead ;
         }
      }
   // Extract value from key
   lpUserName = strstr(lpFormData, "name") ;
   if (! ((LPCTSTR) lpUserName == NULL))          // Adjust for "NAME="
      {
      lpUserName += 5 ;
      // remove special characters
      DecodeURL(lpUserName) ;
      }
   // Send content type
   dwBufferSize = sizeof(szContent) ;
   pECB->ServerSupportFunction(pECB->ConnID,
                               HSE_REQ_SEND_RESPONSE_HEADER,
                               NULL, &dwBufferSize,
                               (LPDWORD) szContent) ;

   // Output "Hello" page
   WriteHTML(TEXT("<HTML><HEAD><TITLE>Hello!</TITLE></HEAD>\r\n"), pECB) ;
```

Example 1 *(continued)*

```
    wsprintf(szString, "<BODY><H2>Hello, %s!</H2><P>\r\n", lpUserName) ;
    WriteHTML(szString, pECB) ;

    wsprintf(szString, "Greetings from %s!<P>\r\n", lpServerName) ;
    WriteHTML(szString, pECB) ;
    WriteHTML(TEXT("Thank you for taking the time out of your\r\n"), pECB) ;
    WriteHTML(TEXT("busy day to visit us!\r\n"), pECB) ;
    WriteHTML(TEXT("</BODY></HTML>\r\n"), pECB) ;

    // Free memory
    HeapFree(hHeap, 0, lpFormData) ;
    // Indicate successful termination
    return HSE_STATUS_SUCCESS ;
    }

// Output HTML string to client
BOOL WriteHTML(LPCTSTR str, EXTENSION_CONTROL_BLOCK *pECB)
    {
    DWORD dwBufferSize = lstrlen(str) ;

    return (pECB->WriteClient(pECB->ConnID, (PVOID) str, &dwBufferSize, 0)) ;
    }

// Replace "+" with spaces
VOID DecodeURL(char *str)
    {
    HANDLE hHeap ;
    unsigned int nPos = 1 ;
    char *charptr, *szBuffer ;
    char *space = "+" ;
    // Create temporary buffer
    hHeap = GetProcessHeap() ;
    szBuffer = HeapAlloc(hHeap, HEAP_ZERO_MEMORY,
                         lstrlen(str)+1) ;
    memset(szBuffer, '\0', sizeof(szBuffer)) ;
    memcpy(szBuffer, str, lstrlen(str)) ;

    charptr = szBuffer ;
    nPos = strcspn(charptr, space) ;
    while (nPos)
        {
        charptr = charptr + nPos ;
        *charptr = ' ' ;
        nPos = strcspn(++charptr, space) ;
        }

    lstrcpy(str, szBuffer) ;
    // Free memory
    HeapFree(hHeap, 0, szBuffer) ;

    return ;
    }
```

As Example 1 suggests, the Web server communicates with the ISAPI application by means of a data structure named an EXTENSION_CONTROL_BLOCK. The data structure includes a number of members, like `lpszMethod`, which indicates the request method, or `lpszQueryString`, which contains any query string included in the requested URL. It also contains pointers to three functions: `GetServerVariable`, to get additional information about the server; `ReadClient`, to retrieve POST data submitted by the client; and `WriteClient`, to respond to the client's request. In many respects, ISAPI is a straightforward extension of standard CGI, except that, rather than using system environment variables to communicate between server and application, it uses a server-defined data structure.

Ordinarily, we'd now present the Visual Basic version of the C application shown in Example 1. But instead, we run up against the first of the limitations of the server APIs: While Win-CGI applications can be created with any of a broad array of development tools, this is not true of applications using server APIs. Visual Basic, one of the more popular tools for Win-CGI development, for instance, cannot be used to create an ISAPI (or any other server API) application for two reasons:

- It does not support the creation of any dynamic link libraries except for in-process OLE automation servers.

- The EXTENSION_CONTROL_BLOCK, the data structure that communicates between server and the ISAPI application, contains three callback functions that are needed to retrieve most of the client's data, as well as to send all data back to the client. VB, however, does not support callbacks or the use of pointers to functions.

Instead, those wishing to develop server API applications have a rather narrow choice of development tools, which for the most part are limited to implementations of C and C++. In other words, when compared to the number of people who are capable of creating Win-CGI applications, the number of people who can develop server API extensions is quite limited.

But not everyone in the already elite audience of C/C++ programmers has the expertise needed to create server API extensions. DLLs in Windows are necessarily multithreaded. In a simple application like the one in Example 1, multithreading is thrown in "for free," since the program is not doing anything sufficiently complex for one thread to interfere with the operation of any other thread. In any "real-world" application, though, this isn't likely to be the case. Threads are almost certain to share a common set of data (like an access counter) or to access a shared set of resources (like a back-end database). In these cases, there's a very real possibility of collisions among threads accessing the same data or the same resource. To handle this possibility, developers using server APIs must be familiar with techniques for multithreaded programming and concurrency synchronization.

In short, developing professional server API extensions requires developers with a high level of skill and expertise. Typically, developers of this caliber don't work for non-technology companies (who usually can't justify the expense of keeping them around on a permanent basis). This means that they must be brought in as consultants. But consultants are rarely familiar with a company's operations, so there's always a fairly large amount of "down time" as consultants learn about a company's business rules. Once consultants are finished with a project, their software is frozen. To make changes to these server extensions, you must bring back the consultant (the preferable alternative) or, if—as often happens—he or she is unavailable, bring in another consultant. The latter is a very unsatisfactory alternative, though, since the new consultant necessarily starts at ground zero both in knowledge of a company's operation *and* in understanding the code of the API extension that the first consultant created. In a nutshell, creating server API applications requires highly specialized, and therefore very expensive, developers.

Server API extensions also suffer from another major limitation, which interestingly, is really the flip side of their major advantage. Because they consist of routines in dynamic link libraries and therefore run in the same process as the server, they can corrupt the server's internal data or, if they fail to clean up properly after themselves, can cause memory or resource leaks. In extreme cases (which are surprisingly easy to achieve), access violations by the server API application can crash the server itself. Preventing this from happening requires that the server API extension be rigorously and exhaustively tested and debugged. This in turn, of course, lengthens the application's development cycle and increases the cost of the project.

Both because they typically depend heavily on the participation of outside consultants and because they require long development cycles, server API extensions are relatively difficult to change and revise as the needs of the underlying business changes. They also have very high life-cycle costs.

Finally, applications developed using server APIs will typically run under one server but not under another. For instance, NSAPI applications run under neither Microsoft servers nor under Web-Site. Similarly, while ISAPI applications can run under Microsoft servers and under WebSite, they cannot run on Netscape servers. This means that the decision to develop an application using a server API also imvolves a long-term commitment to a particular server platform.

This is not to say, though, that the server APIs do not have a place in Internet application development. Because they run in the same process as the server, they are the preferred solution for those relatively rare situations in which performance is absolutely critical, and in which competing technologies are not able to satisfactorily

handle the load placed on a Web server or servers.

Client-Side Scripting

Although it isn't a complete replacement for CGI or Win-CGI applications, Web pages that incorporate client-side scripts (CSS) developed using such languages as VBScript or JavaScript[*] have been offered as at least a partial replacement for CGI. Typically, CGI applications perform one or more of the following four tasks:

- Validate data submitted by the client.

- Perform back-end processing, such as updating a database or a spreadsheet.

- Retrieve data from some source, like a database, to transmit to the client.

- Build pages on the fly to display on the client's browser.

Since client-side scripts consist of static text until they are received and interpreted by the browser, they can't be used to retrieve remote (i.e., from the server or the server's network) data or to perform back-end processing of the data transmitted by the server. They can, however, be used for data validation, as well as to build pages on the fly on the client's browser.

In fact, it's possible to write our earlier "Hello, World!" application so that it relies exclusively on a client-side script and does not involve the server. (The server is responsible only for transmitting the original Web page containing the script.) The HTML and VBScript source code for such a program is shown in Example 2. Because it uses VBScript, the program runs only under Microsoft Internet Explorer versions 3.0 or greater.

Whereas our "Hello, World!" applications written in C and VB relied on a form included in an HTML page to invoke a Win-CGI application, which in turn built a page on the fly based on the

---

[*] See the articles on VBScript and JavaScript by authors Paul Lomax and Nick Heinle, also in this issue.

Example 2

```
<HTML>
<HEAD>
<TITLE>Hello, World!</TITLE>
<SCRIPT LANGUAGE="VBSCRIPT">

Function cmdSubmit_OnClick

dim strName

strName = Document.frmName.txtName.Value
if len(trim(strName)) = 0 then
    Call MsgBox("You forgot to enter your name!" _
                & chr(13) & chr(10) & chr(13) & chr(10) & _
                "Please be sure to enter your name before " & _
                "clicking the OK button!", _
                vbOKOnly, "Missing Name")
else
    Document.Open
    Document.Write("<HTML><HEAD><TITLE>Hello!</TITLE></HEAD>")
    Document.Write("<H2>Hello, " & strName & "!</H2><P>")
    ' Server-side include of server name
    Document.Write("Greetings from <!--#echo var="SERVER_NAME"-->!<P>")
    Document.Write("Thanks for taking the time out of your busy ")
    Document.Write("day to visit us!")
    Document.Close
End If

End Function

</SCRIPT>
</HEAD>
<BODY>
<FORM NAME="frmName">
What is your name? <INPUT TYPE="text" NAME="txtName" SIZE=60><BR>
<INPUT TYPE="Button" VALUE="OK" NAME="cmdSubmit">
<INPUT TYPE="reset"  VALUE="Clear">
</FORM>
</BODY> </HTML>
```

user's action and returned it to the browser, our scripted equivalent of these "Hello, World!" programs uses just a single HTML document. It not only displays the form that asks the user for his or her name, but it also checks the validity of the user's input and displays a greeting if the user input is valid. Because these latter two functions are handled locally on the client, the form's data does not have to be submitted to the server. Because of this, the Web page's <FORM> tag includes only a NAME attribute; it does not include the METHOD or ACTION attributes.

By performing data validation locally, the application has become considerably more user-friendly. In its C and VB variants, if the user fails to provide a name before submitting the form data, the Win-CGI "Hello, World!" application creates a brand new Web page containing the warning message and replaces the Web page containing the original form with it. The validation routine in the VBScript cmdSubmit_

OnClick event procedure, on the other hand, uses the MsgBox function to display a modal dialog informing the user that a name is required. When the user clicks the OK button, the form is immediately accessible; the user does not have to navigate backward to it.

The major purpose of the application, though, is to display a message greeting the user. The C and VB versions of the "Hello, World" application did this by retrieving two Win-CGI variables, one for the user's name that was submitted by the client, and the other for the server name. In the scripted version of the program, of course, the form data is still accessible; the script in Example 2 retrieves it using the Microsoft Internet Explorer object model. The server name, however, is not easily accessible to a client-side script. Instead, a server-side include is used to insert it into the HTML text stream.

Along with its greater friendliness to the user and, quite possibly, its superior performance, a client-side script like the "Hello, World!" Web page is very easy to create and maintain. For example, VBScript's ease of development is comparable to that of Visual Basic when used as a development environment for Win-CGI applications. (On balance, it's probably slightly more difficult to use, since VBScript lacks an IDE, while Visual Basic's IDE makes it considerably easier to code and helps to reduce a wide range of compile and run-time errors.) And the ease with which scripted applications can be tested and debugged probably exceeds that of Win-CGI applications.

Since client-side scripts are still in their infancy, any discussion of the compatibility of scripting languages is subject to change. Currently, the leading scripting language is JavaScript because it runs on both Navigator and Internet Explorer, while VBScript is supported only by Internet Explorer. This situation, however, is likely to change over time, and it seems likely that, within the not too distant future, JavaScript, VBScript, and other scripting languages like Perl will all work on multiple browsers on multiple platforms.

Before we conclude that client-side scripts should replace Win-CGI, however, it's worthwhile taking a closer look at precisely what the Web page in Example 2 does and does not do. Let's begin with what it does not do: it does not do any back-end processing of form data. Typically, Win-CGI applications are developed not merely to parrot back the data that the user has entered into an HTML form but rather to store some or all of that data in a database or another type of file. This, however, is a function that client-side scripting is incapable of performing. Some other method—like Win-CGI or a server API—must be used to retrieve and store incoming data. So client-side scripting and Win-CGI appear to be complementary, rather than competing, technologies.

If we modify our script to submit data to the server for back-end processing, as Example 3 shows, it quickly becomes apparent that there is a second operation that the script does not readily support. Namely, since it builds its own Web page on the fly, it does not allow the server to return data to the client browser without overwriting the Web page created by the script. This problem, however, is readily solved. If the Win-CGI application is developed in Visual Basic, it can simply call the SendNoOp routine in CGI32. BAS. If it's written in C or C++, it can send a "204 No Content" or "204 No Response" status code directly to the browser. (This, incidentally, is what the SendNoOp routine does.) The 204 status code was implemented precisely so that scripts could execute on the client without requiring that the current document be replaced.

Finally, there is clearly one operation that the script in Example 2 or Example 3 performs quite well: it validates the data entered by the user. Before the advent of client-side scripting, data had to be sent to the server for validation; and the server had to send a Web page containing error information back to the browser. Now, however, all validation can be performed on the client, and one round trip between client and server can be saved in cases when an error

Example 3

```
<HTML>
<HEAD>
<TITLE>Hello, World!</TITLE>
<SCRIPT LANGUAGE="VBSCRIPT">

Function frmName_OnSubmit

dim strName

strName = Document.frmName.txtName.Value
if len(trim(strName)) = 0 then
    Call MsgBox("You forgot to enter your name!" _
                & chr(13) & chr(10) & chr(13) & chr(10) & _
                "Please be sure to enter your name before " & _
                "clicking the OK button!", _
                vbOKOnly, "Missing Name")

    frmName_OnSubmit = FALSE' Cancel form submission
else
    Document.Open
    Document.Write("<HTML><HEAD><TITLE>Hello!</TITLE></HEAD>")
    Document.Write("<H2>Hello, " & strName & "!</H2><P>")
    Document.Write("Greetings from <!--#echo var="SERVER_NAME"-->!<P>")
    Document.Write("Thanks for taking the time out of your busy ")
    Document.Write("day to visit us!")
    Document.Close
    frmName_OnSubmit = TRUE' Confirm form submission
End If

End Function

</SCRIPT>
</HEAD>

<BODY>
<FORM ACTION="\cgi-win\helloscr.exe" METHOD=POST NAME="frmName">
What is your name? <INPUT TYPE="text" NAME="txtName" SIZE=60><BR>
<INPUT TYPE="Submit" VALUE="OK" NAME="cmdSubmit">
<INPUT TYPE="reset"  VALUE="Clear">
</FORM>
</BODY> </HTML>
```

occurs. Finally, the server can be freed from the need to validate input data. Or can it?

It's easy enough to use a browser's View Source option to examine the source code for an HTML page and to save it to disk. Thereafter, the code can be run locally, although the form's ACTION attribute still invokes a program or routine on the remote server, assuming, of course, that it uses either an absolute URL or that the user is capable of changing the necessary relative URLs into absolute ones. Along with modifying any URLs contained within the Web page so that they work, the user is free to make additional modifications. With many users suspicious of possible dangers resulting from running scripts on their machines, one of the possible modifications is the elimination of the script containing the data validation routine. In this case, the user can submit invalid data to the server, which then accepts invalid data because all data validation functions have been transferred to scripts running on the client.

So what are the implications of this in terms of the client? Earlier, we argued that client-side scripting complements, rather than replaces, applications running on the server. This is true of data validation as well. Performing data validation on the client offers better performance and less frustration for the user, which makes it the best primary method available for validating data. But in most cases, it is unsafe to assume that data submitted by the client has actually been validated by the client-side data validation scripts. This means that incoming data should be processed on the server in either of two ways:

- By duplicating the same validation procedures on the server as ran on the client. If data has been properly validated on the client, this runs the same procedure needlessly but should not result in error messages or warnings being sent back to the user. If data has not been properly validated on the client, it insures that all data is validated at least once.

- By examining the URL from which a server application was launched and, if it is not an "official" URL, refusing to process the data. In Win-CGI applications, the `Referer` entry in the `[CGI]` section (or, if you're using the Win-CGI framework for VB, the `CGI_Referer` variable) indicates the name of the URL from which the Win-CGI application was launched. If the Win-CGI application was launched interactively, by the user entering its URL into a text box, the `Referer` entry is absent from the `[CGI]` section of the temporary initialization file, and `CGI_Referer` is a null string.

So although client-side scripting is a useful and accessible tool to use in creating interactive Web pages, it by no means replaces solutions on the server. It can be used to improve an application's performance by eliminating some additional trips from the client to the server (the assumption being that the server will perform more efficiently if it simply transmits some extra text—in the form of scripts embedded within a Web page—than if it handles one or more additional requests coming from a client), and can be extremely powerful in enhancing the overall friendliness and attractiveness of an application.

Server-Side Includes

Along with Win-CGI, server-side includes (SSI) is one of the oldest forms of providing dynamic content on the Web. SSI is highly server-dependent and relies on the inclusion of special markers in the HTML document. When the server receives a request, it replaces the markers with the value of variable data before sending the page to the client. Examples 2 and 3, for instance, make use of SSI to insert the name of the server into an HTML page sent by a WebSite server. The `echo` tag instructs the server to insert the value of a predefined variable into the HTML text stream; the `var` argument specifies the variable's name.

As you can see from this limited example, SSI is really a macro language. Like most macro languages, it is extremely easy to learn; a content provider who knows HTML can easily master SSI within a few hours. Web pages that use SSI can be created, tested, and debugged quickly. Since it is very simple, Web applications can be maintained and modified with little effort. Since it is a fairly simple technology that inserts text into the HTML text stream, it cannot jeopardize the operation of the server.

While SSI certainly excels in ease of use, it is distinctly a low-end development methodology that relies extensively on the implementation of SSI on the server that a particular Web site is using. A number of Web servers, like IIS and the Personal Web Servers from Microsoft, do not support SSI. But even on servers, like O'Reilly's WebSite server, that offer full-featured implementations, SSI is strictly limited in the extent to which it adds active content to Web pages. Depending on the implementation of SSI on a particular server, it can be used to include the such variable information as the following into the HTML text stream:

- *Server state variables.* SSI can be used to retrieve a number of items of information about the server, like the server software, the name of the server, or the current date and time on the server.

- *Client request information.* It can include a number of items of information, like the name of the browser or the request method, about the request that the browser submitted to the server.

- *Resource information.* It can gather basic file system information, like the date an HTML document was last updated or its file size, to include in an HTML page.

- *File contents.* It can insert the entire contents of a file into the HTML text stream. This makes it possible to include a uniform header or footer (or a toolbar) on each of a site's Web pages.

- *Hit counters.* It can maintain a hit counter for a particular page and include its current value within the page.

- *Output from a CGI program.* SSI can be used to include the output generated by a CGI application within an HTML page; otherwise, if a CGI application runs by itself, it must output an entire page to the client.

And that's about it. Since SSI is capable of substituting variable information for a predefined set of markers, its flexibility is necessarily limited. It isn't possible to use SSI to retrieve specially formatted data, to display a portion of a file, or to check the validity of a user's form data. Nor do most implementations of SSI support decision making and branching within individual HTML pages.

Server-Side Scripting

A relatively recent development, server-side scripting (SSS), represented by Active Server Pages for the Microsoft family of servers and LiveWire for Netscape servers, brings scripting to the server. This means that the HTML page contains one or more embedded scripts that are executed at the server, and any output from the script is inserted into the HTML text stream. To this extent, server-side scripts sound very much like server-side includes.

In fact, however, server-side scripts possess a flexibility and power that rival that of Win-CGI and server API applications. Unlike SSI, in which the "script" is merely a marker that indicates where variable text is to be inserted, the script in a scripted server-side application is an integration tool that, in the case of Active Server Pages, for instance, can be used to control OLE automation objects (now called ActiveX Server Components) and to access assorted information from the server by using the server's object model. As a result, through the use of assorted add-on components, server-side scripts are very similar in function (although very different in implementation) to Win-CGI applications.

Example 4 contains our complete "Hello, World!" application as an active server page. The application itself is assigned a file extension of .ASP, which indicates to the server that it contains embedded server-side "scripts." When a client requests the document, the server parses the document, compiles and executes any server-side scripts (which are indicated either by the <% and %> tags or by a <SCRIPT RUNAT=server> tag), inserts any text generated by the scripts into the HTML text stream, and transmits the Web page to the client.

For our simple "Hello, World!" example, the HTML page in Example 4 is considerably less complicated and significantly easier to develop than the corresponding Win-CGI, ISAPI, and client-side VBScript applications, largely because the information that we want to extract is imme-

Example 4

```
<HTML>
<HEAD><TITLE>Hello!</TITLE></HEAD>
<BODY>
<H2>Hello, <% Request.Form(Name) %>!</H2><P>
Greetings from <% Request.ServerVariables("SERVER_NAME") %> <P>
Thank you for taking the time out of your busy day
to visit us! <P>
</BODY>
<HTML>
```

diately available using the server's object model. Although most applications developed using server-side scripts will probably be fairly simple, the complexity of professional server-side scripts can nevertheless rival that of Win-CGI applications.

Very much like any of a number of development tools can be used to create a Win-CGI application, a number of scripting languages are available for creating server-side scripts. For instance, currently Active Server Page applications can be developed using VBScript, JavaScript, Perl, and Rexx. Although server-side scripting is accessible to anyone, from the HTML content provider who is intimidated by programming to the Internet application programmer, creating complete server-side applications requires programming skills comparable to those needed by a Win-CGI programmer. Typically, developers who either have or can easily gain the required expertise can be found within most companies.

Given the diversity of server-side scripts, their development time is equally variable. Complex scripted server-side applications, though, can be built in a time frame that's roughly comparable to that of Win-CGI applications. Because they are scripted, they can also be easily changed. In contrast to Win-CGI, though, testing and debugging is slightly more complicated and therefore can be more time-consuming, since server-side scripts can only be tested online, while Win-CGI applications can typically be tested either online or offline.

Typically, errors in server-side scripts or bugs in the scripting engine do not affect the state of the server as a whole. Depending on the exact way in which support for scripting is implemented, though, it is possible for a server-side script to bring down the server. This can occur when the scripting engine runs in the context of the server's own process (as it does for Active Server Page applications) and generates a server-killing fault.

Interestingly, although server-side scripting is now presented as the preferred alternative to Win-CGI, it is a comparatively low-performance alternative. First, server-side scripts are interpreted, and not compiled; interpreting the script at run-time is a comparatively slow process. Typically, the scripting engine must be initialized before interpretation can start; in the case of Active Server Pages, scripting engines are COM objects that must be instantiated using OLE, a comparatively slow process.

The compatibility of scripted applications across multiple servers is potentially a tricky issue. At its most basic level, compatibility requires that there be a version of the scripting engine that's available for a particular server. For instance, JavaScript can currently be used to develop server-side scripts for both the Microsoft and the Netscape families of servers. But even if a scripting language is compatible across multiple servers, complete scripted applications that run one server may not be compatible with the second server. This is the case if the server object models are different, or if the add-on server components that are used in one server application are either unavailable or are implemented differently on another server.

Java

Java is a C++-like object-oriented programming language that produces platform-independent executables. On the client side, it can be used either to produce a Java *applet*, a small application that runs in the context of the Web browser, or a Java *application*, a stand-alone executable that is not dependent on any Web client software for its operation. On the server side, it can be used to create applications that provide much of the functionality of traditional CGI (and Win-CGI) applications. In fact, on some servers, such as the O'Reilly WebSite server, server-side Java applications are implemented as CGI applications. In this case, Java is merely the development language used to create a Win-CGI application.

When viewed as competitors to Win-CGI, client-side Java applets or applications very closely resemble applications that include client-side scripts. In many ways, they supplement, rather than replace, the functionality of CGI and Win-CGI applications. Some of the functions traditionally performed by Win-CGI applications—like data validation and generating certain kinds of Web pages—can now be performed by a Java applet. But for the most part, Java is used to enrich the user's browsing experience by offering features that cannot be implemented by applications running on the server. There's also another sense in which Java strongly resembles server-side scripts: very much like server-side scripts are merely seen as text included in the HTML text stream, Java applets and applications are merely included in the stream of objects transmitted by a server.

Despite the attention that it has received, Java is in many ways very comparable to the server APIs. That is, Java was closely modeled after object-oriented programming languages in general and C++ in particular. This means that Java stands very much outside the "mainstream" of Web development technologies: whereas most technologies emphasize their accessibility and ease of use, Java emphasizes its flexibility and power. So Java applications, like server API applications, require very skilled developers with considerable expertise in Web development.

The Place of Win-CGI

Table 1 summarizes our evaluation of the development technologies that we've discussed in the course of this article. It indicates that, despite the emergence of competing technologies, Win-CGI remains viable as a flexible and powerful tool that at the same time is accessible to large numbers of developers and that permits applications to be developed quickly and efficiently. One of its major strengths is its compatibility across server platforms. As long as a Windows Web server supports Win-CGI, an application developed for another Win-CGI-compliant server should run under it without modification.

Most of the criticism of Win-CGI has focused on its supposedly poor performance: because Win-CGI applications run out of process, so the criticism goes, they quickly become performance bottlenecks that cripple a server and frustrate users attempting to access its resources. Since performance clearly is a major area of concern, let's look more carefully at the performance of Win-CGI applications in relation to that of server API applications and server-side scripts, the two application development technologies that compete most directly with Win-CGI.

Win-CGI and ISAPI

Microsoft Internet Information Server Performance Analysis, [2] a document published by Microsoft's Business Systems Division in March 1996, contains the results of a benchmark that compared an ISAPI application with its CGI counterpart running on Microsoft's Internet Information Server. Figure 1 compares the throughput in megabits per second for two servers with 64 clients, one of which exclusively served HTML documents created by an ISAPI application, while the

Table 1   Evaluating Web Development Technologies

	CGI	API	CSS	SSI	SSS
Flexibility & Power	High	High	Medium	Low	High
Developer Expertise	Medium	High	Medium	Low	Medium
Development & Testing Time	Medium	High	Medium	Low	Medium
Adaptability to Change	High	Low	High	High	High
Life-Cycle Cost	Medium	High	Medium	Low	Medium
Operational Risk	Low	High	Low	Low	Medium
CPU Overhead	High	Low	Low	Medium	High
Compatibility	High	Low	Low	Low	Low

other exclusively served HTML documents created by a CGI application. Figure 2 shows the number of connections per second that the ISAPI and the CGI server were able to support.

This indicates that, in a direct comparison of two identical applications running on identical servers, ISAPI, the server API for Microsoft Internet Information Server, is nearly five times faster than CGI.

Just what does this mean, though? Figure 2, for instance, shows that the server reaches its saturation point when running CGI applications at about 20 connections per second; it reaches saturation with ISAPI, though, at somewhere in the neighborhood of 95 connections per second. On the one hand, that indicates that ISAPI is nearly five times as fast as CGI. It also indicates, though, that CGI is capable of supporting 20 connections per second before reaching saturation; that's 1,200 connections per minute, 72,000 connections per hour, and 1,728,000 connections per day. That's extremely heavy traffic.

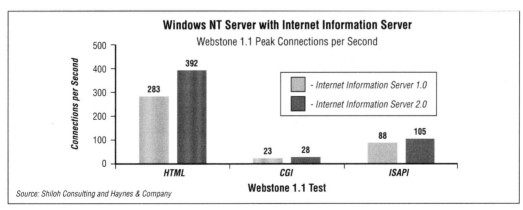

Figure 1   Comparison of ISAPI and CGI throughput

The throughput tells basically the same story. Throughput on the server running ISAPI applications was approximately 625,000 bytes per second (or 5,000,000 megabits per minute), while the throughput on the CGI server was only about 125,000 bytes per second (or 1,000,000 megabits per minute). Here, ISAPI proved to be almost exactly five times faster than CGI. But throughput on the CGI server was still 125,000 bytes per second—which is 7,500,000 bytes per minute, 450,000,000 bytes per hour, or 10,800,000,000 bytes per day. (For purposes of comparison, saturation on a T1 occurs at about 185,000 bytes per second.)

So although these benchmarks are reasonably consistent in showing that an ISAPI application is five times faster than the corresponding Win-CGI application, what this means from the viewpoint of a Web site that is thinking of deploying server API applications rather than Win-CGI applications is unclear. These standard benchmarks measure performance under unrealistically heavy loads that almost no Web server ever attains. And so they allow us to conclude that server API applications are faster than Win-CGI applications (though that general conclusion was never disputed), and they allow us to assess the performance of each application at the point that the server reaches saturation. Since most Web servers

are idle a significant portion of the time (and many are idle *most* of the time), the point at which saturation occurs is really of academic interest only.

In other words, applications developed using server APIs are faster than applications developed Win-CGI. That conclusion, though, is not surprising. How much faster remains open to debate. Although these benchmarks show that ISAPI applications are at least five times faster when tested under unrealistically heavy loads that almost no server ever attains, these standard benchmarks are most useful in measuring the point at which performance is likely to break down because of excessive loads. Interestingly, while the benchmarks establish that Win-CGI is five times slower than ISAPI, they also show that Win-CGI is capable of providing adequate performance when responding to heavy volumes of traffic.

A more meaningful benchmark, perhaps, is one that compares the performance of ISAPI and Win-CGI applications on a server that is comparatively idle. For instance, if we compare the "Hello, World" application written in C with its corresponding ISAPI application (shown earlier in Example 1), the ISAPI application tends to execute about 50 default faster than the Win-CGI

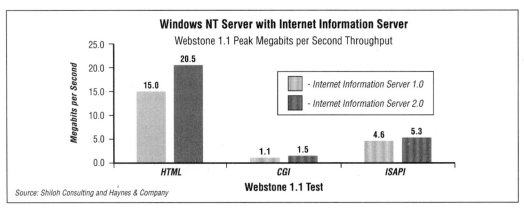

Figure 2   Comparison of ISAPI and CGI connections per second

application on Microsoft's Personal Web Server for Windows 95. Since the Microsoft family of servers doesn't actually offer native support for Win-CGI ("Win-CGI" applications for Microsoft Web servers are actually ISAPI applications that create a Win-CGI-compatible framework before launching a Win-CGI application), this figure should be adjusted downward slightly. But it nevertheless serves as a reasonable indicator of the "superiority" of server API applications over Win-CGI applications.

Note that, though server API applications offer 50 percent better performance than Win-CGI applications, their total development and maintenancecost is likely to be far more than twice that of a Win-CGI application. As we've seen, developing server API applications require substantial expertise and exhaustive testing, and the applications themselves are relatively difficult to modify. As a result, it makes the most sense to rely on server APIs for developing applications on Web servers with extremely high access rates.

Win-CGI and Server-Side Scripting

While the development costs of ISAPI applications clearly put them out of the reach of most Web sites, that clearly isn't true of server-side scripting. Instead, server-side scripting is designed to be accessible not only to programmers, but to HTML authors and Web content providers as well. Although the appearance of development tools for the scripted languages has lagged behind the appearance of the languages themselves, it nevertheless is probably fair to say that the ease with which scripted applications can be developed roughly parallels the ease of development of Win-CGI applications. And very much like the developer of a Win-CGI application can choose from among a wide array of languages, development tools and development environments, the creator of scripted applications can choose from a growing range of scripted languages.

But although server-side scripts can offer an ease of use that is comparable to that of Win-CGI, they

frequently do so at the expense of performance. Ordinarily, servers simply parse requests to determine which resource is needed, and then transmit that resource which, from the viewpoint of the server, is nothing more than a collection of bytes. Server-side scripting is considerably more expensive: the server must not only parse client requests to determine what resources they want; it must now parse HTML documents—which previously it was able to handle only as a collection of bytes—to determine whether they contain embedded scripts to be run at the server. If they do, it must interpret and execute the script. The result is an HTML document—the collection of bytes—built on the fly that the server can transmit to fill the client's request. That this need to parse and build an HTML page before serving it is very expensive in terms of performance is clearly indicated by Active Server Pages, Microsoft's general framework for server-side scripting. Internet Information Server requires that Web pages containing embedded script have a special .ASP file extension to differentiate them from non-scripted Web pages, which continue to have an .HTM or . HTML extension. This saves the Web server the degradation of performance that would result from having to parse and interpret every single HTML document that it serves.

The overhead of parsing and serving, rather than simply serving, documents, though, is not the only performance hit that is involved in server-side scripting. The scripting engine itself, which in the case of Microsoft's family of Web servers is an OLE server component, must also be instantiated or initialized. Although the overhead involved for initializing the scripting engine is probably lower than that for starting up a Win-CGI application, compiled Win-CGI applications, once they are running, involve less CPU overhead than interpreted scripted applications.

Server-side scripting is a technology still in its infancy. And as a young technology, it has two significant disadvantages that Win-CGI does not have:

- *Platform dependence.* Although the same scripting languages (JavaScript, VBScript, Perl) are available for server-side scripting as for client-side scripting, the real power of a scripted application on the server comes from accessing server components through the server's object model. Since no *de facto* standards for server-side scripting have emerged, however, the object models of the two major families of script-enabled servers, from Microsoft and Netscape, are not compatible. Other Windows servers do not yet support scripting. This means that, unlike Win-CGI applications, scripted applications cannot easily be ported from one server to another. In other words, at least at this point, if you make a commitment to application development using server-side scripting, you're simultaneously making a long-term commitment to a particular line of Web server products.

- *Absence of development tools.* Although this situation is certain to change rapidly over time, the development of server-side scripted applications currently lacks the kind of powerful, integrated IDE that is typical of Win-CGI programming. A Visual Basic programmer, for instance, develops Win-CGI applications within Visual Basic's integrated environment. The most common tool for a VBScript programmer developing an Active Server Pages application, however, is Notepad or a similar text editor. This means that, although potentially server-side scripting offers an ease of development that parallels that of Win-CGI programming, realizing this potential depends on the availability of new development tools.

Summary

Despite the emergence of a number of competing technologies, Win-CGI remains a viable technology for developing applications that enhance and extend Web servers. In our assessment of Win-CGI and its relationship to other methods for developing Web applications, we've seen the following:

- Applications developed using server APIs, though they offer superior performance because they run in the same process as the server, are far more costly to develop than Win-CGI applications. They require very skilled programmers, have a longer development cycle, require more extensive debugging and testing, and are difficult to maintain or modify.

- Server-side scripting is a new and promising technology that is still in its infancy. Scripted applications still involve some performance overhead," since the Web server must now have the intelligence to parse documents, rather than to simply serve them, and since the scripting engine itself must be instantiated. In addition, there is currently a lack of development tools for scripted applications that run on the server, and the applications themselves are not portable.

- Server-side includes allow the Web server to insert certain items of information—like the time or the server's name—into the HTML text stream. However, they offer limited flexibility—server-side includes allow you to access only a relatively limited subset of information. Moreover, HTML documents that use server-side includes are of limited portability: not all servers support server-side includes, those that do support it diverge in the kinds of information that can be included in the text stream, and those that support the inclusion of similar items of information typically differ in the syntax required to include them.

- Client-side scripting is another relatively new technology that complements, rather than replaces, Web server applications. The major advantage of client-side scripts are that they perform on the client some of the data validation that currently is typically performed on the server and that often requires repeated round trips between the client and the server.

- Like scripted applications, Java applets can run either on the client or the server. Client-side Java applets, like client-side scripts, complement, rather than supplant, Win-CGI applications. Server-side Java applets, on the other hand, are frequently implemented as Win-CGI applications. ■

References

1. Dr. GUI can be accessed from the Developer Network News page at *http://www.microsoft.com/devnews*

2. Microsoft Internet Information Server Performance Analysis is available on the Web at *http://www.graphcomp.com/info/specs/isapi/iisperf.htm*

About the Author

Ron Petrusha
5250 Country Club Drive
Rohnert Park, CA 94928
ron@ora.com

Ron Petrusha began working with computers in the mid '70s, programming in SPSS (a programmable statistical package) and FORTRAN on the IBM 370 family. Since then, he has been a computer book buyer, editor of a number of books on Windows and UNIX, and a consultant on projects written in dBASE, Clipper, and Visual Basic. Ron also has a background in quantitative labor history, specializing in Russian labor history, and holds degrees from the University of Michigan and Columbia University. He is currently writing an O'Reilly book entitled *Build Your Own Win-CGI Programs.*

Introduction to the LWP Library for Perl

Clinton Wong

Abstract

This document is an excerpt from Web Client Programming with Perl, published by O'Reilly & Associates, Inc. It is written for Perl programmers who want to write Web robots and other programs for automating tasks using HTTP. This article introduces LWP and describes the syntax for some of its modules.

The Library modules for WWW access in Perl, known as LWP, is a set of modules for Perl 5 that encapsulate common functions for a Web client or server. Using LWP, you can write specialized clients that go beyond the capabilities of a graphical browser.

The LWP library is available at all CPAN archives. CPAN is a collection of Perl libraries and utilities, freely available to all. There are many CPAN mirror sites; you should use the one closest to you, or just go to *http://www.perl.com/CPAN/* to have one chosen for you at random. LWP was developed by several people, but its primary driving force is Gisle Aas. It is based on the libwww library developed for Perl 4 by Roy Fielding.

This article concentrates on using LWP for writing simple client applications.

Some Simple Examples

LWP is distributed with a very helpful—but very short—"cookbook" tutorial, designed to get you started. This section serves much the same function: to show you some simpler applications using LWP.

Retrieving a File

To give you an idea of how simple LWP can make things, here's a program that retrieves the URL in the command line and prints it to standard output:

```
#!/bin/perl
use LWP::Simple;

print (get $ARGV[0]);
```

The first line, starting with #!, is the standard line that calls the Perl interpreter. If you want to try this example on your own system, it's likely you'll have to change this line to match the location of the Perl 5 interpreter on your system.

The second line, starting with **use** declares that the program will use the LWP::Simple class. This class of routines defines the most basic HTTP commands, such as **get**.

The third line uses the **get()** routine from LWP::Simple on the first argument from the command line, and applies the result to the **print()** routine.

Can it get much easier than this? Actually, yes. There's also a **getprint()** routine in LWP::Simple for getting and printing a document in one fell swoop. The third line of the program could also read:

```
getprint($ARGV[0]);
```

That's it. Obviously there's some error checking that you could do, but if you just want to get your feet wet with a simple Web client, this example will do. You can call the program **geturl** and make it executable. For example on UNIX:

```
% chmod +x geturl
```

Windows NT users may want to use the **pl2bat** program, included with the Perl distribution, to make the `geturl.pl` executable from the command line:

```
C:\your\path\here> pl2bat geturl
```

You can then call the program to retrieve any URL from the Web:

```
% geturl http://www.ora.com/
<HTML>
<HEAD>
<LINK REV=MADE
    HREF="mailto:webmaster@ora.com">
<TITLE>O'Reilly &amp; Associates</
    TITLE>
</HEAD>
<BODY bgcolor=#ffffff>
...
```

Parsing HTML

Since HTML is hard to read in text format, instead of printing the raw HTML, you could strip it of HTML codes for easier reading. You could try to do it manually:

```perl
#!/bin/perl

use LWP::Simple;

foreach (get $ARGV[0]) {
    s/<[^>]*>//g;
    print;
}
```

But this only does a little bit of the job. Why reinvent the wheel? There's something in the LWP library that does this for you. To parse the HTML, you can use the HTML module:

```perl
#!/bin/perl

use LWP::Simple;
use HTML::Parse;

print parse_html(get ($ARGV[0]))-
    >format;
```

In addition to LWP::Simple, we include the HTML::Parse class. We call the `parse_html()` routine on the result of the `get()`, and then format it for printing.

You can save this version of the program under the name `showurl`, make it executable, and see what happens:

```
% showurl http://www.ora.com/
O'Reilly & Associates

    About O'Reilly -- Feedback --
    Writing for O'Reilly

    What's New -- Here's a sampling
    of our most recent postings...

      * This Week in Web Review:
    Tracking Ads
        Are you running your Web
    site like a business? These
    tools can help.

      * Traveling with your dog?
    Enter the latest Travelers'
    Tales
            writing contest and
    send us a tale.


    New and Upcoming Releases
    ...
```

Extracting Links

To find out which hyperlinks are referenced inside a HTML page, you could go to the trouble of writing a program to search for text within angle brackets (`<...>`), parse the enclosed text for the `<A>` or `<IMG>` tag, and extract the hyperlink that appears after the HREF or SRC parameter. LWP simplifies this process down to two function calls. Let's take the `geturl` program from before and modify it:

```perl
#!/usr/local/bin/perl
use LWP::Simple;
use HTML::Parse;
use HTML::Element;

$html         = get $ARGV[0];
$parsed_html = HTML::Parse::parse_
    html($html);
```

```
for (@{ $parsed_html->extract_
    links( ) }) {
    ($link) = @$_;
    print "$link\n";
}
```

The first change to notice is that in addition to LWP::Simple and HTML::Parse, we added the HTML::Element class.

Then we get the document and pass it to `HTML::Parse::parse_html()`. Given HTML data, the `parse_html()` function parses the document into an internal representation used by LWP.

```
$parsed_html = HTML::Parse::parse_
    html($html);
```

Here, the `parse_html()` function returns an instance of the HTML::TreeBuilder class that contains the parsed HTML data. Since the HTML::TreeBuilder class inherits the HTML::Element class, we make use of `HTML::Element::extract_links()` to find all the hyperlinks mentioned in the HTML data:

```
for (@{ $parsed_html->
    extract_links( ) }) {
```

`extract_links()` returns a list of array references, where each array in the list contains a hyperlink mentioned in the HTML. Before we can access the hyperlink returned by `extract_links()`, we dereference the list in the for loop:

```
for (@{ $parsed_html->extract_
    links( ) }) {
```

and dereference the array within the list with:

```
($link) = @$_;
```

After the deferencing, we have direct access to the hyperlink's location and we print it out:

```
print "$link\n";
```

Save this program into a file called showlink and run it:

```
% showlink http://www.ora.com/
```

You'll see something like this:

```
graphics/texture.black.gif
/maps/homepage.map
/graphics/headers/homepage-anim.gif
http://www.oreilly.de/o/comsec/
    satan/index.html
/ads/international/satan.gif
http://www.ora.com/catalog/pperl2
. . .
```

Expanding Relative URLs

From the previous example, the links from showlink printed out the hyperlinks exactly as they appear within the HTML. But in some cases, you want to see the link as an absolute URL, with the full glory of a URL's scheme, hostname, and path. Let's modify showlink to print out absolute URLs all the time:

```
#!/usr/local/bin/perl
use LWP::Simple;
use HTML::Parse;
use HTML::Element;
use URI::URL;

$html       = get $ARGV[0];
$parsed_html = HTML::Parse::parse_
    html($html);

for (@{ $parsed_html->extract_
    links( ) }) {
    ($link) = @$_;
    $url      = new URI::URL $link;
    $full_url = $url->abs($ARGV[0]);
    print "$full_url\n";
}
```

In this example, we've added URI::URL to our ever-expanding list of classes. To expand each hyperlink, we first define each hyperlink in terms of the URL class:

```
$url = new URI::URL $link;
```

Then we use a method in the URL class to expand the hyperlink's URL, with respect to the location of the page it was referenced from:

```
$full_url = $url->abs($ARGV[0]);
```

Save the program in a file called fulllink, make it executable, and run it:

```
% fulllink http://www.ora.com/
```

You should see something like this:

```
http://www.ora.com/graphics/texture.
    black.gif
http://www.ora.com/maps/homepage.map
http://www.ora.com/graphics/headers/
    homepage-anim.gif
http://www.oreilly.de/o/comsec/
    satan/index.html
http://www.ora.com/ads/
    international/satan.gif
http://www.ora.com/catalog/pperl2
...
```

Now let's talk a little more about the more interesting modules, so you know what's possible under LWP and how everything ties together.

Listing of LWP Modules

There are eight main modules in LWP: LWP, File, Font, HTML, HTTP, MIME, URI, and WWW. Figure 1 sketches out the top-level hierarchy within LWP.

- The File module parses directory listings.

- The Font module handles Adobe Font Metrics.

- In the HTML module, HTML syntax trees can be constructed in a variety of ways. These trees are used in rendering functions that translate HTML to PostScript or plain text.

- The HTTP module describes client requests, server responses, and dates, and computes a client/server negotiation.

- The LWP module is the core of all Web client programs. It allows the client to communicate over the network with the server.

- The MIME module converts to/from base 64 and quoted printable text.

- In the URI module, one can escape a URI or specify or translate relative URLs to absolute URLs.

- Finally, in the WWW module, the client can determine if a server's resource is accessible via the robot exclusion standard.

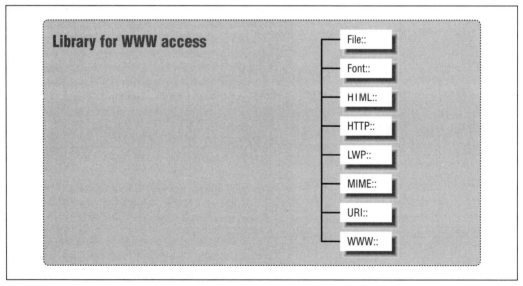

Figure 1   The top-level LWP hierarchy

In the context of Web clients, some modules in LWP are more useful than others. In this book, we cover LWP, HTML, HTTP, and URI. HTTP describes what we're looking for, LWP requests what we're looking for, and the HTML module is useful for interpreting HTML and converting it to some other form, such as PostScript or plain text. The URI module is useful for dissecting fully constructed URLs, specifying a URL for the HTTP or LWP module, or performing operations on URLs, such as escaping or expanding.

In this section, we'll give you an overview of the some of the more useful functions and methods in the LWP, HTML, HTTP, and URI modules. The other methods, functions, and modules are beyond the scope of this article.

The LWP Module

The LWP module, in the context of Web clients, performs client requests over the network. There are 10 classes in all within the LWP module (as shown in Figure 2), but we're mainly interested in the Simple, UserAgent, and RobotUA classes.

LWP::Simple

When you want to quickly design a Web client, but robustness and complex behavior are of secondary importance, the LWP::Simple class comes in handy. Within it, there are seven functions:

get($url)
> Returns the contents of the URL specified by $url. Upon failure, get() returns undef. Other than returning undef, there is no way of accessing the HTTP status code or headers returned by the server.

head($url)
> Returns header information about the URL specified by $url in the form of: ($content_ type, $document_length, $modified_

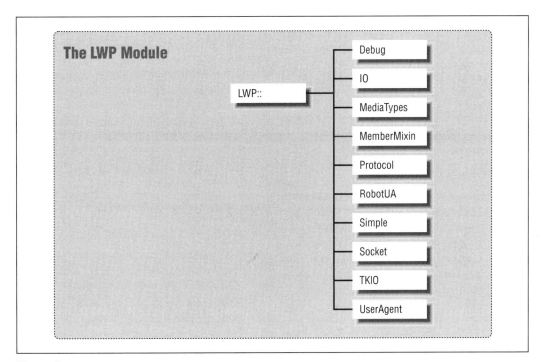

Figure 2   Structure of the LWP classes

time, $expires, $server). Upon failure, head() returns an empty list.

getprint($url)

Prints the contents of the URL on standard output, where the URL is specified by $url. The HTTP status code given by the server is returned by getprint().

getstore($url, $file)

Stores the contents of the URL specified by $url into a file named by $file. The HTTP status code is returned by getstore().

mirror($url, $file)

Copies the contents of the URL specified by $url into a file named by $file, when the modification time or length of the online version is different from that of the file.

is_success($rc)

Given a status code from getprint(), getstore(), or mirror(), returns true if the request was successful.

is_error($rc)

Given a status code from getprint(), getstore(), or mirror(), returns true if the request was not successful.

LWP::UserAgent

Requests over the network are performed with the LWP::UserAgent module. To create an LWP::UserAgent object, you would do:

    $ua = new LWP::UserAgent;

The most useful method in this module is request(), which contacts a server and returns the result of your query. Other methods in this module change the way request() behaves. You can change the timeout value, customize the value of the User-Agent header, or use a proxy server. Here's an overview of most of the useful methods:

$ua->request($request [, $subroutine [, $size]])

Performs a request for the resource specified by $request, which is an HTTP::Request

object. Normally, doing a $result=$ua->request($request) is enough. On the other hand, if you want to request data as it becomes available, you can specify a reference to a subroutine as the second argument, and request() will call the subroutine whenever there are data to be processed. In that case, you can specify an optional third argument that specifies the desired size of the data to be processed. The subroutine should expect chunks of the entity-body data as a scalar as the first parameter, a reference to an HTTP::Response object as the second argument, and a reference to an LWP::Protocol object as the third argument.

$ua->request($request, $file_path)

When invoked with a file path as the second parameter, this method writes the entity-body of the response to the file, instead of the HTTP::Response object that is returned. However, the HTTP::Response object can still be queried for its response code.

$ua->credentials($netloc, $realm, $uname, $pass)

Use the supplied username and password for the given network location and realm. To use the username webmaster and password of yourguess with the admin realm at www.ora.com, you would do this:

    $ua->credentials('www.ora.com',
        'admin', 'webmaster',
        'yourguess').

$ua->get_basic_credentials ($realm, $url)

Returns ($uname, $pass) for the given realm and URL. get_basic_credentials() is usually called by request(). This method becomes useful when creating a subclass of LWP::UserAgent with its own version of get_basic_credentials(). From there, you can rewrite get_basic_credentials() to do more flexible things, like asking the user for the account information, or referring to authentication information in a file, or whatever. All you need to do is return a list, where the first element is a username and the second element is a password.

`$ua->agent([$product_id])`

When invoked with no arguments, this method returns the current value of the identifier used in the User-Agent HTTP header. If invoked with an argument, the User-Agent header will that identifier in the future. The User-Agent header tells a Web server what kind of client software is performing the request.)

`$ua->from([$email_address])`

When invoked with no arguments, this method returns the current value of the email address used in the From HTTP header. If invoked with an argument, the From header will use that email address in the future. (The From header tells the Web server the email address of the person running the client software.)

`$ua->timeout([$secs])`

When invoked with no arguments, the `time-out()` method returns the timeout value of a request. By default, this value is three minutes. So if the client software doesn't hear back from the server within three minutes, it will stop the transaction and indicate that a timeout occurred in the HTTP response code. If invoked with an argument, the time-out value is redefined to be that value.

`$ua->use_alarm([$boolean])`

Retrieves or defines the ability to use `alarm()` for timeouts. By default, timeouts with `alarm()` are enabled. If you plan on using `alarm()` for your own purposes, or `alarm()` isn't supported on your system, it is recommended to disable alarm by calling this method with a value of 0 (zero).

`$ua->is_protocol_supported($scheme)`

Given a scheme, this method returns a true or false (nonzero or zero) value. A true value means that LWP knows how to handle a URL with the specified scheme. If it returns a false value, LWP does not know how to handle the URL.

`$ua->mirror($url, $file)`

Given a URL and file path, this method copies the contents of `$url` into the file when the length or modification date headers are different. If the file does not exist, it is created. This method returns an HTTP::Response object, where the response code indicates what happened.

`$ua->proxy( (@scheme | $scheme), $proxy_url)`

Defines a URL to use with scheme(s). The first parameter can be an array of scheme names or a scalar that defines a single scheme. The second argument defines the proxy's URL to use with the scheme.

`$ua->env_proxy( )`

Defines a scheme/proxy URL mapping by looking at environment variables. For example, to define the HTTP proxy, one would define the `http_proxy` environment variable with the proxy's URL. To define a domain to avoid the proxy, one would define the `no_proxy` environment variable with the domain that doesn't need a proxy.

`$ua->no_proxy($domain,...)`

Do not use a proxy server for the domains given as parameters.

LWP::RobotUA

The Robot User Agent (LWP::RobotUA) is a subclass of LWP::UserAgent. User agent applications directly reflect the actions of the user. For example, in a user agent application, when a user clicks on a hyperlink, the user expects to see the data associated with the hyperlink. On the other hand, a robot application requests resources in an automated fashion. Robot applications cover such activities as searching, mirroring, or surveying. Some robots collect statistics, while others wander the Web and summarize their findings for a search engine. For this type of application, a robot application should use LWP::RobotUA instead of LWP::UserAgent. The LWP::RobotUA module observes the robot exclusion standards, which Web server administrators can define on their Web site to keep robots away from certain (or all) areas of the Web site. To create a new LWP::RobotUA object, one could do:

```
$ua = LWP::RobotUA->new($agent_
    name, $from, [$rules])
```

where the first parameter is the identifier that defines the value of the UserAgent header in the request, the second parameter is the email address of the person using the robot, and the optional third parameter is a reference to a WWW::RobotRules object. If you omit the third parameter, the LWP::RobotUA module requests the robots.txt file from every server it contacts, and generates its own WWW::RobotRules object.

Since LWP::RobotUA is a subclass of LWP::UserAgent, the LWP::UserAgent methods are also available in LWP::RobotUA. In addition,, LWP::RobotUA has the following robot related methods:

`$ua->delay([$minutes])`

Returns the number of minutes to wait between requests. If a parameter is given, the time to wait is redefined to be the time given by the parameter. Upon default, this value is 1 (one). It is generally not very nice to set a time of zero.

`$ua->rules([$rules])`

Returns or defines a the WWW:RobotRules object to be used when determining if the module is allowed access to a particular resource.

`$ua->no_visits($netloc)`

Returns the number of visits to a given server. $netloc is of the form user: password@host:port. The user, password, and port are optional.

`$ua->host_wait($netloc)`

Returns the number of seconds the robot must wait before it can request

another resource from the server. $netloc is of the form user:password@host:port. The user, password, and port are optional.

`$ua->as_string( )`

Returns a human-readable string that describes the robot's status.

The HTTP Module

The HTTP module specifies HTTP requests and responses, plus some helper functions to interpret or convert data related to HTTP requests and responses. There are eight classes within the HTTP module, as shown in Figure 3, but we're mainly interested in the Request, Response, Header, and Status classes.

The two main modules that you'll use in the HTTP module are HTTP::Request and HTTP::Response. HTTP::Request allows one to specify a request method, URL, headers, and entity-body. HTTP::Response specifies a HTTP response code, headers, and entity-body. Both HTTP::Request and HTTP::Response are subclasses of HTTP::Message and inherit HTTP::Message's facility to handle headers and an entity-body.

For both HTTP::Request and HTTP::Response, you might want to define the headers in your request or look at the headers in the response. In this case, you can use HTTP::Headers to poke around with your HTTP::Request or HTTP::Response object.

In addition to HTTP::Headers for looking at HTTP::Response headers, HTTP::Status includes functions to classify response codes into the categories of informational, successful, redirection, error, client error, or server error. It also exports symbolic aliases of HTTP response codes; one could refer to the status code of 200 as RC_OK, and refer to 404 as RC_NOT_FOUND.

The Date module converts date strings from and to machine time.

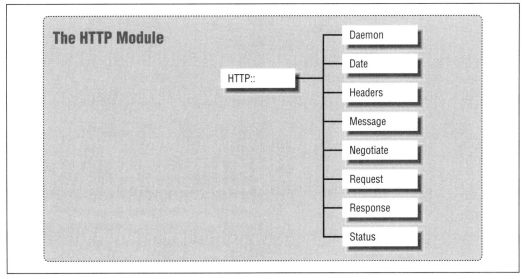

Figure 3   Structure of the HTTP module

HTTP::Request

This module summarizes a Web client's request. For a simple GET or HEAD request, you could define the GET method and a URL to apply it to, and the headers would be filled in by LWP. For a POST or PUT, you might want to specify a custom HTTP::Headers object at the third parameter, or the $content parameter for an entity-body. Since HTTP::Request inherits everything in IITTP::Messagc. You can use the header and enti-tyon methods from HTTP::Message in HTTP::Request objects.

`$r = new HTTP::Request $method, $url, [$header, [$content]]`

The first parameter, $method, expects an HTTP method, like GET, HEAD, POST, PUT, etc. The second parameter, $url, is the URL to apply the method to. This can be a string, like www.ora.com, or a reference to a URI::URL object. To specify your own headers, you can specify an optional third parameter as a reference to an HTTP::Headers object. The fourth parameter, also optional, is a scalar that specifies the HTTP entity-body of the request. If omitted, the entity-body is empty.

`$r->method([$val])`

To see what the HTTP::Request object has as its HTTP method, call the object's `method()` method without any parameters, and it will return the object's current HTTP method. To define a new HTTP method for the HTTP::Request object, call the object's `method()` method with your new HTTP method.

`$r->url([$val])`

To see what the HTTP::Request object has as its request URL, call the object's `url()` method without any parameters, and it will return the object's current URL. To define a new URL, call `url()` with your new URL as a parameter, like `$myobject->url( www. ora.com )`.

`$r->header($field [=> $val],...)`

When called with just an HTTP header as a parameter, this method returns the current value for the header. For example, `$myob-ject->('content- type )` would return the value for the object's content-type header. To define a new header value, invoke **header()** with an associative array with header => value pairs, where the value is a scalar or reference to an array. For example, to define the content-type header, you would do this:

```
$r->header('content-type' => 'text/
    plain')
```

By the way, since HTTP::Request inherits HTTP::Message, and HTTP::Message contains all the methods of HTTP::Headers, you can use all the HTTP::Headers methods within an HTTP::Request object. See HTTP::Headers later in this section.

$r->content([$content])

To get the entity-body of the request, call the **content()** method without any parameters, and it will return the object's current entity-body. To define the entity-body, invoke **content()** with a scalar as its first parameter. This method, by the way, is inherited from HTTP::Message.

$r->add_content($data)

Appends $data to the end of the object's current entity-body.

$r->as_string( )

This returns a text version of the request, useful for debugging purposes. For example,

```
use HTTP::Request;

$request = new HTTP::Request 'PUT',
    'http://www.ora.com/example/ hi.
    text';
$request->header('content-length'
    => 2);
$request->header('content-type' =>
    'text/plain');
$request->content('hi');
print $request->as_string( );
```

would look like this:

```
--- HTTP::Request=HASH(0x68148) ---
```

```
PUT http://www.ora.com/example/hi.
    text
Content-Length: 2
Content-Type: text/plain

hi
----------------------------------
```

HTTP::Response

Responses from a Web server are described by HTTP::Response objects. If LWP has problems fulfilling your request, it internally generates an HTTP::Response object and fills in an appropriate response code. In the context of Web client programming, you'll usually get an HTTP::Response object from LWP::UserAgent and LWP::RobotUA. If you plan to write extensions to LWP or a Web server or proxy server, you might use HTTP::Response to generate your own responses.

$r = new HTTP::Response ($rc, [$msg, [$header, [$content]]])

In its simplest form, an HTTP::Response object can contain just a response code. If you would like to specify a more detailed message than "OK" or "Not found", you can specify a human-readable description of the response code as the second parameter. As a third parameter, you can pass a reference to an HTTP::Headers object to specify the response headers. Finally, you can also include an entity-body in the fourth parameter as a scalar.

$r->code([$code])

When invoked without any parameters, the **code()** method returns the object's response code. When invoked with a status code as the first parameter, **code()** defines the object's response to that value.

$r->is_info( )

Returns true when the response code is 100 through 199.

$r->is_success( )

Returns true when the response code is 200 through 299.

`$r->is_redirect( )`

Returns true when the response code is 300 through 399.

`$r->is_error( )`

Returns true when the response code is 400 through 599. When an error occurs, you might want to use `error_as_HTML()` to generate an HTML explanation of the error.

`$r->message([$message])`

Not to be confused with the entity-body of the response. This is the human-readable text that a user would usually see in the first line of an HTTP response from a server. With a response code of 200 (RC_OK), a common response would be a message of "OK" or "Document follows". When invoked without any parameters, the `message()` method returns the object's HTTP message. When invoked with a scalar parameter as the first parameter, `message()` defines the object's message to the scalar value.

`$r->header($field [=> $val],...)`

When called with just an HTTP header as a parameter, this method returns the current value for the header. For example, `$myobject->('content- type')` would return the value for the object's Content-type header. To define a new header value, invoke `header()` with an associative array of header => value pairs, where value is a scalar or reference to an array. For example, to define the Content-type header, one would do this:

```
$r->header('content-type' => 'text/
    plain')
```

By the way, since HTTP::Request inherits HTTP::Message, and HTTP::Message contains all the methods of HTTP::Headers, you can use all the HTTP::Headers methods within an HTTP::Request object. See "HTTP::Headers" later in this section.

`$r->content([$content])`

To get the entity-body of the request, call the `content()` method without any parameters, and it will return the object's current entity-body. To define the entity-body, invoke `content()` with a scalar as its first parameter. This method, by the way, is inherited from HTTP::Message.

`$r->add_content($data)`

Appends `$data` to the end of the object's current entity-body.

`$r->error_as_HTML( )`

When `is_error()` is true, this method returns an HTML explanation of what happened. LWP usually returns a plain text explanation.

`$r->base( )`

Returns the base of the request. If the response was hypertext, any links from the hypertext should be relative to the location specified by this method. LWP looks for the BASE tag in HTML and Content-base/Content-location HTTP headers for a base specification. If a base was not explicitly defined by the server, LWP uses the requesting URL as the base.

`$r->as_string( )`

This returns a text version of the response. Useful for debugging purposes. For example:

```
use HTTP::Response;
use HTTP::Status;

$response = new HTTP::Response(RC_
    OK, 'all is fine');
$response->header('content-length'
    => 2);
$response->header('content-type' =>
    'text/plain');
$response->content('hi');
print $response->as_string( );
```

would look like this:

```
--- HTTP::Response=HASH(0xc8548) ---
RC: 200 (OK)
Message: all is fine

Content-Length: 2
Content-Type: text/plain
```

hi

$r->current_age

Returns the numbers of seconds since the response was generated by the original server. This is the current_age value as described in section 13.2.3 of the HTTP 1.1 spec 07 draft.

$r->freshness_lifetime

Returns the number of seconds until the response expires. If expiration was not specified by the server, LWP will make an informed guess based on the Last-modified header of the response.

$r->is_fresh

Returns true if the response has not yet expired. Returns true when (freshness_ lifetime > current_ age).

$r->fresh_until

Returns the time when the response expires. The time is based on the number of seconds since January 1, 1970, UTC.

HTTP::Headers

This module deals with HTTP header definition and manipulation. You can use these methods within HTTP::Request and HTTP::Response.

$h = new HTTP::Headers([$field => $val],...)

Defines a new HTTP::Headers object. You can pass in an optional associative array of header => value pairs.

$h->header($field [=> $val],...)

When called with just an HTTP header as a parameter, this method returns the current value for the header. For example, $myob-ject->('content- type') would return the value for the object's Content-type header. To define a new header value, invoke header() with an associative array

of header => value pairs, where the value is a scalar or reference to an array. For example, to define the Content-type header, one would do this:

```
$h->header('content-type' => 'text/
    plain')
```

$h->push_header($field, $val)

Appends the second parameter to the header specified by the first parameter. A subsequent call to header() would return an array. For example:

```
$h->push_header(Accept => 'image/
    jpeg');
```

$h->remove_header($field,...)

Removes the header specified in the parameter(s) and the header's associated value.

HTTP::Status

This module provides functions to determine the type of a response code. It also exports a list of mnemonics that can be used by the programmer to refer to a status code.

is_info( )

Returns true when the response code is 100 through 199.

is_success( )

Returns true when the response code is 200 through 299.

is_redirect( )

Returns true when the response code is 300 through 399.

is_client_error( )

Returns true when the response code is 400 through 499.

is_server_error( )

Returns true when the response code is 500 through 599.

is_error( )

Returns true when the response code is 400 through 599. When an error occurs, you might want to use **error_as_HTML()** to generate an HTML explanation of the error.

There are some mnemonics exported by this module. You can use them in your programs. For example, you could do something like:

```
if ($rc = RC_OK) {....}
```

Here are the mnemonics:

```
RC_CONTINUE (100)
RC_SWITCHING_PROTOCOLS (101)
RC_OK (200)
RC_CREATED (201)
RC_ACCEPTED (202)
RC_NON_AUTHORITATIVE_INFORMATION
    (203)
RC_NO_CONTENT (204)
RC_RESET_CONTENT (205)
RC_PARTIAL_CONTENT (206)
RC_MULTIPLE_CHOICES (300)
RC_MOVED_PERMANENTLY (301)
RC_MOVED_TEMPORARILY (302)
RC_SEE_OTHER (303)
RC_NOT_MODIFIED (304)
RC_USE_PROXY (305)
RC_BAD_REQUEST (400)
RC_UNAUTHORIZED (401)
RC_PAYMENT_REQUIRED (402)
RC_FORBIDDEN (403)
RC_NOT_FOUND (404)
RC_METHOD_NOT_ALLOWED (405)
RC_NOT_ACCEPTABLE (406)
RC_PROXY_AUTHENTICATION_ REQUIRED
    (407)
RC_REQUEST_TIMEOUT (408)
RC_CONFLICT (409)
RC_GONE (410)
RC_LENGTH_REQUIRED (411)
RC_PRECONDITION_FAILED (412)
RC_REQUEST_ENTITY_TOO_LARGE (413)
RC_REQUEST_URI_TOO_LARGE (414)
RC_UNSUPPORTED_MEDIA_TYPE (415)
RC_INTERNAL_SERVER_ERROR (500)
RC_NOT_IMPLEMENTED (501)
RC_BAD_GATEWAY (502)
RC_SERVICE_UNAVAILABLE (503)
```

```
RC_GATEWAY_TIMEOUT (504)
RC_HTTP_VERSION_NOT_ SUPPORTED (505)
```

HTTP::Date

The HTTP::Date module is useful when you want to process a date string.

time2str([$time])

Given the number of seconds since machine epoch,[*] this function generates the equivalent time as specified in RFC 1123, which is the recommended time format used in HTTP. When invoked with no parameter, the current time is used.

str2time($str [, $zone])

Converts the time specified as a string in the first parameter into the number of seconds since epoch. This function recognizes a wide variety of formats, including RFC 1123 (standard HTTP), RFC 850, ANSI C **asctime()**, common log file format, UNIX **ls -l**, and Windows **dir**, among others. When a time zone is not implicit in the first parameter, this function will use an optional time zone specified as the second parameter, such as -0800 or +0500 or **GMT**. If the second parameter is omitted and the time zone is ambiguous, the local time zone is used.

The HTML Module

The HTML module provides an interface to parse HTML into an HTML parse tree, traverse the tree, and convert HTML to other formats. There are eleven classes in the HTML module, as shown in Figure 4.

We're mostly interested in parsing the HTML into an HTML syntax tree, extracting links, and converting the HTML into text or PostScript. As a

---

[*] Which is January 1, 1970, UTC on UNIX Systems.

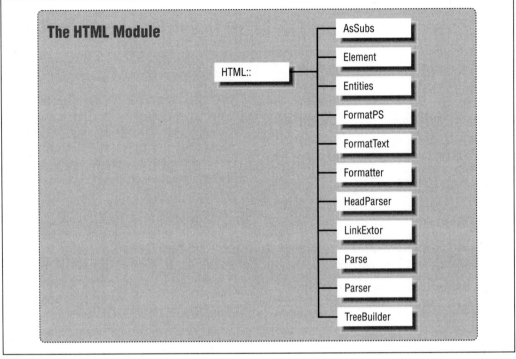

Figure 4   Structure of the HTML module

warning, chances are that you will need to explicitly do garbage collection when you're done with an HTML parse tree.[*]

HTML::Parse

`parse_html($html, [$obj])`

Given a scalar variable containing HTML as a first parameter, this function generates an HTML syntax tree and returns a reference to an object of type HTML::TreeBuilder. When invoked with an optional second parameter of type HTML::TreeBuilder,[†] the syntax tree is constructed with that object, instead of a new object. Since HTML::TreeBuilder inherits HTML::Parser and HTML::Element, methods

from those classes can be used with the returned HTML::TreeBuilder object.

`parse_htmlfile($file, [$obj])`

Same as `parse_html()`, except that the first parameter is a scalar containing the location of a file containing HTML.

With both `parse_html()` and `parse_html-file()`, you can customize some of the parsing behavior with some flags:

`$HTML::Parse::IMPLICIT_TAGS`

Assumes certain elements and end tags when not explicitly mentioned in the HTML. This flag is on by default.

---

[*] Since HTML syntax trees use circular references, the Perl garbage collector does not currently dispose of the memory used by the tree. You'll have to call the `delete()` method for the root node in an HTML syntax tree to manually deallocate memory used by the tree. Future versions of Perl or LWP may handle this automatically. See online documentation at *www.perl.com* for up-to-date information.

[†] Or a subclass of HTML::Parser, which HTML::TreeBuilder happens to be.

`$HTML::Parse::IGNORE_UNKNOWN`

Ignores unknown tags. On by default.

`$HTML::Parse::IGNORE_TEXT`

Ignores the text content of any element. Off by default.

`$HTML::Parse::WARN`

Calls `warn()` when there's a syntax error. Off by default.

`HTML::Element`

The HTML::Element module provides methods for dealing with nodes in an HTML syntax tree. You can get or set the contents of each node, traverse the tree, and delete a node. We'll cover `delete()` and `extract_links()`.

`$h->delete( )`

Deallocates any memory used by this HTML element and any children of this element.

`$h->extract_links([@wantedTypes])`

Returns a list of hyperlinks as a reference to an array, where each element in the array is another array. The second array contains the hyperlink text and a reference to the HTML::Element that specifies the hyperlink. If invoked with no parameters, `extract_links()` will extract any hyperlink it can find. To specify certain types of hyperlinks, one can pass in an array of scalars, where the scalars are: body, base, a, img, form, input, link, frame, applet, and area.

For example:

```
use HTML::Parse;

$html='<img src="dot.gif">';
$html.='<img src="dot2.gif">';
$tree=HTML::Parse::parse_
    html($html);

$link_ref = $tree->extract_links( );
@link = @$link_ref; # dereference
    the array reference
```

```
for ($i=0; $i <= $#link; $i++) {
  print "$link[$i][0]\n";
}
prints out:
dot.gif
dot2.gif
```

HTML::FormatText

The HTML::FormatText module converts an HTML parse tree into text.

`$formatter = new HTML::FormatText`

Creates a new HTML::FormatText object.

`$formatter->format($html)`

Given an HTML parse tree, as returned by `HTML::Parse::parse_html()`, this method returns a text version of the HTML.

HTML::FormatPS

The HTML::FormatPS module converts an HTML parse tree into PostScript.

`$formatter = new HTML::FormatPS (parameter, ...)`

Creates a new HTML::FormatPS object with parameters of PostScript attributes. Each attribute is an associative array. One can define the following attributes:

PaperSize

Possible values of 3, A4, A5, B4, B5, Letter, Legal, Executive, Tabloid, Statement, Folio, 10x14, and Quarto. The default is A4.[*]

PaperWidth

Width of the paper in points.

PaperHeight

Height of the paper in points.

LeftMargin

Left margin in points.

RightMargin

Right margin in points.

---

[*] A4 is the standard paper size in Europe. Americans will probably want to change this to Letter.

HorizontalMargin

Left and right margin. Default is 4 cm.

TopMargin

Top margin in points.

BottomMargin

Bottom margin in points.

VerticalMargin

Top and bottom margin. Default is 2 cm.

PageNo

Boolean value to display page numbers. Default is 0 (off).

FontFamily

Font Family to use on the page. Possible values are Courier, Helvetica and Times. Default is Times.

FontScale

Scale factor for the font.

Leading

Space between lines, as a factor of the font size. Default is 0.1.

For example, you could do:

```
$formatter = new
    HTML::FormatPS('papersize' =>
    'A4').
```

$formatter->format($html);

Given an HTML syntax tree, returns the HTML representation as a scalar with Post-Script content.

The URI Module

The URI module contains functions and modules to specify and convert URIs. (URLs are a type of URI.) There are only two classes within the URI module, as shown in Figure 5.

We'll talk about escaping and unescaping URIs, as well as specifying URLs in the URI::URL module.

URI::Escape

uri_escape($uri, [$escape])

Given a URI as the first parameter, returns the equivalent URI with certain characters replaced with % followed by two hexadecimal digits. The first parameter can be a text string, like *http://www.ora.com*, or an object of type URI::URL. When invoked without a second parameter, `uri_escape()` escapes characters specified by RFC 1738. Otherwise, one can pass in a regular expression (in the context of [ ]) of characters to escape as the second parameter. For example:

```
$escaped_uri = uri_escape($uri,
    'aeiou')
```

Escapes all lowercase vowels in $uri and returns the escaped version. You might wonder why one would want to escape certain characters in a URI. Here's an example: If a file on the server happens to contain a question mark, you would want to use this function to escape the question mark in the URI before sending the request to the server. Otherwise, the question mark would be interpreted by the server to be a query string separator.

uri_unescape($uri)

Substitutes any instance of % followed by two hexadecimal digits back into its original

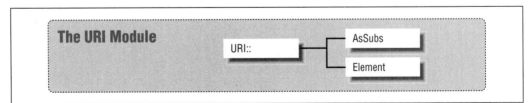

Figure 5   Structure of the URI module

form and returns the entire URI in unescaped form.

URI::URL

new URI::URL($url_string [, $base_url])
Creates a new URI::URL object with the URL given as the first parameter. An optional base URL can be specified as the second parameter and is useful for generating an absolute URL from a relative URL.

URI::URL::strict($bool)
When set, the URI::URL module calls croak() upon encountering an error. When disabled, the URI::URL module may behave more gracefully. The function returns the previous value of strict().

$url->base ([$base])
Gets or sets the base URL associated with the URL in this URI::URL object. The base URL is useful for converting a relative URL into an absolute URL.

$url->abs([$base, [$allow_scheme_in_ relative_urls]])
Returns the absolute URL, given a base. If invoked with no parameters, any previous definition of the base is used. The second parameter is a boolean that modifies abs()'s behavior. When the second parameter is nonzero, abs() will accept a relative URL with a scheme but no host, like http:index.html. By default, this is off.

$url->rel($base)
Given a base as a first parameter or a previous definition of the base, returns the current object's URL relative to the base URL.

$url->crack( )
Returns an array with the following data:

```
(scheme, user, password, host,
    port, epath, eparams, equery,
    frag)
```

$url->scheme([$scheme])
When invoked with no parameters, this returns the scheme in the URL defined in the object. When invoked with a parameter, the object's scheme is assigned to that value.

$url->netloc( )
When invoked with no parameters, this returns the network location for the URL defined in the object. The network location is a string composed of user:password@host:port, where user, password, and port may be omitted when not defined. When netloc() is invoked with a parameter, the object's network location is defined to that value. Changes to the network location are reflected in the user(), password(), host(), and port() method.

$url->user( )
When invoked with no parameters, this returns the user for the URL defined in the object. When invoked with a parameter, the object's user is assigned to that value.

$url->password( )
When invoked with no parameters, this returns the password in the URL defined in the object. When invoked with a parameter, the object's password is assigned to that value.

$url->host( )
When invoked with no parameters, this returns the hostname in the URL defined in the object. When invoked with a parameter, the object's hostname is assigned to that value.

$url->port( )
When invoked with no parameters, this returns the port for the URL defined in the object. If a port wasn't explicitly defined in the URL, a default port is assumed. When invoked with a parameter, the object's port is assigned to that value.

$url->default_port( )
When invoked with no parameters, this returns the default port for the URL defined in the object. The default port is based on the scheme used. Even if the port for the

URL is explicitly changed by the user with the `port()` method, the default port is always the same.

$url->epath( )

When invoked with no parameters, this returns the escaped path of the URL defined in the object. When invoked with a parameter, the object's escaped path is assigned to that value.

$url->path( )

Same as `epath()` except that the path that is set/returned is not escaped.

$url->eparams( )

When invoked with no arguments, this returns the escaped parameter of the URL defined in the object. When invoked with an argument, the object's escaped parameter is assigned to that value.

$url->params( )

Same as `eparams()` except that the parameter that is set/returned is not escaped.

$url->equery( )

When invoked with no arguments, this returns the escaped query string of the URL defined in the object. When invoked with an argument, the object's escaped query string is assigned to that value.

$url->query( )

Same as `equery()` except that the parameter that is set/returned is not escaped.

$url->frag( )

When invoked with no arguments, this returns the fragment of the URL defined in the object. When invoked with an argument, the object's fragment is assigned to that value.

$url->full_path( )

Returns a string consisting of the escaped path, escaped parameters, and escaped query string.

$url->eq($other_url)

Returns true when the object's URL is equal to the URL specified by the first parameter.

$url->as_string( )

Returns the URL as a scalar string. All defined components of the URL are included in the string.

Using LWP

Let's try out some LWP examples and glue a few functions together to produce something useful. First, let's revisit a program from the beginning of the paper.

```perl
#!/usr/local/bin/perl
use LWP::Simple;

print (get ($ARGV[0]));
```

Because this is a short and simple example, there isn't a whole lot of flexibility here. For example, when `LWP::Simple::get()` fails, it doesn't give us a status code to use to figure out what went wrong. The program doesn't identify itself with the User-Agent header, and it doesn't support proxy servers. Let's change a few things.

Using LWP::UserAgent

LWP::UserAgent has its advantages when compared to LWP::Simple. With only a few more lines for code, one can follow HTTP redirections, authenticate requests, use the User-Agent and From headers, set a timeout, and use a proxy server. For the remainder of this article, we'll experiment with various aspects of LWP::User-Agent to show you how everything fits together.

First, let's convert our LWP::Simple program into something that uses LWP::UserAgent.

```perl
use LWP::UserAgent;
use HTTP::Request;
use HTTP::Response;

my $ua = new LWP::UserAgent;

my $request = new
    HTTP::Request('GET', $ARGV[0]);
```

```
my $response = $ua-
    >request($request);
if ($response->is_success) {
    print $response->content;
} else {
    print $response->error_as_HTML;
}
```

Lets try it out:

> **hcat_plain http://www.ora.com/**

By converting to LWP::UserAgent, we've instantly gained the ability to report error messages and follow a URL redirection. Let's go through the code line by line, just to make sure you see how the different objects interact.

First, we include the modules that we plan to use in our program.

```
use LWP::UserAgent;
use HTTP::Request;
use HTTP::Response;
```

Then we create a new LWP::UserAgent object:

```
my $ua = new LWP::UserAgent;
```

We construct an HTTP request by creating a new HTTP::Request object. Within the constructor, we define the HTTP GET method and use the first argument ($ARGV[0]) as the URL to get.

```
my $request = new
    HTTP::Request('GET', $ARGV[0]);
```

We pass the HTTP::Request object to $ua's request() method. In other words, we're passing an HTTP::Request object to the LWP::User-Agent->request() method, where $ua is an instance of LWP::UserAgent. LWP::UserAgent performs the request and fetches the resource specified by $ARGV[0]. It returns a newly created HTTP::Response object, which we store in $response.

```
my $response = $ua-
    >request($request);
```

We examine the HTTP response code with HTTP::Response->is_success() by calling the is_success() method from the $response object. If the request was successful, we use HTTP::Response::content() by invoking $response's content() method to retrieve the

entity-body of the response and print it out. Upon error, we use HTTP::Response::error_as_HTML by invoking $response s error_as_HTML() method to print out an error message as HTML.

In a nutshell, we create a request with an HTTP::Request object. We pass that request to LWP::UserAgent's request method, which does the actual request. It returns an HTTP::Response object, and we use methods in HTTP::Response to determine the response code and print out the results.

Adding Proxy Server Support

Let's add some more functionality to the previous example. In this case, we'll add support for a proxy server. A proxy server is usually used in firewall environments, where the HTTP request is sent to the proxy server, and the proxy server forwards the request to the real Web server. If your network doesn't have a firewall, and you don't plan to have proxy support in your programs, then you can safely skip over this part now and come back when you eventually need it.

To show how flexible the LWP library is, we've added only two lines of code to the previous example, and now the Web client knows that it should use the proxy at *proxy.ora.com* at port 8080 for HTTP requests, but to avoid using the proxy if the request is for a Web server in the *ora.com* domain.

```
use LWP::UserAgent;
use HTTP::Request;
use HTTP::Response;

my $ua = new LWP::UserAgent;

$ua->proxy('http', 'http://proxy.
    ora.com:8080/');
$ua->no_proxy('ora.com');

my $request = new
    HTTP::Request('GET', $ARGV[0]);
my $response = $ua-
    >request($request);
if ($response->is_success) {
    print $response->content;
```

```
    } else {
        print $response->error_as_HTML;
    }
```

The invocation of this program is exactly the same as the previous example. If you downloaded this program from the O'Reilly Web site, you could then use it like this:

```
(intense) /usr/home/apm> hcat_
    proxy http://www.ora.com/
```

Adding Robot Exclusion Standard Support

Let's do one more example. This time, let's add support for robot exclusion standards. As discussed in the LWP::RobotUA section, the Robot Exclusion Standard give Webmasters the ability to block off certain areas of the Web site from automated "robot" type of Web clients. It is arguable that the programs we've gone through so far aren't really robots; chances are that the user invoked the program by hand and is waiting for a reply. But for the sake of example, and to show how easy it is, let's add support for the Robot Exclusion Standard to our previous example.

```
use LWP::RobotUA;
use HTTP::Request;
use HTTP::Response;

my $ua = new LWP::RobotUA('hcat_
    RobotUA', 'examples@ora.com');

$ua->proxy('http', 'http://proxy.
    ora.com:8080/');
$ua->no_proxy('ora.com');

my $request = new
    HTTP::Request('GET', $ARGV[0]);
my $response = $ua-
    >request($request);
```

```
    if ($response->is_success) {
        print $response->content;
    } else {
        print $response->error_as_HTML;
    }
```

Since LWP::RobotUA is a subclass of LWP::UserAgent, LWP::RobotUA contains all the methods as LWP::UserAgent. So we replaced the use LWP::UserAgent line with use LWP::Robot:UA. Instead of declaring a new LWP::UserAgent object, we declare a new LWP::RobotUA object.

LWP::RobotUA's constructor is a little different, though. Since we're programming a Web robot, the name of the robot and the email address of the user are mandatory. So, we pass that information to the LWP::RobotUA object through the constructor. In practice, one would determine the email address of the client user in advance. The *examples@ora.com* is provided for illustration purposes only. ∎

About the Author

Clinton Wong
Intel Corporation
1900 Prairie City Road
FM1-58
Folsom, CA 95630
clinton_d_wong@ccm.fm.intel.com

Clinton Wong works in the Internet/Web Engineering group at Intel Corporation, where his work focuses on protocol analysis, proxy servers, and Intranet solutions. Clinton graduated from Purdue University in 1996 and is the author of the O'Reilly & Associates book entitled *HTTP Programming with Perl*.

WEB GATEWAYS

INCREASING THE POWER OF THE WEB

Shishir Gundavaram

Abstract

Dozens of servers already exist on the Internet that a Web programmer may want to interact with: mail and news programs, relational databases, search utilities, and so on. If you know the protocol used by the server (the expected input and output), you can implement a gateway to create a Web page offering a pleasant and powerful interface to the server. The key is to understand the input and output (including error messages). This article illustrates the process by creating a program that uses the Common Gateway Interface (CGI) to displays Usenet News.

If you surf the Web at all, you'll come across all kinds of neat resources, ranging from powerful search engines and interesting applications that analyze your diet, to cool utilities that allow you to participate in a virtual chat room. These are just a few examples of the types of applications that are possible on the Web through the use of *gateways.*

A gateway is analogous to a foreign language translator. Imagine, for a moment, that you are in beautiful Switzerland, away from the hustle and bustle of your everyday life, and you are giddy with joy at the sight of so many beautiful restaurants. You decide to take a break from your tourist activities and take a bite to eat. Unfortunately, you run into a problem: you can't communicate with anyone in the restaurant. What to do? Ahhhh Haaa! You pull out your trusty English/Swiss electronic language converter, and you're well on your way to happiness.

You can think of the Web in the same manner. There are a vast number of "foreign" applications, such as system utilities, relational database engines and Internet information servers, which you cannot access directly though the Web. The only way to tie these resources to the Web is by developing "converters" or gateways. Figure 1 illustrates this concept..

Gateways can be written using Java, ActiveX, Server-Side JavaScript, or the Common Gateway Interface (CGI). One of Web's best kept secrets is that CGI is astoundingly simple, yet powerful. An example of its simplicity and flexibility is that we can use any programming language we desire.

In this article, we will develop a CGI gateway to the Network News Transfer Protocol, or NNTP (Usenet News) information server. Our Web browser will act as an NNTP client through which you can read news articles from a variety of newsgroups. But before we get to that, let's briefly look at the nuts and bolts of how clients and servers work on the Net.

Internet Clients and Servers

Let's start by looking at how a server works. Take an electronic mail application (though the theory can apply to any other server). Most mail programs save the user's messages in a particular file, typically in the */var/spool/mail* directory. When you send mail to someone on a different host, the mail program must find the recipient's mail file on that machine and append the message to it. How exactly does the mail program achieve this task, since it cannot manipulate files on a remote host directly?

The answer to this question is *interprocess communication* (IPC). A process on the remote host acts as a messenger for the mail process on that machine. The local process communicates with this remote agent across a network to "deliver" mail. As a result, the remote process is called a

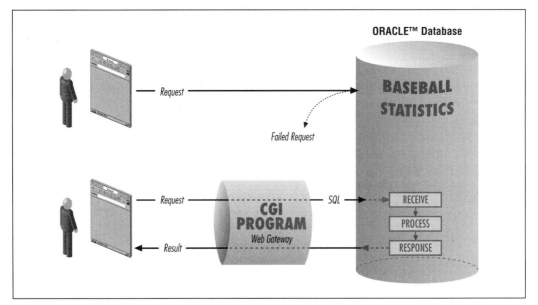

Figure 1

server (it "services" an issued request), and the local process is referred to as a *client*. The Web works along the same philosophy: the browser is the client that issues a request to an HTTP server that interprets and executes the request.

The most important thing to remember here is that the client and the server must "speak the same language." In other words, a particular client is designed to work with a specific server. So, for example, an Archie client cannot communicate with a Web server. But if you know the stream of data expected by a server, and the stream produced as output, you can write a CGI program that communicates with it, as you will see later in this article.

Okay, now it's finally time to develop our gateway.

Usenet News on the Web

NNTP is the most popular software used to transmit Usenet news over the Internet. It lets the receiving (client) system tell the sending (server) system which newsgroups to send, and which articles from each group. NNTP accepts commands in a fairly simple format. It sends back a stream of text consisting of the articles posted and occasional status information.

This CGI gateway communicates with an NTTP server directly by using socket I/O. The program displays lists of newsgroups and articles for the user to choose from. You will be able to read news from the specified newsgroups in a threaded fashion (i.e., all the replies to each article are grouped together).

```
#!/usr/bin/perl

use CGI_Lite;
use Easy_Sockets;
```

The `CGI_Lite` module provides us with a set of functions to quickly and easily parse CGI information and data. And the `Easy_Sockets` module makes it easy for us to communicate with servers. Both of these modules are available at your nearest CPAN mirror.* Or, you can use Tom Chris-

---

* The current list of CPAN, the Comprehensive Perl Archive Network, can be found at *http://perl.com/CPAN*.

tiansen's CPAN multiplexer in the following manner to locate these modules:

```
http://www.perl.com/CPAN/authors/
     Shishir_Gundavaram
```

Let's continue with the code:

```
sub print_header;
sub print_footer;
sub escape;
sub check_nntp;
sub set_newsgroup;
sub show_article;
sub show_all_articles;
sub by_article_number;
sub display_newsgroups;
sub return_error;
```

Unlike other languages, most notably C and C++, Perl does not require us to declare subroutine (or function) prototypes. But we do so for readability (as shown in Example 1).

We store a list of the newsgroups that the user is allowed to access in the %Groups associative array, or hash table. Keep in mind that all capitalized variables represent global variables.

There is no form front end to this CGI gateway. Instead, all parameters are passed as query information (GET method). If you access this application without a query, a document listing all the newsgroups is listed. Once you select a newsgroup from this list, the program is invoked again, this time with a query that specifies the newsgroup you want. For instance, if you want the newsgroup whose key is images, the following query is passed to the program:

```
http://some.machine/cgi-bin/nntp.
     pl?group=images
```

The string "images" is associated with the actual newsgroup name in the %Groups hash. This is a more secure way of handling things, as opposed to passing the entire newsgroup name. If the program receives a query like the previous one, it displays a list of the articles in the newsgroup. When the user chooses an article, the query information will look like this:

```
http://some.machine/cgi-bin/nntp.
     pl?group=images&article=18721
```

This program will then display the article.

```
$cgi      = new CGI_Lite;
%data   = $cgi->parse_form_data;

$group_name      = $data{'group'};
$article_number = $data{'article'};
```

We create a new instance of the CGI_Lite object and store it in $cgi. The parse_form_data method parses the query information and stores it in the %data hash. For convenience, we store the passed group name and article number in $group_name and $article_number, respectively.

```
$all_groups =
     '(cgi|html|porters|misc|perl)';
```

The $all_groups variable contains a regular expression listing all of the keys of the %Groups hash. This ensures that a valid newsgroup is specified by the user.

```
$nntp_server = 'nntp.ora.com';
```

We will access the NNTP server at *nntp.ora.com*. If you do not want users from domains other

Example 1

```
$Webmaster      = "Shishir Gundavaram (shishir\@ora\.com)";
$Gateway_Error = "CGI NNTP Gateway Error";

%Groups = ('cgi'        =>      'comp.infosystems.www.authoring.cgi',
           'html'       =>      'comp.infosystems.www.authoring.html',
           'porters'    =>      'perl.porters-gw',
           'misc'       =>      'comp.infosystems.www.authoring.misc',
           'perl'       =>      'comp.lang.perl.misc');
```

than *ora.com* to access this gateway, you can set up a simple authentication scheme like this:

```
$allowed_domain = 'ora.com';
$remote_host = $ENV{'REMOTE_HOST'};
($remote_domain) = ($remote_host =~
    /([^.]+\.[^.]+)$/);

if ($remote_domain ne $allowed_
    domain) {
    return_error (500, $Gateway_
    Error,

    "Sorry! You are not allowed to
    read news!");
}.
```

The regular expression used above extracts the domain name from an IP name or address. Or, you can allow multiple domains, as follows:

```
$allowed_domains = '(ora.com|mit.
    edu|perl.com)';
$remote_host = $ENV{'REMOTE_HOST'};

if ($remote_host !~ /$allowed_
    domains$/o) {
    return_error (500, $Gateway_
    Error,

    "Sorry! You are not allowed to
    read news!");
}
```

Let's continue with the program:

```
if ($group_name =~ /\b$all_groups\b/
    o) {
    $selected_group = $Groups{$group_
    name};
```

This block of code will be executed only if the group field in the query string consists of a valid newsgroup name, as stored in $all_groups. The $selected_group variable contains the actual newsgroup name, as extracted from the %Groups hash.

```
$socket = new Easy_Sockets (NNTP,
    $nntp_server, "nntp");
$socket->open_connection ||
    return_error (500, $Gateway_
    Error,
    "Could not connect to NNTP server.
    ");
```

We use the `Easy_Sockets` module to try to communicate with the NNTP server at "nntp.ora.com". If the `open_connection` method returns an error, we proceed to call the `return_error` subroutine to display an error.

```
check_nntp;
```

The `check_nntp` subroutine checks the header information that is returned by the NNTP server upon connection. If the server issues any error messages, the script terminates.

```
($first, $last) = set_newsgroup
    ($selected_group);
```

The NNTP server keeps track of all the articles in a newsgroup by numbering them in ascending order, starting at some arbitrary number. The `set_newsgroup` subroutine returns the identification number for the first and last articles.

```
if ($article_number) {
    if (($article_number < $first)||
        ($article_number > $last)) {
        return_error (500, $Gateway_
        Error,
            "The article number
            you specified is not
            valid.");
    } else {
        show_article ($selected_group,
            $article_number);
    }
```

If the user selected an article from the list that was dynamically generated when a newsgroup is selected, this branch of code is executed. The article number is checked to make sure that it lies within the valid range. You might wonder why we need to check this, since the list that is presented to the user is based on the range generated by the set_newsgroup subroutine. The reason for this is that the NNTP server lets articles expire periodically, and articles are sometimes deleted by their author. If sufficient time passes between the time the list is displayed and the time the user makes a selection, the specified article number could be invalid. In addition, I like to handle the possibility that a user hardcoded a query.

```
    } else {
        show_all_articles ($group_name,
            $selected_group, $first, $last);
    }
```

If no article is specified, which happens when the user selects a newsgroup from the main HTML document, the **show_all_articles** subroutine is called to display a list of all the articles for the selected newsgroup.

```
    print NNTP "quit\n";
    $socket->close_connection;
```

Finally, the *quit* command is sent to the NNTP server, and the socket is closed.

```
    } else {
        display_newsgroups;
    }

    exit (0);
```

If this program is accessed without any query information, or if the specified newsgroup is not among the list stored in the **%Groups** hash, the **display_newsgroups** subroutine is invoked to display a list of the valid newsgroups.

The following two subroutines, **print_header** and **print_footer**, are for convenience. The **print_header** subroutine displays the **text/html** MIME type as well as HTML header information. And the **print_footer** subroutine displays the footer for the document.

```
sub print_header
{
    my $title = shift;

    print <<End_of_Header;
Content-type: text/html

<HTML>
<HEAD>
    <TITLE>$title</TITLE>
</HEAD>
<BODY>
<H1>$title</H1>
<HR>
<BR>

End_of_Header
}
```

```
sub print_footer
{
    print <<End_of_Footer;
<HR>
<ADDRESS>$Webmaster</ADDRESS>
</BODY>
</HTML>

End_of_Footer
}
```

The **escape** subroutine "escapes" all characters with the exception of alphanumeric characters and whitespace. This ensures that all characters are displayed properly by the Web browser.

```
sub escape
{
    my $string = shift;

    $string =~ s/([^\w\s])/sprintf
    ("&#%d;", ord ($1))/ge;

    return ($string);
}
```

For example, if an article in a newsgroup contains the following:

```
From: joe@test.net (Joe Test)
Subject: I can't get the <H1>
    headers to display correctly
```

The browser will actually interpret the "<H1>" as HTML, and the rest of the document will not be displayed properly. The **escape** subroutine escapes the text so that it looks like the following:

```
From&#58; joe&#64;test&#46;net
    &#40;Joe Test&#41;
Subject&#58; I can&#39;t get the
    &#60;H1&#62; headers to display
    correctly
```

A Web client can interpret any string in the form &#ascii; where ascii is the ASCII code of the character. This might slow down the display slightly but is much safer than taking a chance.

The **check_nntp** subroutine continuously reads the output from the NNTP server (see Example 2) until the return status is either a success (200 or 201) or a failure (4xx or 5xx). You might have noticed that these status codes are very similar to

Example 2

```
sub check_nntp
{
    while (<NNTP>) {
        if (/^(200|201)/) {
            last;
        } elsif (/^4|5\d+/) {
            return_error (500, $Gateway_Error,
                                "The NNTP server retured an error.");
        }
    }
}
```

the HTTP status codes. In fact, most Internet servers that follow a standard use these codes.

The **set_newsgroup** subroutine returns the first and last article numbers for the newsgroup.

```
sub set_newsgroup
{
    my $group = shift;
    my ($group_info, $status, $first_
        post, $last_post);

    print NNTP "group $group\n";
```

In response to the *group* command, the NNTP server sets its current newsgroup to the one specified, and returns the following piece of information:

```
group comp.infosystems.www.
    authoring.cgi
211 1289 4776 14059 comp.
    infosystems.www.authoring.cgi
```

The first column indicates the status of the operation 211 (success), followed by the total number of articles, the first and last articles, and the newsgroup name. As you can clearly see, the number of articles is not equal to the numerical difference of the first and last articles. This is due to article expiration and deletion (as mentioned previously).

```
$group_info = <NNTP>;
($status, $first_post, $last_
    post) = (split (/\s+/, $group_
    info))[0, 2, 3];
```

The server output is split on whitespace, and the first, third, and fourth elements are stored in

$status, $first_post, and $last_post, respectively. Remember, arrays are zero based in Perl; the first element is zero, not one.

```
if ($status != 211) {
    return_error (500, $Gateway_
        Error,
                Could not get group
                information for
                $group");
    } else {
    return ($first_post, $last_post);
    }
}
```

If the status is not 211, an error message is returned. Otherwise, we proceed to return the first and last article numbers.

We use the **show_article** subroutine to retrieve and output the actual news article.

```
sub show_article
{
    my ($group, $number) = @_;
    my ($useful_headers, $header_
    line);

    $useful_headers =
    '(From:|Subject:|
        Date:|Organization:)';

    print NNTP "head $number\n";
    $header_line = <NNTP>;
```

The *head* command displays the headers for the specified article. Here is the format of the NNTP output:

```
221 14059 <47hh6767ghe1$d09@nntp.
    test.net> head
```

```
Path: news.bu.edu!decwrl!nntp.test.
    net!usenet
From: joe@test.net (Joe Test)
Newsgroups: comp.infosystems.www.
    authoring.cgi
Subject: I can't get the <H1>
    headers to display correctly
Date: Thu, 05 Oct 1995 05:19:03 GMT
Organization: Joe's Test Net
Lines: 17
Message-ID: <47hh6767ghe1$d09@nntp.
    test.net>
Reply-To: joe@test.net
NNTP-Posting-Host: my.news.test.net
X-Newsreader: Joe Windows Reader v1.
    28
.
```

The first line contains the status, the article number, the article identification, and the NNTP command, respectively. The status of 221 indicates success. All of the other lines constitute the various article headers, and are based on how, when, and where the article was posted. The header body ends with the dot character (.).

```
if ($header_line =~ /^221/) {
    print_header ($group);
    print "<PRE>\n";
```

If the server returns a success status of 221, the **print_header** subroutine is called to display the MIME header, followed by the usual HTML.

```
while (<NNTP>) {
  if (/^$useful_headers/) {
      $_ = escape ($_);
      print "<B>$_</B>";

  } elsif (/^\.\s*$/) {
      last;
    }
}
```

This loop iterates through the header body, and escapes and displays the *From, Subject, Date,* and *Organization* headers.

```
print "\n";
print NNTP "body $number\n";
<NNTP>;
```

If everything is successful up to this point, the *body* command is sent to the server. In response,

the NNTP server outputs the body of the article in the following format:

```
body 14059
222 14059 <47hh6767ghe1$d09@nntp.
    test.net> body
I am trying to display headers
    using the <H1> tag, but it does
    not seem to be working. What
    should I do? Please help.

Thanks in advance,
-Joe
.
```

There is no need to check the status of this command if the *head* command executed successfully. In case you're curious, the server returns a status of 222 to indicate success.

```
while (<NNTP>) {
    last if (/^\.\s*$/);
    $_ = escape ($_);
    print;
}
```

The **while** loop iterates through the body, escapes all the lines, and displays them. If the line starts with a period and contains nothing but whitespace, the loop terminates.

```
    print "</PRE>\n";
    print_footer;

} else {
  return_error (500, $Gateway_
  Error,
                "Article number
                $number could
                not be
                retrieved.");
  }
}
```

If the specified article is not found, an error message is returned.

The following subroutine reads all of the articles for a particular group into memory, threads them—all replies to a specific article are grouped together for reading convenience—and displays the article numbers and subject lines.

```
sub show_all_articles
{
```

```
my ($id, $group, $first_article,
    $last_article) = @_;
my ($this_script, %all, $count,
    @numbers, $article, $subject,
        @threads, $query);

$this_script = $ENV{'SCRIPT_
    NAME'};
$count = 0;
```

This is the most complicated (but the most interesting) part of the program. Before your eyes, you will see a nice Web interface grow from some fairly primitive output from the NNTP server.

```
print NNTP "xhdr subject $first_
    article-$last_article\n";
<NNTP>;
```

The *xhdr subject* command lists all the articles in the specified range in the following format:

```
xhdr subject 4776-14059
221 subject fields follow
4776 Re: CGI Scripts (guestbook ie)
4831 Re: Access counter for CERN
    server
12769 Re: Problems using sendmail
    from Perl script
12770 File upload, Frames and BSCW
-
- (More Articles)
-
.
```

The first line contains the status. Again, there is no need to check this, as we know the news group exists. Each article is listed with its number and subject.

```
print_header ("Newsgroup: $group");
print "<UL>\n";

while (<NNTP>) {
    last if (/^\.\s*$/);
    $_ = escape ($_);

    ($article, $subject) = split
        (/\s+/, $_, 2);

    $subject =~ s/^\s*(.*)\b\s*/ $1/
        ;
    $subject =~ s/^[Rr][Ee]:\s*//;
```

The loop iterates through all of the subjects. The *split* command separates each entry into the article number and subject. Leading and trailing spaces, as well as "Re:" at the beginning of the line are removed from the subject for sorting purposes.

```
if (defined ($all{$subject})) {
    $all{$subject} = join ("-",
        $all{$subject}, $article);
} else {
    $count++;
    $all{$subject} = join ("\0",
        $count, $article);
    }
}
```

This group of code is responsible for threading the articles. Each new subject is stored in the $all hash, keyed by the subject. The $count variable gives a unique number to start each value in the array. If the article already exists, the article number is simply appended to the end to the element with the same subject. For example, if the subjects look like this:

```
2020 What is CGI?
2026 How do you create counters?
2027 Please help with file
    locking!!!
2029 Re: What is CGI?
2030 Re: What is CGI?
2047 Re: How do you create counters?
.
.
.
```

This is how the associative array will look:

```
$all{'What is CGI?'} = "1\02020-
    2029-2030";
$all{'How do you create counters?'}
    = "2\02026-2047";
$all{'Please help with file
    locking!!!'} = "3\02027";
```

Note that we assigned a $count of 1 to the first thread we see ("What's CGI?"), 2 to the second thread, and so on. Later we sort by these numbers, so the user will see threads in the order that they were posted to the newsgroup. We could have certainly used Perl's references to create a complex data structure to store the threads, but this is much simpler.

```
@numbers = sort by_article_number
    keys (%all);
```

What you see here is a common Perl technique for sorting. The *sort* command invokes a subroutine repeatedly (in this case, a very simple one that I wrote called **by_article_number**). Using a fast algorithm, it passes pairs of elements from the $all hash to the subroutine.

```
foreach $subject (@numbers) {
  $article = (split ("\0",
    $all{$subject}))[1];
```

The loop iterates through all of the subjects. The list of article numbers for each subject is stored in article. Thus, the $article variable for "What is CGI?" would be: 2020-2029-2030.

Now, we work on the string of articles.

```
@threads = split (/-/, $article);
```

The string containing all of the articles for a particular subject are split on the – delimiter and stored in the @threads array.

```
foreach (@threads) {
  $query = "$this_script?group=
      id&article=$_";
  print qq|<LI><A HREF=
    "$query">$subject</A>\n|;
  }
}

  print "</UL>\n";
  print_footer;
}
```

The loop iterates through each article number (or thread), and builds a hypertext link containing the newsgroup name and the article number (see Figure 2).

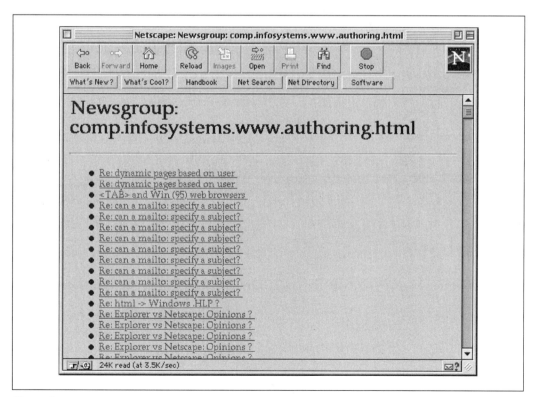

Figure 2

The following is the **sort** subroutine, which is responsible for comparing the values in the hash.

```
sub by_article_number
{
    $all{$a} <=> $all{$b};
}
```

This one line statement is identical to the following:

```
if ($all{$a} < $all{$b}) {
    return (-1);
} elsif ($all{$a} == $all{$b}) {
    return (0);
} elsif ($all{$a} > $all{$b}) {
    return (1);
}
```

The $a and $b constitute two values in the hash. In this case, Perl uses this logic to compare and sort all the values.

The **display_newsgroups** subroutine creates a dynamic HTML document that lists all the newsgroups contained in the **%Groups** hash.

```
sub display_newsgroups
{
    my ($script_name, $keyword,
    $newsgroup, $query);

    print_header ("CGI NNTP
    Gateway");
    $script_name = $ENV{'SCRIPT_
    NAME'};

    print "<UL>\n";

    foreach $keyword (keys %Groups)
    {
        $newsgroup =
    $Groups{$keyword};
        $query = "$script_
    name?group=$keyword";

        print qq|<LI><A
    HREF="$query">$newsgroup</A>\n|;
    }

    print "</UL>";
    print_footer;
}
```

Each newsgroup is listed as an unordered list, with the query consisting of the specific key from the hash. Remember, the qq|...| notation is exactly like the ... notation, except for the fact that | is the delimiter, instead of the double quotation marks (").

The last subroutine we will look at is **return_error** (see Example 3). Its job is to simply display the error message and exit.

As you will see in this example, gateways can be quite complex and powerful. As long as you know what type of data the external application expects, you can communicate and interface with it. However, there will be times when it won't be that simple.

Let's take a look at a hypothetical airline reservation system, one that allows you to perform transactions such as booking a reservation, deleting a reservation in case of a change in travel plans, checking for alternate flights, and electronically purchasing your ticket. The system will be even more useful to a potential customer if he/she is able to search for resorts around the area of interest, reserve motel rooms, and view the various entertainment facilities.

What's involved in developing such a system? For simplicity sake, let's divide the system into two parts: the transactional part, and the part responsible for providing various pieces of information. The transactional part is more difficult than we first thought. Remember, the Web protocol is stateless! What this means is that the protocol treats each request from a Web client separately from the others. This presents a major challenge: keeping track of requests in such a way as to identify "sessions," so as to maintain "state" between our transactions.[*] In addition to that, the transactional part of our gateway must also interface and communicate with some type of database system in order to provide reservation information to the customer.

---

[*] See the Fall 1996 issue of the *World Wide Web Journal*, *Building an Industrial Strength Web*, for the article entitled "Using Cookies With CGI: Maintaining State on the Web," by Shishir Gundavaram.

Example 3

```
sub return_error
{
    my ($status, $keyword, $message) = @_;

    print <<End_of_Error;
Content-type: text/html
Status: $status $keyword

<HTML>
<HEAD>
    <TITLE>CGI Program - Unexpected Error</TITLE>
</HEAD>
<BODY>
<H1>$keyword</H1>
<HR>
$message
<P>
Please contact $Webmaster for more information.
</BODY>
</HTML>

End_of_Error

    exit (1);
}
```

Now, let's look at the second major part of our gateway: one that provides various pieces of information. What's involved here? Our gateway must be able to perform a variety of complex data lookups, sometimes in multiple databases, coordinate the data and images, and present that to the user. As you can see, this type of gateway is much more complicated than the one presented here.

There is really no limitation to the type of information you can present on the Web, thanks largely to the fact that we can develop gateways that interface with nearly any type of resource. ■

About the Author

Shishir Gundavaram
22 McGrath Highway, Suite 1
Somerville, MA 02143
shishir@ora.com

Shishir Gundavaram is the Chief Technical Architect at JKoss Technologies in Cambridge, Massachusetts, where he is responsible for the development of software products for electronic commerce over the World Wide Web. Shishir graduated from Boston University with a BS in Biomedical Engineering in 1995, and is the author of the O'Reilly & Associates publication *CGI Programming on the World Wide Web.*

Shishir loves to run . . . *fast*. He is looking forward to competing against the world's fastest sprinters in the international Grand Prix, and possibly at the 2000 Olympics in Sydney!

WEB DATABASE CONNECTIVITY WITH SCRIPTING LANGUAGES

Z. Peter Lazar and Peter Holfelder

Abstract

As Web database development moves into the mainstream of corporate software development, inexpensive Web database connectivity becomes a crucial business issue. Scripting languages play an important role in Web database interfacing due to their simplicity and portability. This paper compares three fundamentally different scripting language approaches to interfacing databases and the Web: traditional CGI programming with Perl, Netscape LiveWire 1.0 applications based on JavaScript, and NeXT WebObjects 3.0 applications based on WebScript. These three particular tool sets were chosen because they highlight key design aspects of most Web database tool sets. These aspects include the level of Web server integration, the level of dynamic database integration, the extent to which code is generated automatically, and the code structure. Likewise, the conclusions we draw for these products about performance, data maintainability, portability, extendability and code maintainability are also applicable to other similar products. We first discuss the architecture of the three systems, then based on an example program, we compare the source code and development tool sets required for each system.

System Architecture

This section describes how traditional CGI, LiveWire, and WebObjects applications connect to Web servers and relational databases. Also, it compares and contrasts these system architectures based on performance and data maintainability. Performance, in this context, can be measured by the speed that the Web server can serve Web pages to the browser under light as well as heavy usage. Varying memory, CPU, and file I/O demands of the described Web database systems can affect performance. Data maintainability can be measured by the amount of effort required to ensure that database data seen by Web users is up to date. Data is more maintainable when it is centralized and can be more conveniently updated.

Traditional CGI-Based System Using Perl

CGI programming with Perl is probably the most prevalent method for displaying relational database data on the Web. Perl, by itself, does not contain built-in database connectivity features, but extension products facilitate indirect or direct

database access from Perl. Some of these extensions offer dynamic database access and are quite efficient. In this paper, though, we will discuss the less efficient but more common technique in which the Perl script retrieves database information indirectly from a text file (see Figure 1).

In this approach, the database periodically dumps a table or a view into a tab-delimited text file. The database schedules this dump regularly or triggers it whenever data in the underlying tables change. Unchanging Web pages are implemented by static HTML files, but Perl scripts use tab-delimited text files to dynamically generate any HTML pages based on database data.

This static CGI approach suffers from poor performance because the Web server loads, executes and terminates a new CGI program for each user access. Also, the approach involves extra processing and file I/O whenever data updates require rebuilding the text file.

Large data sets and complex queries especially burden the system because data querying must take place in the CGI program instead of in the database. Rather than delegate complex queries

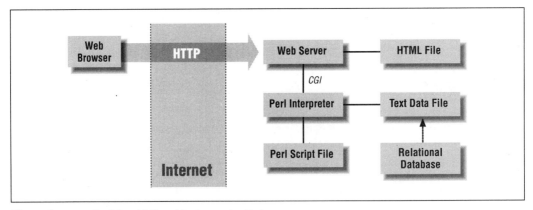

Figure 1   Traditional CGI architecture using Perl

to a relational database on another machine, the CGI program itself must perform such complex operations based on the text file data.

The human time and effort required to maintain data using the static CGI approach presents problems more serious than poor performance, which is usually alleviated by "throwing hardware" at the system. At any time, the copy of the database used by the Perl script may be out of date. Also, the architecture does not allow for direct database update via the Web. Inevitably, system maintainers will need to manually update data

and resolve problems resulting from unsynchronized data.

WebObjects-Based System Using WebScript

Because WebObjects generates HTML dynamically from the database as requested by the browser, it interfaces databases to the Web more effectively than the traditional CGI approach. As shown in Figure 2, the browser requests Web pages from the Web server. Using ISAPI (Internet Server Application Programming Interface),

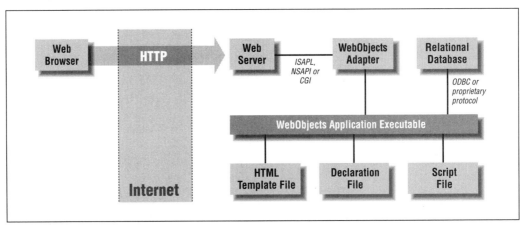

Figure 2   WebObject's architecture

NSAPI (Netscape Server Application Programming Interface), or CGI, the Web server passes the request along to a small program, called the WebObjects Adaptor. The WebObjects adaptor, in turn, starts up the appropriate WebObjects application executable if it is not already running. The WebObjects adaptor serves as a communications bridge between the Web server and the application executable. Finally, the application executable generates HTML based on live data from the database, a user interface defined in the HTML template file, and application objects and logic defined in the declaration and script files. The declaration and script files are written in WebScript, which is a proprietary scripting language based on Objective C.

This approach improves performance because the adaptor and application executable can be distributed over more than one machine. Also, the application executable remains running for multiple user accesses and only the relatively smaller Adaptor program is instantiated with each user access. The lifetime of an application executable is called a *user session*. Developers can configure user sessions to last for a single Web page access or multiple accesses. The application executable helps minimize processing overhead by keeping database connections open for the duration of a session.

Unlike the traditional CGI approach, WebObjects improves data maintenance by directly translating database data to HTML as requested by the browser. If database data changes, the subsequent Web access immediately sees this change. Furthermore, WebObjects improves data maintainability because it enables direct database updating via the Web.

LiveWire-Based System Using JavaScript

LiveWire also dynamically connects databases to the Web, but the architecture is less complex than that of WebObjects (see Figure 3). The user interface in HTML and application logic in JavaScript reside in the same file. LiveWire's JavaScript is identical to the industry-standard client-side JavaScript developed by Netscape and Sun except that it contains database connectivity, state maintenance, and other back-end features. At run-time, the LiveWire manager interprets these files, incorporates live database data, and sends HTML back to the Web browser.

The LiveWire manager runs in the Netscape Web server process and shares a configurable number of open database connections among all users. This requires fewer system resources than WebObjects' multiple short-lived processes. Also, as long as the Web server and database are running, there is no need to establish and terminate costly

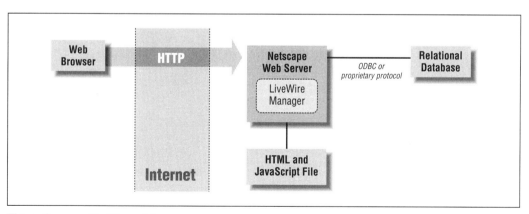

Figure 3   LiveWire architecture

database connections. Of the three discussed Web database connectivity approaches, LiveWire most tightly integrates with the Web server and relational database.

From a data maintainability perspective, LiveWire is superior to the traditional CGI approach but equivalent to WebObjects because both LiveWire and WebObjects dynamically interact with the database.

In summary, tight integration with the Web server and relational database improves performance of a Web database solution. Traditional CGI, WebObjects, and LiveWire represent increasing degrees of integration. Traditional CGI is the least integrated because each Web access spawns a new process and establishes a new database connection. LiveWire is the most integrated because the LiveWire engine runs in the Web server process and shares database connections across all Web accesses.

Traditional CGI, WebObjects, and LiveWire also incur different levels of data maintenance effort. Maintaining database data using the traditional CGI approach can be very expensive because it requires managing and synchronizing multiple copies of data. WebObjects and LiveWire reduce data maintenance costs because data is stored in only one place and accessed dynamically by the Web browser.

Development Tool Set

Traditional CGI, WebObjects, and LiveWire development all involve scripting languages; however, the nature of these scripting languages and their database interfacing roles are quite varied. This section describes these varied development approaches and contrasts them based on portability, extendability, and code maintainability.

Four aspects of portability affect the cost-effectiveness of a particular development tool for Web database connectivity:

- Portability of the development tool across platforms

- Ease of development tool installation

- Portability of the development tool across Web servers

- Portability of the application source code across platforms.

Extendability in this context is a function of the ease with which more sophisticated database operations can be added to an application, and the ease with which a developer can precisely control the format of the output HTML.

The maintainability issues that we examine for this class of applications are the ease of source code maintenance and the ease of splitting work between graphic designers and programmers.

Description of Example Program

In the following sections, we will implement a simple three-page dynamic Web site using Perl, WebObjects, and LiveWire. The first page of the site will be a static HTML page that serves as the home page for the site. It links to the category page, which contains a dynamically generated list of hyperlinked categories such as colors, shapes, and sizes. Each hyperlink contains a key/value pair where the value corresponds to the category ID of the hyperlinked phrase. The item page is reached by following one of the hyperlinks on the second page. It contains a list of items, which is dynamically generated based on the value of the category ID passed to the application. For instance, if the user follows the colors hyperlink, the browser will send an HTTP request with a category ID of 1 back to the application, which will then generate a list of all colors.

The database that underlies the program consists of two tables, CATEGORY and ITEM. The CATEGORY table consist of two fields, CategoryID and CategoryName. CategoryID is a numeric field that is the primary key for the CATEGORY table; Cate-

Example 1   Perl.html

```
<HTML><HEAD>
<!--
///////////////////////////////////////////////////////////////////////
//      Perl.html - Initial Perl Page                                  //
///////////////////////////////////////////////////////////////////////
-->
<TITLE> Initial Perl Page </TITLE></HEAD>
<BODY>
<H2>List Generated Dynamically from Database Using Perl</H2>
<P>Click <A HREF=category.pl>here</A> to generate a list of hyperlinks from the
    CATEGORY table.
</BODY>
</HTML>
```

goryName is a string that describes the category, such as colors, shapes, sizes, etc. The ITEM table consists of three fields, ItemID, CategoryID, and ItemName. ItemID is the key field of the ITEM table, CategoryID is a foreign key to the CATEGORY table, and ItemName is a string that describes an individual item in the category.

Traditional CGI-Based System Using Perl

Perl source code is plain text and thus can be created with any text editor. No special server configuration is needed to run a Perl script under CGI. The Perl version of the site contains three files: a static HTML file for the home page (see

Example 1); *category.pl* (see Example 2), a Perl script to generate the category page; and *item.pl* (Example 3), a Perl script to generate the item page. The scripts obtain data from two tab-delimited text files, which correspond to the two tables used in the WebObjects and LiveWire environments.

category.pl prints the header of an HTML page. Note that the programmer must send the `Content-type: text/html` line explicitly; this is done automatically in WebObjects and LiveWire. After sending the header, the script opens the text file containing the category data. It reads each line of the file, splits the "record" into two

Example 2   category.pl

```
#!/usr/bin/perl
# category.pl - Perl implementation of category page

&print_HTML_header();
# Open the category.dat file.
open (CATEGORY, "category.dat") || &print_error("Error: cannot open CATEGORY table.");

# Read each line of the file, checking for bad records.
$records = -1;
while (!eof(CATEGORY)) {
    $line = <CATEGORY>;
    ($ID, $Category) = split ('\t', $line);
    if (($ID ne "") && ($Category ne "")) {
        $records++;
        $IDs[$records] = $ID;
        $Categories[$records] = $Category;
    }
    else {
```

Example 2 *(continued)*   category.pl

```perl
      $records = -1;
      $errMessage = "Error: bad record in CATEGORY table.";
      last;
   }
}
# Close the category.dat file.
close (CATEGORY);
# Make sure we found some records. If we did, print instructions
# for following the links.
if ($records > -1) {
   print
      "<H2>List of Categories</H2>
      <P>Follow any of the hyperlinks in the list to view a list
         of items in that category.
      <UL>\n";
}
else {
   &print_error($errMessage);
}
# Generate hyperlinks for each of the records.
for ($a = 0; $a <= $records; $a++) {
   print "   <LI><A HREF=\"http://localhost/cgi-bin/w3j/item.pl?ID=",
         $IDs[$a],
         "\">",
         $Categories[$a],
         "</A>\n";
}
# If there were any records to print, close the unordered list, and
# print the HTML footer.
if ($records > -1) {
   print "</UL>\n";
}
&print_HTML_footer();
return 0;

sub print_HTML_header {
   print
      "Content-type: text/html

      <HTML>
      <HEAD>
         <TITLE>A simple database application in Perl: Category page</TITLE>
      </HEAD>
      <BODY>\n";
}

sub print_error {
   $errString = @_;
   print "$errString\n";
   &print_HTML_footer;
   exit;
}
```

Example 2 *(continued)* category.pl

```perl
sub print_HTML_footer {
   print "</BODY>
           </HTML>\n";
}
```

"fields" on the tab character, and checks that each "field" exists. It then places the category ID and category name into separate arrays and closes the text file. If any line contains an error, the script writes an error message to the output HTML and quits. If the data in the file was read successfully, the script dynamically creates a hyperlink for each category. The hyperlinks point to the *item.pl* script and include a category ID value that *item.pl*

will use to select the items to display. Finally, the script prints an HTML footer.

item.pl also prints the header of an HTML page. It then obtains the query string from the CGI QUERY_STRING environment variable and parses it; this is an automatic process in Web-Objects and LiveWire. If the query string parses correctly, the script opens the text file containing the item data. It reads each line of the file, splits

Example 3 item.pl

```perl
#!/usr/bin/perl
# item.pl - Perl implementation of item page
#
# This page displays a list of items that correspond with the category selected
#        from the category page.
&print_HTML_header();
# Retrieve the query string.
$query = $ENV{'QUERY_STRING'};
if ($query eq "") {
   &print_error ("Error: no query sent to script.");
}
# Parse the query string. We are doing the most minimal parsing,
# assuming that there is only one key/value pair, that the key is
# the proper key, and that there are no escaped characters in
# the key or value.
($dummy, $queryID) = split ('=', $query);
if ($dummy ne 'ID' || $queryID eq "") {
   &print_error ("Error: incorrect query.");
}


# Open the item.dat file.
open (ITEM, "item.dat") || print "Error: cannot open ITEM table. \n";
# Read each line of the file, checking for bad records.
$records = -1;
while (!eof(ITEM)) {
   $line = <ITEM>;
   ($ID, $Item) = split ('\t', $line);
   if (($ID ne "") && ($Item ne "")) {
      if ($ID == $queryID) {
         $records++;
         $IDs[$records] = $ID;
         $Items[$records] = $Item;
      }
```

Example 3 *(continued)*   item.pl

```perl
    }
    else {
       $errMessage = "Error: bad record in ITEM table.\n";
       $records = -1;
       last;
    }
}

# Close the category.dat file.
close (ITEM);

# Make sure we found some records. If we did, print instructions
# for following the links.
if ($records > -1) {
   print
       "<H2>List of Items</H2>
       <UL>;
}
else {
    &print_error ('Error: no records found in the ITEM table.');
}

# Generate hyperlinks for each of the records.
for ($a = 0; $a <= $records; $a++) {
    print "   <LI>$Items[$a]\n";
}
print "</UL>\n";
&print_HTML_footer();
return 0;

sub print_HTML_header {
 print
    "Content-type: text/html

    <HTML>
    <HEAD>
       <TITLE>A simple database application in Perl: Item page</TITLE>
    </HEAD>
    <BODY>\n";
}
sub print_error{
    $errString = @_;
    print "$errString\n";
    &print_HTML_footer();
    exit;
}

sub print_HTML_footer {
    print "</BODY>
           </HTML>";
}
```

the "record" into three "fields" on the tab character, and checks that the "fields" exist. If the category ID field matches the category ID passed to the script via the CGI, the item's name is placed into an array. If the data in the file was read successfully, the script creates a list element for each matching item, then prints an HTML footer.

Perl as a development tool has clear advantages in terms of portability. It can be installed on all popular versions of UNIX. This includes the freeware Linux and FreeBSD, which commercial products generally do not support. Perl is also available for 32- and 16-bit versions of Windows, MacOS, VMS, and the IBM AS400. Perl installs automatically on UNIX and many other operating systems, but the installation can be time consuming compared to LiveWire and WebObjects. Perl scripts and other traditional CGI applications have a very high portability across Web servers. Practically all commercial and freeware Web servers in common use have implemented CGI, which is an open standard. Portability of application source code is also very high with Perl. Two issues stand out: ports of Perl to non-UNIX systems may not support Perl features that are closely tied to that operating system (not a major concern with a text-file database), and the specification of pathnames may need to be changed to meet the conventions of the local system.

Using Perl with character-delimited copies of database tables limits its extendability. Without built-in SQL support provided by specialized database connectivity extensions, database operations such as JOINs and complex SELECT statements spanning multiple tables require complex programming. The indirect database access method also makes it difficult to extend the system so that Web users can update database data. Extendability in terms of formatting output HTML is high, however, since traditional CGI programs do not separate HTML formatting from the program itself.

Code is easy to follow in the traditional CGI approach because there are few components and concepts. This simplicity enhances maintainabil-ity—especially when the maintainer is different than the original developer. Developers must pay attention to the internals of the CGI in this approach, however, either by writing the code themselves or selecting a third party library. The maintainability of a traditional CGI application will depend on the features of the language used to implement it. In the case of Perl, its functions and objects aid maintainability. Its main maintainability drawbacks are the somewhat cryptic regular expression matching statements and predefined variables in versions 4 and earlier. In the traditional CGI environment, formatting is not distinct from functionality. The HTML created by the script is partially or completely embedded in the scripts. Consequently, a graphic artist cannot use his or her favorite WYSIWYG editor to modify the user interface layout.

WebObjects-Based System in WebScript

Figure 4 depicts the WebObjects user interface. It provides a visual means of generating WebObjects' underlying template files (*.html), declarations files (*.wod), script files (*.wos), and other underlying data definition files. The partially obscured window in the upper right is the Application window. It is used to create, modify, or delete HTML templates as well as application or session variables. The window in the top middle is the Script window used for editing .wos files. The window in the upper left is the Static Elements panel used to generate static HTML elements. The window in the middle left is the main WebObjects Builder panel. At the top, it allows visually specifying static and dynamic HTML elements. At the bottom, it facilitates creating and modifying bindings. Bindings for a given element can be edited in greater detail using the Inspector at the bottom right. The window at the bottom left is used to define and modify classes of components. In summary, a developer can visually construct a dynamic Web site using the windows displayed in Figure 4 along with a collection of other windows and pop-ups. The format and functionality is stored by the system in automati-

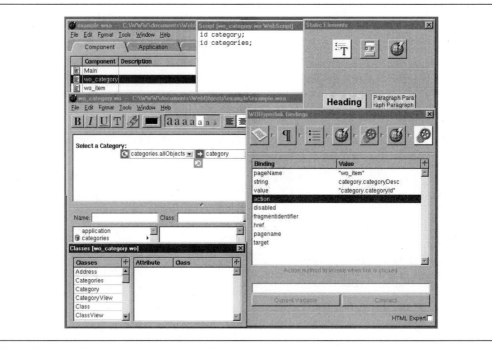

Figure 4   WebObjects developer's interface

cally generated WebScript files such as those listed below.

Main.html (shown in Example 4) is the first page of the WebObjects example application. It is an HTML template that is processed and sent to the browser by the application executable (shown earlier in Figure 2). The *Main.wod* declarations file defines the `CategoryPage` object referenced

in *Main.html* and maps it to the action `WOHyperlink`:

```
CategoryPage: WOHyperlink {string =
    "here"; pageName = "wo_
    category"; };
```

`WOHyperlink` refers to the next dynamic page, wo_category. The *wo_category.html* template file (shown in Example 5) defines the static user

Example 4   Main.html

```
<HTML>
<HEAD>
  <TITLE>Initial WebObjects Page </TITLE>
</HEAD>
<BODY>
<H2>List Generated Dynamically from Database Using WebObjects</H2>
<P>Click <WEBOBJECT NAME=CategoryPage></WEBOBJECT> to generate a list of hyperlinks
    from the CATEGORY table.</P>
</BODY>
</HTML>
```

Example 5   wo_category.html

```
<HTML><HEAD>
<!--

////////////////////////////////////////////////////////////////////////////
// wo_category.html - WebObjects Implementation                            //
//                                                                          //
//   This page displays a list of categories from the CATEGORY table.      //
//   The category names are hyperlinked and lead to a page with associated//
//   items from the ITEM table.                                            //
////////////////////////////////////////////////////////////////////////////

-->
<TITLE>Categories</TITLE>
</HEAD><BODY>
<P> <B>Select a Category:</B>
<CENTER>
<UL>
<WEBOBJECT item=category list=categorys.allObjects name=CategoryList
    wbwebobjectclass=WORepetition>
<WEBOBJECT name=ItemPage value=category.categoryId wbwebobjectclass=WOString>
    </WEBOBJECT><BR>
</WEBOBJECT>
</UL>
</CENTER>
</BODY>
</HTML>
```

interface components of the next page in the example application.

It references two objects defined in the *wo_category.wod* declarations file:

```
CategoryList: WORepetition {item =
    category; list = categorys.
    allObjects; };
ItemPage: WOHyperlink {string =
    category.categoryName; pageName
    = "wo_item"; };
```

The *wo_category.html* template file also references two variables defined in the *wo_category.wos* script file:

```
id category;
id categorys;
```

CategoryList in *wo_category.wod* is the list of "categories" containing the element "item." ItemPage is a hyperlink attribute of the category variable that references the next Web page, *wo_item.*

The *wo_category.wos* script file contains declarations for the category and categories variables. Script files for more sophisticated WebObjects applications usually also contain functions that interact with objects defined in the declarations files.

The two listings *wo_category.woo* (see Example 6) and *category.plist* (Example 7) are also automatically generated by WebObjects, but it is unlikely that a developer would modify these files manually. They define the relationships and interface between the category and categories objects and the corresponding database table

WebObjects systems are portable across Windows NT, several UNIX platforms, OPENSTEP, and NEXTSTEP. They support ODBC as well as the proprietary database protocols of Oracle, Sybase, Informix, and DB2. Installation of the development tool is straightforward, but it contains many elements. Like the traditional CGI approach, but unlike LiveWire, WebObjects will

Example 6   wo_category.woo

```
{
    NameCounts = {WORepetition = 2; WOString = 4; };
    Types = {};
    encoding = NSWindowsCP1252StringEncoding;
    variables = {
        category = {TypeName = Category; };
        categorys = {
            AutoInitialized = 1;
            TypeName = Categories;
            initialValue = {
                class = WODisplayGroup;
                dataSource = {
                    class = EODatabaseDataSource;
                    editingContext = session.defaultEditingContext;
                    fetchSpecification = {class = EOFetchSpecification; entityName =
    Category; isDeep = YES; };
                };
                fetchesOnLoad = YES;
                formatForLikeQualifier = "%@*";
                numberOfObjectsPerBatch = 0;
                selectsFirstObjectAfterFetch = YES;
            };
        };
    };
}
```

work with its own built-in Web server as well as with Netscape, Microsoft IIS, NCSA, and CERN servers. The application source code, being an interpreted scripting language, is very portable across platforms. In short, WebObjects is very portable.

WebObjects functionality is system generated. Therefore, extendability is limited by the features and versatility of the code generator. Developers can program features unsupported by the code generator directly into the WebScript definition and script files, but this circumvents the code generator and reduces its usefulness.

Another extendability weakness is inflexible data formatting due to lack of conditional logic or looping constructs in the HTML template files. Other than HTML, the template files contain only placeholders that are filled in at runtime by the

Example 7   category.plist

```
{
    attributes = (
        {
            allowsNull = Y;
            columnName = category_name;
            externalType = TEXT;
            name = categoryName;
            valueClassName = NSString;
            width = 220;
        },
        {
            allowsNull = Y;
```

Example 7 *(continued)* category.plist

```
            columnName = category_id;
            externalType = COUNTER;
            name = categoryId;
            precision = 10;
            valueClassName = NSNumber;
            valueType = i;
        }
    );
    attributesUsedForLocking = (categoryId, categoryName);
    classProperties = (categoryId, categoryName);
    externalName = CATEGORY;
    name = Category;
    primaryKeyAttributes = (categoryId);
}
```

application executable. Only a limited number of automatically generated functions for filling in the placeholder exist, and they support only a limited number of display formats. Any variations must be programmed manually, outside the code generator.

The WebObjects application generator's purpose is to improve maintainability by reducing the need to manually code. In practicality, however, the application generator transfers the complexity of coding to the code generator's user interface. Consequently, a developer needs to become an expert at the complex user interface or else try to decipher machine-generated code to understand an unfamiliar WebScript system. This lessens system maintainability. Additionally, WebObjects user interface and functionality components are defined across separate user interface panels and WebScript files. This reduces maintainability by making it necessary to look in many different places to understand how one part of the system operates.

Unlike the CGI-Perl approach, WebObjects does separate "look and feel" from functionality by providing its own WYSIWYG HTML editor. This improves maintainability because the graphic artist can modify content without knowing how to code. However, it requires that the graphic artist use WebObjects' WYSIWYG editor rather than other commercially available products.

LiveWire-Based System in JavaScript

LiveWire source code, like Perl, is plain text. It is either embedded within special tags in an otherwise standard HTML file or placed by itself in plain text files. LiveWire source code must be compiled into a proprietary format to be used by the application manager of the Netscape server, which requires some simple configuration.

The LiveWire source code is divided into four HTML files, one for each of the three pages that the user will see, plus a LiveWire "initial page." The initial page (see Example 8) is processed by

Example 8   project.html

```
<SERVER>
////////////////////////////////////////////////////////////////////////
//      project.html - LiveWire Implementation                         //
//                                                                      //
//  Example applications project file.  Establishes database connection //
//  shared for all users of example application.                        //
////////////////////////////////////////////////////////////////////////
```

Example 8 *(continued)*   project.html

```
//  Establish a Connection to the EXAMPLE Database for ALL Clients
if ( !database.connected() ) {
        project.lock();
        database.connect("ODBC","EXAMPLE","admin","","");
        if(!database.connected()) {
                write("<p>Database connection failed");
        }
        project.unlock();
}
</SERVER>
```

the Web server when the application is first accessed by a user. It typically contains code to connect to databases and definitions for properties of LiveWire's Project object, which exists as long as the application is running on the server. LiveWire applications run in a separate server thread and are not terminated when there are no connections, so the Project object persists as long as the Web server is running. The initial page consists entirely of server-side JavaScript code. It checks for an existing database connection. If none exists, which is the expected result, it locks the Project object, so that no other clients can change any properties of the Project object. The application then establishes the connection to the database (in this case via an ODBC connection to a SQL Server database running on a dedicated server) and unlocks the Project object. The initial page generates HTML only if the connection to the database fails.

The home page for our application (shown in Example 9) is a static HTML page that contains a single hyperlink to the category page. The category page (Example 10) contains server-side JavaScript between a static HTML header and footer. After serving the header, the application checks for the existence of a database connection. If a connection exists, the application begins a database transaction and executes a predefined SQL query. LiveWire places the results of the query into a database cursor object. The application then dynamically generates a hyperlink for each record returned in the cursor. Finally, the application closes the cursor, commits the database transaction, and sends the rest of the static HTML.

When the item page is accessed, LiveWire automatically decodes the key-value pairs in the CGI transaction and makes them properties of its Request object. The item page uses the value of

Example 9   LiveWire.html

```
<HTML><HEAD>
<!--
/////////////////////////////////////////////////////////////////////////////
//      LiveWire.html - LiveWire Application's Home Page                    //
/////////////////////////////////////////////////////////////////////////////
-->
<TITLE> Initial LiveWire Page </TITLE></HEAD>
<BODY>
<H2>List Generated Dynamically from Database Using LiveWire</H2>
<P>Click <A HREF=lw_category.html>here</A> to generate a list of hyperlinks from the
    CATEGORY table.
</BODY>
</HTML>
```

Example 10   lw_category.html

```
<HTML><HEAD>
<SERVER>
////////////////////////////////////////////////////////////////////////////
//  lw_category.html - LiveWire Implementation
//
//  This page displays displays a list of categories from the CATEGORY table.
//  The category names are hyperlinked and lead to a page with associated
//  items from the ITEM table.
////////////////////////////////////////////////////////////////////////////
</SERVER>
<TITLE>Categories</TITLE>
</HEAD><BODY>
<P> <B>Select a Category:</B>
<CENTER><UL>
<SERVER>
if ( database.connected() ) {
        database.beginTransaction();
        qs = "SELECT category_id, category_name from CATEGORY";
        results = database.cursor( qs );
        while(results.next())
        {
          write( "<LI><A HREF=\"lw_item.html?category_id="+results.category_
    id+"\">"+results.category_name+"</A>\n");
        }
        results.close();
        database.commitTransaction();
}
else {
        write("<p>Database connection failed");
}
</SERVER></UL>
</CENTER>
</BODY></HTML>
```

the Request object's CategoryID property (which directly corresponds to the CategoryID passed to the item page via the URL on the category page) to generate a SQL query. LiveWire places the result of the query into a cursor object and dynamically generates an item in an unordered list for each record returned in the cursor. Finally, the application closes the cursor, commits the database transaction, and sends the rest of the static HTML.

The LiveWire application environment is portable between Windows NT and several UNIX platforms. It installs quickly and automatically, and configuring and running applications under the environment is a simple process. In addition, the JavaScript source code is fully portable between all supported platforms (but pathname references must adhere to local pathnaming conventions). LiveWire's only portability drawback is that it can be used only with the Netscape Enterprise and FastTrack servers.

LiveWire's sophisticated database features and programmatic development approach make it very extendable. SQL support gives LiveWire developers the ability to perform sophisticated database functions, including JOINs, complex multi-table SELECTs, INSERTs, UPDATEs, and DELETEs. Integration of database cursors, functions, and looping constructs into the HTML file give LiveWire programmers detailed control over the HTML formatting of database data. Powerful database functionality combined with precise control of the appearance of HTML output enhances extendability.

LiveWire's support of JavaScript functions and user-defined objects helps developers produce clear, maintainable code. Also, in LiveWire, HTML formatting is distinct from functionality. All JavaScript code is embedded in <SERVER> and </SERVER> tags so that it does not interfere with WYSIWYG HTML editors. Consequently, a graphic artist does not have to use coding tools or know how to code in JavaScript in order to modify user interface layout.

All three discussed approaches to Web database connectivity require a minimum of code modification when ported to other platforms, and while ease of development tool installation varies, it is a one-time cost. A traditional CGI application using Perl can be run on a large number of platforms with a wide variety of Web servers. WebObjects applications run on a smaller number of platforms but can also run on a wide variety of Web servers. LiveWire applications run on a number of platforms (more than WebObjects and less than Perl) but can only be used with Netscape servers.

CGI applications using Perl are difficult to extend with complex database operations, but it is easier to extend the formatting of data output, since the developer has complete control over where and how HTML output is generated within the script. WebObjects built-in database functionality makes it easy to extend the database capabilities of an application, but the lack of flow control in HTML templates makes data output formats difficult to extend. LiveWire shows good extendability in both areas, with both built-in database functionality and precise control over data output.

Perl, as a structured programming language, has all of the features necessary to write clear, maintainable code. In Perl, however, there is no clear boundary between static and dynamic HTML in the script, making it difficult to split tasks between developers and graphics professionals. WebObjects, as a visual application development environment, requires code maintainers to learn a user interface and search several different types of files to understand an application. WebObjects places a clear boundary between static and dynamic HTML, but forces both developers and graphics professionals to learn a proprietary tool. LiveWire features both structured programming and a clear boundary between static and dynamic HTML.

Conclusion

An effective Web database architecture should exhibit the characteristics of high performance and data maintainability; and its source code should show portability, extendability, and code maintainability.

Tighter integration of the Web server and application improves performance but at the cost of portability. However, it does not restrict portability among the supported platforms. For example, the LiveWire manager performs well due to its tight integration with the Netscape Web server but is not portable to other servers. Perhaps more importantly, persistent database connections improve performance since they reduce the high costs of establishing and terminating database connections.

Consolidation of source code into fewer files, with a clear demarcation between static HTML and executable code, aids code maintainability and promotes the separation of tasks between graphic artists programmers. Consolidation of source code and formatting also enhances extendability compared to the HTML template/placeholder approach used by WebObjects. The ability to pass native SQL and stored procedures directly to a database engine and retrieve results also improves extendability and, when combined with live database connections, results in high data maintainability. ∎

References

1. Deep, J., and P. Holfelder. *Developing CGI Applications with Perl,* John Wiley and Sons: New York, 1996.

2. Varela, C., D. Nekhayev, P. Chandrasekharan, C. Krishnan, V. Govindan, D. Modgil, S. Siddiqui, and D. Lebedenko. DB: Browsing Object-Oriented Databases over the Web. *World Wide Web Journal,* vol. 1, issue 1(Winter 1996). Available at *http://www.w3.org/pub/WWW/Journal/1/ varela.282/paper/282.html*

3. Netscape Communications Corporation. "Netscape Enterprise Server. A WWW Server," work in progress, available at *http://www.netscape.com/ comprod/server_central/index.html*

4. NeXT Corporation. "WebObjects Documentation," work in progress, available at *http://www. next.com/Pubs/Documents/WebObjects/ WebObjectsTOC.html*

5. Netscape Communications Corporation. "Netscape DevEdge—Support," work in progress, available at *http://developer.netscape.com/support/faqs/ index.html*

6. Morgan, M. "Special Edition: Using Netscape LiveWire," Que Corporation, 1996.

7. NeXT Corporation. "Federal WebObjects Enterprise Seminar Notes."

About the Authors

Z. Peter Lazar

BTG Incorporated
3877 Fairfax Ridge Road, 3K
Fairfax, VA 22030-7448
plazar@btg.com
http://www.btg.com/~plazar/

Z. Peter Lazar is a senior engineer with BTG and the designer of many Web systems. He received a Master of Computer Science degree from the University of Virginia in 1992.

Peter Holfelder

BTG Incorporated
3877 Fairfax Ridge Road, 3K
Fairfax, VA 22030-7448
pholfelder@btg.com

Peter Holfelder is a Web developer at BTG who builds Web back-ends in Perl and JavaScript. He received a B.S. degree in Physics from the Rensselaer Polytechnic Institute in 1990.

More Titles from O'Reilly

Developing Web Content

Building Your Own WebSite

By Susan B. Peck & Stephen Arrants
1st Edition July 1996
514 pages, ISBN 1-56592-232-8

This is a hands-on reference for Windows® 95 and Windows NT™ desktop users who want to host their own site on the Web or on a corporate intranet. You'll also learn how to connect your web to information in other Windows applications, such as word processing documents and databases. Packed with examples and tutorials on every aspect of Web management. Includes the highly acclaimed WebSite™ 1.1 on CD-ROM.

Web Client Programming with Perl

By Clinton Wong
1st Edition March 1997 (est.)
250 pages (est.), ISBN 1-56592-214-X

Web Client Programming with Perl teaches you how to extend scripting skills to the Web. This book teaches you the basics of how browsers communicate with servers and how to write your own customized Web clients to automate common tasks. It is intended for those who are motivated to develop software that offers a more flexible and dynamic response than a standard Web browser.

JavaScript: The Definitive Guide, Second Edition

By David Flanagan
2nd Edition January 1997
672 pages, ISBN 1-56592-234-4

In this second edition, the author of the best-selling, *Java in a Nutshell* describes the server-side JavaScript application, LiveWire, developed by Netscape and Sun Microsystems.

Using LiveWire, developers can easily convert JavaScript applications and any HTML pages containing JavaScript code, into platform-independent byte codes ready to run on any Netscape 2.0 Server. The book describes the version of JavaScript shipped with Navigator 2.0, 2.0.1, and 2.0.2, and also the much-changed version of JavaScript shipped with Navigator 3.0. LiveConnect, used for communication between JavaScript and Java applets, and addresses commonly encountered bugs on JavaScript objects.

HTML: The Definitive Guide, Second Edition

By Chuck Musciano & Bill Kennedy
2nd Edition April 1997 (est.)
520 pages (est.), ISBN 1-56592-235-2

The second edition covers the most up-to-date version of the HTML standard (the proposed HTML version 3.2), Netscape 4.0 and Internet Explorer 3.0, plus all the common extensions, especially Netscape extensions. The authors address all the current version's elements, explaining how they work and interact with each other. Includes a style guide that helps you to use HTML to accomplish a variety of tasks, from simple online documentation to complex marketing and sales presentations. Readers of the first edition can find the updates for the second edition on the Web at www.ora.com.

Designing for the Web: Getting Started in a New Medium

By Jennifer Niederst with Edie Freedman
1st Edition April 1996
180 pages, ISBN 1-56592-165-8

Designing for the Web gives you the basics you need to hit the ground running. Although geared toward designers, it covers information and techniques useful to anyone who wants to put graphics online. It explains how to work with HTML documents from a designer's point of view, outlines special problems with presenting information online, and walks through incorporating images into Web pages, with emphasis on resolution and improving efficiency.

WebMaster in a Nutshell

By Stephen Spainhour & Valerie Quercia
1st Edition October 1996
378 pages, ISBN 1-56592-229-8

Web content providers and administrators have many sources of information, both in print and online. *WebMaster in a Nutshell* pulls it all together into one slim volume—for easy desktop access.

This quick-reference covers HTML, CGI, Perl, HTTP, server configuration, and tools for Web administration.

O'REILLY™

TO ORDER: **800-998-9938** • **order@ora.com** • **http://www.ora.com/**
OUR PRODUCTS ARE AVAILABLE AT A BOOKSTORE OR SOFTWARE STORE NEAR YOU.
FOR INFORMATION: **800-998-9938** • **707-829-0515** • **info@ora.com**

Security

Practical UNIX & Internet Security, 2nd Edition

By Simson Garfinkel & Gene Spafford
2nd Edition April 1996
1004 pages, ISBN 1-56592-148-8

This second edition of the classic *Practical UNIX Security* is a complete rewrite of the original book. It's packed with twice the pages and offers even more practical information for UNIX users and administrators. In it you'll find coverage of features of many types of UNIX systems, including SunOS, Solaris, BSDI, AIX, HP-UX, Digital UNIX, Linux, and others. Contents include UNIX and security basics, system administrator tasks, network security, and appendixes containing checklists and helpful summaries.

Building Internet Firewalls

By D. Brent Chapman & Elizabeth D. Zwicky
1st Edition September 1995
546 pages, ISBN 1-56592-124-0

More than a million systems are now connected to the Internet, and something like 15 million people in 100 countries on all seven continents use Internet services. More than 100 million email messages are exchanged each day, along with countless files, documents, and audio and video images. Although businesses are rushing headlong to get connected to the Internet, the security risks have never been greater.

Some of these risks have been around since the early days of networking—password attacks (guessing them or cracking them via password dictionaries and cracking programs), denial of service, and exploiting known security holes. Some risks are newer and even more dangerous—packet sniffers, IP (Internet Protocol) forgery, and various types of hijacking. Firewalls are a very effective way to protect your system from these Internet security threats.

Building Internet Firewalls is a practical guide to building firewalls on the Internet. If your site is connected to the Internet, or if you're considering getting connected, you need this book. It describes a variety of firewall approaches and architectures and discusses how you can build packet filtering and proxying solutions at your site. It also contains a full discussion of how to configure Internet services (e.g., FTP, SMTP, Telnet) to work with a firewall, as well as a complete list of resources, including the location of many publicly available firewall construction tools.

PGP: Pretty Good Privacy

By Simson Garfinkel
1st Edition January 1995
430 pages, ISBN 1-56592-098-8

PGP is a freely available encryption program that protects the privacy of files and electronic mail. It uses powerful public key cryptography and works on virtually every platform. This book is both a readable technical user's guide and a fascinating behind-the-scenes look at cryptography and privacy. It describes how to use PGP and provides background on cryptography, *PGP*'s history, battles over public key cryptography patents and U.S. government export restrictions, and public debates about privacy and free speech.

Computer Crime

By David Icove, Karl Seger & William VonStorch
(Consulting Editor Eugene H. Spafford)
1st Edition August 1995
462 pages, ISBN 1-56592-086-4

This book is for anyone who needs to know what today's computer crimes look like, how to prevent them, and how to detect, investigate, and prosecute them if they do occur. It contains basic computer security information as well as guidelines for investigators, law enforcement, and system administrators. It includes computer-related statutes and laws, a resource summary, detailed papers on computer crime, and a sample search warrant.

Computer Security Basics

By Deborah Russell & G.T. Gangemi, Sr.
1st Edition July 1991
464 pages, ISBN 0-937175-71-4

Computer Security Basics provides a broad introduction to the many areas of computer security and a detailed description of current security standards. This handbook uses simple terms to describe complicated concepts like trusted systems, encryption, and mandatory access control, and it contains a thorough, readable introduction to the "Orange Book."

Network Administration

Getting Connected:
The Internet at 56K and Up

By Kevin Dowd
1st Edition June 1996
424 pages, ISBN 1-56592-154-2

Getting Connected is a complete guide for businesses, schools, and other organizations who want to connect their computers to the Internet. This book covers everything you need to know to make informed decisions, from helping you figure out which services you really need to providing down-to-earth explanations of telecommunication options, such as frame relay, ISDN, and leased lines. Once you're online, it shows you how to set up basic Internet services, such as a World Wide Web server. Tackles issues for PC, Macintosh, and UNIX platforms.

DNS and BIND, 2nd Edition

By Paul Albitz & Cricket Liu
2nd Edition December 1996
446 pages, ISBN 1-56592-236-0

This book is a complete guide to the Internet's Domain Name System (DNS) and the Berkeley Internet Name Domain (BIND) software, the UNIX implementation of DNS. This second edition covers Bind 4.8.3, which is included in most vendor implementations today, as well as Bind 4.9.3, the potential future standard.

Using & Managing UUCP

By Ed Ravin, Tim O'Reilly, Dale Dougherty & Grace Todino
1st Edition September 1996
424 pages, ISBN 1-56592-153-4

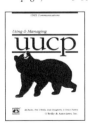

Using & Managing UUCP describes, in one volume, this popular communications and file transfer program. UUCP is very attractive to computer users with limited resources, a small machine, and a dial-up connection. This book covers Taylor UUCP, the latest versions of HoneyDanBer UUCP, and the specific implementation details of UUCP versions shipped by major UNIX vendors.

TCP/IP Network Administration

By Craig Hunt
1st Edition August 1992
502 pages, ISBN 0-937175-82-X

TCP/IP Network Administration is a complete guide to setting up and running a TCP/IP network for practicing system administrators. The book covers setting up your network, configuring important network applications including sendmail, and issues in troubleshooting and security. It covers both BSD and System V TCP/IP implementations.

Networking Personal Computers with TCP/IP

By Craig Hunt
1st Edition July 1995
408 pages, ISBN 1-56592-123-2

This book offers practical information as well as detailed instructions for attaching PCs to a TCP/IP network and its UNIX servers. It discusses the challenges you'll face and offers general advice on how to deal with them, provides basic TCP/IP configuration information for some of the popular PC operating systems, covers advanced configuration topics and configuration of specific applications such as email, and includes a chapter on NetWare, the most popular PC LAN system software.

sendmail, 2nd Edition

By Bryan Costales, with Eric Allman
2nd Edition Winter 1997
950 pages (est.), ISBN 1-56592-222-0

This second edition of the *sendmail* Nutshell Handbook covers sendmail version 8.8. This cross-referenced edition offers an expanded tutorial, solution-oriented examples, and new topics such as the #error delivery agent, sendmail's exit values, MIME headers, and how to set up and use the user database, mailertable, and smrsh.

Software

WebSite Professional ™

By O'Reilly & Associates, Inc.
Documentation by Susan Peck
1st Edition June 1996
Includes 3 books, ISBN 1-56592-174-7

Designed for the sophisticated user, *WebSite Professional*™ is a complete Web server solution. *WebSite Professional* contains all of *WebSite*'s award-winning features, including remote administration, virtual servers for creating multiple home pages, wizards to automate common tasks, a search tool for Web indexing, and a graphical outline fo Web documents and links for managing your site. New with *WebSite Professional:* support for SSL and S-HTTP, the premier Web encryption security protocols; the WebSite Application Programming Interface (WSAPI); Cold Fusion Standard, a powerful development tool for dynamic linking of database information into your Web documents; and support for client and server-side Java programming.

PolyForm™

By O'Reilly & Associates, Inc.
Documentation by John Robert Boynton
1st Edition May 1996
Two diskettes & 146-pg book
ISBN 1-56592-182-8

PolyForm™ is a powerful 32-bit Web forms tool that helps you easily build and manage interactive Web pages. *PolyForm*'s interactive forms make it easy and fun for users to respond to the contents of your Web with their own feedback, ideas, or requests for more information. *PolyForm*™ lets you collect, process, and respond to each user's specific input. Best of all, forms that once required hours of complicated programming can be created in minutes because *PolyForm*™ automatically handles all of the CGI programming for processing form contents.

Statisphere™

By O'Reilly & Associates, Inc.
Documentation by Jay York
1st Edition May 1997 (est.)
2 diskettes & a 135-page book,
ISBN 1-56592-233-6

Statisphere™ is a Web traffic analyzer that provides precise, graphical reporting on your Web server's usage. Easy-to-read, browser-based reports deliver real-time profiles and long-term trend analysis on who's visiting your site and what they're reading. Whether you're tracking traffic rates for advertising, or steering Web development efforts to where they'll have the most impact, Statisphere gives you the answers you need to make the right decisions about your Web site.

Building Your Own WebSite™

By Susan B. Peck & Stephen Arrants
1st Edition July 1996, 514 pages, 1-56592-232-8

Building Your Own WebSite™ is a hands-on reference for Windows® 95 and Windows NT™ users who want to host a site on the Web or on a corporate intranet. This step-by-step guide will have you creating live web pages in minutes. You'll also learn how to connect your web to information in other Windows applications. *Building Your Own WebSite* is packed with examples and tutorials on every aspect of web management. You also get the highly acclaimed WebSite 1.1 on CD-ROM.

Building Your Own Web Conferences™

By Susan B. Peck & Beverly Murray Scherf
1st Edition March 1997
270 pages, Includes CD-ROM, 1-56592-279-4

Web-based conferencing is rapidly gaining converts from the ranks of computer bulletin board subscribers and members of online service discussion forums. Why? Because web conferences offer any user with a web browser a richer, more accessible set of discussion tools without the hassle of newsreader programs or the cost of proprietary online service memberships. Web conference administrators can easily create an unlimited number of free Internet- or intranet-accessible discussions, allowing anyone on the Web — or just a select few — to participate. *Building Your Own Web Conferences* is a complete guide for Windows 95 and Windows NT webmasters on how to set up and manage dynamic web discussion groups that will keep users coming back to your site.

Building Your Own Win-CGI Programs

By Robert Denny, Andrew Schulman &
Ron Petrusha
1st Edition April 1997 (est.) 350 pages (est.),
Includes CD-ROM, 1-56592-215-8

CGI (Common Gateway Interface) is the "glue" between web servers and custom web-server applications. This book takes an in-depth look at the Windows CGI, or Win-CGI. Win-CGI lets you create a web interface between Windows-based applications, such as relational databases or spreadsheets, and Windows web servers like WebSite Professional and Microsoft IIS. Win-CGI programs can be written in a variety of languages, including Visual Basic, C++, and C. Co-written by Bob Denny, the inventor of Win-CGI, this book provides numerous examples and sample code for these languages.

O'REILLY™

TO ORDER: **800-998-9938** • order@ora.com • http://www.ora.com/
OUR PRODUCTS ARE AVAILABLE AT A BOOKSTORE OR SOFTWARE STORE NEAR YOU.
FOR INFORMATION: **800-998-9938** • **707-829-0515** • info@ora.com

Web Server Administration

Apache: The Definitive Guide

By Ben Laurie & Peter Laurie
1st Edition Winter 1997
300 pages (est.), ISBN 1-56592-250-6

Despite all the hype about Netscape, Apache is far and away the most widely used Web server platform in the world. It runs on about half the world's existing Web sites and is rapidly increasing market share. *Apache: The Definitive Guide* is the only complete guide on the market today describing how to obtain, set up, and secure the Apache software. Officially authorized by the Apache Group, this book is the definitive documentation for the world's most popular Web server.

Contents include:

- The history of the Apache Group
- Obtaining and compiling the server
- Configuring and running Apache, including such topics as directory structures, virtual hosts, and CGI programming
- The Apache Module API
- Apache security
- The Apache manuals
- A complete list of configuration directives
- A complete demo of a sample Web site

UNIX Web Server Administration

By John Leavitt
1st Edition Winter 1997
325 pages (est.), ISBN 1-56592-217-4

With our increasing dependence on Web sites for our daily work, the Web server has emerged as one of the most crucial services a company can offer. When the server is slow, customers are frustrated. When the server or network is down, customers are turned away.

UNIX Web Server Administration tells Web administrators how to keep a server running smoothly. This book not only covers Apache, the most popular server on the Internet, but also the NCSA, CERN, and Netscape servers.

Managing Internet Information Services

By Cricket Liu, Jerry Peek, Russ Jones, Bryan Buus & Adrian Nye
1st Edition December 1994
668 pages, ISBN 1-56592-062-7

Managing Internet Information Services describes how to create services for the millions of Internet users. By setting up Internet servers for World Wide Web, Gopher, FTP, Finger, Telnet, WAIS (Wide Area Information Services), or email services, anyone with a suitable computer and Internet connection can become an "Internet Publisher."

Services on the Internet allow almost instant distribution and frequent updates of any kind of information. You can provide services to employees of your own company (solving the information distribution problems of spread-out companies), or you can serve the world. Perhaps you'd like to create an Internet service equivalent to the telephone company's directory assistance. Or maybe you're the Species Survival Commission, and you'd like your plans online; this book describes a prototype service the authors created to make SSC's endangered species Action Plans viewable worldwide. Whatever you have in mind can be done. This book tells you how.

Creating a service can be a big job, involving more than one person. This book separates the setup and maintenance of server software from tdata management, so that a team can divide responsibilities. Sections and chapters on data management, a role we call the Data Librarian, are marked with a special icon.

"Excellent book . . . carefully written, informative and readable . . . [well] organized. . . . I 'm enjoying it considerably. I picked it up to flip through—I'm a writer of Internet books myself, and I do a lot of 'been there, done that' when I approach an Internet book—and after an hour or so, I discovered I was actually reading the book. I have even taken the step of . . . using my post-it-notes tabs to mark the good stuff."
—Jill Ellsworth, Ph.D., Author of *The Internet Business Book, Education on the Internet, and Marketing on the Internet*

How to stay in touch with O'Reilly

1. Visit Our Award-Winning Web Site

http://www.ora.com/

★ "Top 100 Sites on the Web" —*PC Magazine*
★ "Top 5% Web sites" —*Point Communications*
★ "3-Star site" —*The McKinley Group*

Our web site contains a library of comprehensive product information (including book excerpts and tables of contents), downloadable software, background articles, interviews with technology leaders, links to relevant sites, book cover art, and more. File us in your Bookmarks or Hotlist!

2. Join Our Email Mailing Lists

New Product Releases
To receive automatic email with brief descriptions of all new O'Reilly products as they are released, send email to: **listproc@online.ora.com**
Put the following information in the first line of your message (*not* in the Subject field):
subscribe ora-news "Your Name" of "Your Organization" (for example: subscribe ora-news Kris Webber of Fine Enterprises)

O'Reilly Events
If you'd also like us to send information about trade show events, special promotions, and other O'Reilly events, send email to: **listproc@online.ora.com**
Put the following information in the first line of your message (*not* in the Subject field):
subscribe ora-events "Your Name" of "Your Organization"

3. Get Examples from Our Books via FTP

There are two ways to access an archive of example files from our books:

Regular FTP
- ftp to:
  ftp.ora.com
  (login: anonymous
  password: your email address)
- Point your web browser to:
  ftp://ftp.ora.com/

FTPMAIL
- Send an email message to:
  ftpmail@online.ora.com
  (Write "help" in the message body)

4. Visit Our Gopher Site
- Connect your gopher to:
  gopher.ora.com

- Point your web browser to:
  gopher://gopher.ora.com/

- Telnet to:
  gopher.ora.com
  login: gopher

5. Contact Us via Email

order@ora.com
To place a book or software order online. Good for North American and international customers.

subscriptions@ora.com
To place an order for any of our newsletters or periodicals.

books@ora.com
General questions about any of our books.

software@ora.com
For general questions and product information about our software. Check out O'Reilly Software Online at **http://software.ora.com/** for software and technical support information. Registered O'Reilly software users send your questions to: **website-support@ora.com**

cs@ora.com
For answers to problems regarding your order or our products.

booktech@ora.com
For book content technical questions or corrections.

proposals@ora.com
To submit new book or software proposals to our editors and product managers.

international@ora.com
For information about our international distributors or translation queries. For a list of our distributors outside of North America check out:
http://www.ora.com/www/order/country.html

O'Reilly & Associates, Inc.
101 Morris Street, Sebastopol, CA 95472 USA
TEL   707-829-0515 or 800-998-9938
           (6am to 5pm PST)
FAX   707-829-0104

O'REILLY™

Titles from O'Reilly

Please note that upcoming titles are displayed in italic.

WEBPROGRAMMING

Apache: The Definitive Guide
Building Your Own Web Conferences
Building Your Own Website
Building Your Own Win-CGI Programs
CGI Programming for the World Wide Web
Designing for the Web
HTML: The Definitive Guide
JavaScript: The Definitive Guide, 2nd Ed.
Learning Perl
Programming Perl, 2nd Ed.
Mastering Regular Expressions
WebMaster in a Nutshell
Web Security & Commerce
Web Client Programming with Perl
World Wide Web Journal

USING THE INTERNET

Smileys
The Future Does Not Compute
The Whole Internet User's Guide & Catalog
The Whole Internet for Win 95
Using Email Effectively
Bandits on the Information Superhighway

JAVA SERIES

Exploring Java
Java AWT Reference
Java Fundamental Classes Reference
Java in a Nutshell
Java Language Reference
Java Network Programming
Java Threads
Java Virtual Machine

SOFTWARE

WebSite™ 1.1
WebSite Professional™
Building Your Own Web Conferences
WebBoard™
PolyForm™
Statisphere™

SONGLINE GUIDES

NetActivism   *NetResearch*
Net Law   *NetSuccess*
NetLearning   *NetTravel*
Net Lessons

SYSTEM ADMINISTRATION

Building Internet Firewalls
Computer Crime: A Crimefighter's Handbook
Computer Security Basics
DNS and BIND, 2nd Ed.
Essential System Administration, 2nd Ed.
Getting Connected: The Internet at 56K and Up
Internet Server Administration with Windows NT
Linux Network Administrator's Guide
Managing Internet Information Services
Managing NFS and NIS
Networking Personal Computers with TCP/IP
Practical UNIX & Internet Security. 2nd Ed.
PGP: Pretty Good Privacy
sendmail, 2nd Ed.
sendmail Desktop Reference
System Performance Tuning
TCP/IP Network Administration
termcap & terminfo
Using & Managing UUCP
Volume 8: X Window System Administrator's Guide
Web Security & Commerce

UNIX

Exploring Expect
Learning VBScript
Learning GNU Emacs, 2nd Ed.
Learning the bash Shell
Learning the Korn Shell
Learning the UNIX Operating System
Learning the vi Editor
Linux in a Nutshell
Making TeX Work
Linux Multimedia Guide
Running Linux, 2nd Ed.
SCO UNIX in a Nutshell
sed & awk, 2nd Edition
Tcl/Tk Tools
UNIX in a Nutshell: System V Edition
UNIX Power Tools
Using csh & tsch
When You Can't Find Your UNIX System Administrator
Writing GNU Emacs Extensions

WEB REVIEW STUDIO SERIES

Gif Animation Studio
Shockwave Studio

WINDOWS

Dictionary of PC Hardware and Data Communications Terms
Inside the Windows 95 Registry
Inside the Windows 95 File System
Win95 & WinNT Annoyances
Windows NT File System Internals
Windows NT in a Nutshell

PROGRAMMING

Advanced Oracle PL/SQL Programming
Applying RCS and SCCS
C++: The Core Language
Checking C Programs with lint
DCE Security Programming
Distributing Applications Across DCE & Windows NT
Encyclopedia of Graphics File Formats, 2nd Ed.
Guide to Writing DCE Applications
lex & yacc
Managing Projects with make
Mastering Oracle Power Objects
Oracle Design: The Definitive Guide
Oracle Performance Tuning, 2nd Ed.
Oracle PL/SQL Programming
Porting UNIX Software
POSIX Programmer's Guide
POSIX.4: Programming for the Real World
Power Programming with RPC
Practical C Programming
Practical C++ Programming
Programming Python
Programming with curses
Programming with GNU Software
Pthreads Programming
Software Portability with imake, 2nd Ed.
Understanding DCE
Understanding Japanese Information Processing
UNIX Systems Programming for SVR4

BERKELEY 4.4 SOFTWARE DISTRIBUTION

4.4BSD System Manager's Manual
4.4BSD User's Reference Manual
4.4BSD User's Supplementary Documents
4.4BSD Programmer's Reference Manual
4.4BSD Programmer's Supplementary Documents
X Programming
Vol. 0: X Protocol Reference Manual
Vol. 1: Xlib Programming Manual
Vol. 2: Xlib Reference Manual
Vol. 3M: X Window System User's Guide, Motif Edition
Vol. 4M: X Toolkit Intrinsics Programming Manual, Motif Edition
Vol. 5: X Toolkit Intrinsics Reference Manual
Vol. 6A: Motif Programming Manual
Vol. 6B: Motif Reference Manual
Vol. 6C: Motif Tools
Vol. 8 : X Window System Administrator's Guide
Programmer's Supplement for Release 6
X User Tools
The X Window System in a Nutshell

CAREER & BUSINESS

Building a Successful Software Business
The Computer User's Survival Guide
Love Your Job!
Electronic Publishing on CD-ROM

TRAVEL

Travelers' Tales: Brazil
Travelers' Tales: Food
Travelers' Tales: France
Travelers' Tales: Gutsy Women
Travelers' Tales: India
Travelers' Tales: Mexico
Travelers' Tales: Paris
Travelers' Tales: San Francisco
Travelers' Tales: Spain
Travelers' Tales: Thailand
Travelers' Tales: A Woman's World

O'REILLY™

TO ORDER: **800-998-9938** • **order@ora.com** • **http://www.ora.com/**
OUR PRODUCTS ARE AVAILABLE AT A BOOKSTORE OR SOFTWARE STORE NEAR YOU.
FOR INFORMATION: **800-998-9938** • **707-829-0515** • **info@ora.com**

International Distributors

UK, Europe, Middle East and Northern Africa (except France, Germany, Switzerland, & Austria)

INQUIRIES
International Thomson Publishing
Europe
Berkshire House
168-173 High Holborn
London WC1V 7AA, United Kingdom
Telephone: 44-171-497-1422
Fax: 44-171-497-1426
Email: itpint@itps.co.uk

ORDERS
International Thomson Publishing
Services, Ltd.
Cheriton House, North Way
Andover, Hampshire SP10 5BE,
United Kingdom
Telephone: 44-264-342-832
  (UK orders)
Telephone: 44-264-342-806
  (outside UK)
Fax: 44-264-364418 (UK orders)
Fax: 44-264-342761 (outside UK)
UK & Eire orders: itpuk@itps.co.uk
International orders: itpint@itps.co.uk

France

Editions Eyrolles
61 bd Saint-Germain
75240 Paris Cedex 05
France
Fax: 33-01-44-41-11-44

FRENCH LANGUAGE BOOKS
All countries except Canada
Phone: 33-01-44-41-46-16
Email: geodif@eyrolles.com

ENGLISH LANGUAGE BOOKS
Phone: 33-01-44-41-11-87
Email: distribution@eyrolles.com

Australia

WoodsLane Pty. Ltd.
7/5 Vuko Place, Warriewood NSW 2102
P.O. Box 935, Mona Vale NSW 2103
Australia
Telephone: 61-2-9970-5111
Fax: 61-2-9970-5002
Email: info@woodslane.com.au

Germany, Switzerland, and Austria

INQUIRIES
O'Reilly Verlag
Balthasarstr. 81
D-50670 Köln
Germany
Telephone: 49-221-97-31-60-0
Fax: 49-221-97-31-60-8
Email: anfragen@oreilly.de

ORDERS
International Thomson Publishing
Königswinterer Straße 418
53227 Bonn, Germany
Telephone: 49-228-97024 0
Fax: 49-228-441342
Email: order@oreilly.de

Asia (except Japan & India)

INQUIRIES
International Thomson Publishing Asia
60 Albert Street #15-01
Albert Complex
Singapore 189969
Telephone: 65-336-6411
Fax: 65-336-7411

ORDERS
Telephone: 65-336-6411
Fax: 65-334-1617
thomson@signet.com.sg

New Zealand

WoodsLane New Zealand Ltd.
21 Cooks Street (P.O. Box 575)
Wanganui, New Zealand
Telephone: 64-6-347-6543
Fax: 64-6-345-4840
Email: info@woodslane.com.au

Japan

O'Reilly Japan, Inc.
Kiyoshige Building 2F
12-Banchi, Sanei-cho
Shinjuku-ku
Tokyo 160 Japan
Telephone: 81-3-3356-5227
Fax: 81-3-3356-5261
Email: kenji@ora.com

India

Computer Bookshop (India) PVT. LTD.
190 Dr. D.N. Road, Fort
Bombay 400 001
India
Telephone: 91-22-207-0989
Fax: 91-22-262-3551
Email: cbsbom@giasbm01.vsnl.net.in

The Americas

O'Reilly & Associates, Inc.
101 Morris Street
Sebastopol, CA 95472 U.S.A.
Telephone: 707-829-0515
Telephone: 800-998-9938 (U.S. & Canada)
Fax: 707-829-0104
Email: order@ora.com

Southern Africa

International Thomson Publishing
Southern Africa
Building 18, Constantia Park
240 Old Pretoria Road
P.O. Box 2459
Halfway House, 1685 South Africa
Telephone: 27-11-805-4819
Fax: 27-11-805-3648

O'REILLY™

TO ORDER: **800-998-9938** • **order@ora.com** • **http://www.ora.com/**
OUR PRODUCTS ARE AVAILABLE AT A BOOKSTORE OR SOFTWARE STORE NEAR YOU.
FOR INFORMATION: **800-998-9938** • **707-829-0515** • **info@ora.com**